GUNS AND GANGS

THE INSIDE STORY OF THE WAR ON OUR STREETS

GRAEME McLAGAN

Allison & Busby Limited
13 Charlotte Mews
London W1T 4EJ
www.allisonandbusby.com

Hardcover published in Great Britain in 2005.
Previous paperback edition published
in 2006 (ISBN 9780749082185).
This paperback edition published in 2009.

A CIP catalogue record for this book is available from
the British Library.

10 9 8 7 6 5 4 3 2 1

ISBN 978-0-7490-0767-6

The paper used for this Allison & Busby publication
has been produced from trees that have been legally sourced
from well-managed and credibly certified forests.

Printed in the UK by CPI Bookmarque, Croydon, CR0 4TD

GRAEME MCLAGAN has specialised in long-term investigations for BBC news and current affairs programmes. The BBC's expert on police corruption for more than twenty years, he presented three *Panorama* programmes on the subject as well as several major stories for *Newsnight*. He won the Royal Television Society prize for his scoops while covering the 'Arms for Iraq' scandal and was commended in 1998 for *Bent*, the second of his *Panorama* programmes on police corruption. He wrote the bestselling *Bent Coppers* and is the co-author of *Mr Evil*, the story of David Copeland, the neo-Nazi nail-bomber. London born, Graeme McLagan is married with two grown-up children. He is now a freelance writer and broadcaster.

CONTENTS

This book is about gun crime across the UK, but it focuses on London where the black communities are adversely affected, as they are in other areas, particularly Manchester, Bristol, the West Midlands and Nottingham. Some argue that it is wrong to concentrate on particular ethnic minorities – that doing so unfairly stigmatises whole communities. However, it is a sad reality that about seventy per cent of the capital's gun murders and shootings involve so-called black-on-black violence, and Scotland Yard set up the successful and highly regarded Operation Trident to deal specifically with gun crime in the black community, whether by Jamaicans, Africans or British-born blacks.

Of course, only a tiny minority of people in these communities are gun criminals. But the effect they have on other people is immense in terms of lives lost, injuries, and devastated families. Black people across the country are now cooperating with police in an attempt to reject the gunmen. Large amounts of public money are being spent on tackling the problem, either through funding community projects aimed at preventing young people turning to the gun, or on the detectives hunting down the gunmen.

It is a largely untold story – the interaction of police, gunmen and the wider black community. For those upholding the law, it is the most challenging detective work possible. Not without reason is this kind of gun crime described as disorganised and chaotic. Most of the gunmen are totally callous, valuing lives cheaply, including their own. Some will kill because they have been shown disrespect. Others behave like Mafia gangsters of old, styling themselves as 'dons'. In one case described in this book, a man was greeted as an old friend with a big hug, and then, a couple of minutes later, hit with five bullets, eventually dying. But there are other surprises. In a trial at the Old Bailey, the defendant, a big man described as 'the baddest gunman' in his area, sat through much of his trial behaving like a vulnerable young child. For hours on end, in the dock, he could be seen sucking vigorously on his thumb.

My deep thanks go out to the very many police who helped

'tell it like it is', and to all those in the black community who are trying to do something about the gun crime problem. Grateful thanks also to several journalists, including Jason Benneto of the *Independent*, Kurt Barling, and to reporters working at the Old Bailey. The following books were also very useful for background: Laurie Gunst – *Born Fi' Dead* (Canongate); Jon Silverman – *Crack of Doom* (Headline); Tony Thompson – *Gangs* (Hodder & Stoughton) and Peter Walsh – *Gang War* (Milo Books).

The ring on the doorbell of a maisonette in the summer of 1998 was to change attitudes to gun crime forever. Until then the police and black communities had been at each other's throats in south London. But what happened at that address near Brixton was so horrific, and was followed by such brute terror across the capital, that it shocked police and blacks into working together to beat the gunmen.

It was just after ten o'clock at night on Friday 25th June when Kirk Johnson went to answer the door of his family's maisonette in Cressingham Gardens, Tulse Hill. As he went downstairs, he heard someone outside shout 'next door neighbour'. He opened the door and was confronted by three men, one of them armed. They barged their way inside, the man with the gun shouting 'what money you got?' and 'I'll kill you'. They grabbed Johnson, forcing him upstairs to a bedroom where his wife Avril was watching television with their daughters, eighteen-month-old Zhane and Ashanti, aged six.

The youngest of the intruders was told to turn up the sound on the television. It looked as though something terrible was about to happen. 'Don't move' shouted the excited gunman, pushing the weapon into Johnson's face. But bravely, Johnson disobeyed. 'I grabbed hold of it,' he said. 'Then I was attacked by his friend.' The second man was wielding a knife and jabbed him in the neck, causing blood to flow profusely. His attackers then warned: 'If you don't give us the money, we'll kill you.' They tore rings from the couple's fingers. A terrified Johnson blurted out that there was about £200 in a cupboard drawer downstairs.

As the two young children were bundled under the bedding, a very frightened Avril told her husband to give the men whatever they wanted. Then they tied up the Johnsons, binding their hands and feet with electrical flex. Avril – who was a successful DJ known as Miss Irie and the sister of 1980s reggae singer Tippa Irie – was forced to lie on the bed, with her husband forced to lie next to her. Johnson saw the gunman hand his weapon to the man with the knife. 'He was pointing the gun over us,' said Johnson. 'I put my head a bit lower. I heard two shots fired.' He played dead, and somehow survived, although he was left with a vivid scar on his neck where the knife had cut. Avril had no such luck. The gunman had held his weapon to her forehead and fired. Then he fired a second time, almost certainly aiming for her husband on the other side of the bed. He missed, and the bullet passed through the edge of the mattress, ending up in the bedroom wall. Avril Johnson died later in hospital.

The police had no idea who the killers were. Detectives had been running a secret intelligence cell gathering information about black murders and shootings in south London. But none of their regular 'grasses' came up with anything useful. The officer put in charge of the investigation was Detective Chief Inspector Steve Kupis who appealed for help from criminals to 'give up' the people responsible. 'If robbery was the motive, this was a most callous act – a horrendous thing,' he said. 'They had already stolen some property and the victims were powerless. For this woman to be shot in the head like that is beyond comprehension.'

It was not disclosed then that police were linking the attack with a terrible rape and attempted murder ten days before in nearby Clapham. There was no security or entry-phone system to the block of flats where a 24-year-old man lived on the third floor. He lay on the sofa in the living room, chatting with his girlfriend, aged eighteen, when there was a knock on the door. The young woman went to answer it. She could see through the glass that the person on the other side was black. Although she did not recognise him, she opened the door. A man wearing a black baseball cap grabbed her wrists, forcing her arms behind her back, propelling her back towards the living room. Two other men entered: one wore a red and black baseball cap, the other had a gun in his hand.

The gunman went towards the sofa where the man still lay and ordered him to 'get up and lie on the floor'. He picked up the man's mobile phone, put it in his pocket and said, 'You have something for me.' The man replied that he did not know what he was talking about. His feet were tied with electrical flex but he struggled as they tried to tie his hands, and was hit on the back of his head with the gun. The intruders then searched the flat, throwing things around, apparently looking for either large amounts of cash or drugs. They found a small amount of money but threatened the man, saying: 'I'll shoot you if you don't give me more.' After telling them there was some more cash in a wardrobe, he was dragged into the bedroom and they took what was there, still believing there was more to be found.

Meanwhile, the man's girlfriend was dragged into the kitchen where she lay on the floor while one of the men searched her, finding a £20 note. He then pulled out his penis. She pleaded with him not to rape her, but he was undeterred. After finishing with her, he pulled her to her feet and dragged her back to the living room where her hands were tied with flex. To her horror another of the men dragged her back to the kitchen and, after hitting her in the face, forced her to perform oral sex on him. Her boyfriend, still in the bedroom, was being kicked and punched by the men who were frustrated at finding so little cash and no drugs. As he lost consciousness he saw that one of them had a knife. After the attackers left, the young woman managed to free her hands to find that her boyfriend had been stabbed, once in the back and once in the chest. The wound at his front had pierced a lung. The couple staggered to an upstairs flat where a friend called an ambulance.

When police arrived, the couple demanded that no details of their ordeal should be given. Detectives agreed to conduct a low-key investigation, believing then that it was an isolated attack. What had happened to the couple was only revealed after the men struck a third time. They were lucky not to have been killed. The victim of the third attack, ten miles away across London, was a thirty-year-old woman. She was not so fortunate.

Four days after Avril Johnson was shot dead, Michelle Carby was murdered at her home in Stratford, east London. Exactly what happened to this mother of three is not known because there were no witnesses, but the police pieced together a likely sequence of events. Michelle Carby was dressed for bed when her killers struck at night. She was hit in the mouth, kicked on her legs, and her hands and feet tied with electrical flex. She was then gagged and bound to a chair in her living room and shot twice in the back of the head. Her three young children were upstairs in bed but they slept through the attack without hearing anything. They discovered their mother's body when they came downstairs the next morning, and running outside alerted the neighbours by shouting, 'We can't wake mummy up'. The house had been ransacked, rings were missing from her fingers and other jewellery had been stolen.

Eighteen days later, on the other side of London, came another murder. Patrick Ferguson lived with his partner, Primrose Johnbaptiste, and their two-year-old daughter Tiana in a house in Highfield Avenue, Kingsbury, Brent. Ferguson was out when the doorbell rang at about 8.30 in the evening. Primrose answered the door and the two men standing outside asked if 'Fergie' was there. She told them he was out but she expected him back a little later and asked if she could take a message. The older of the two men asked her to tell Fergie that Tony had called. Ferguson, a drug dealer, returned three-quarters of an hour later, and she told him the men had called. He seemed uneasy and left the house, but came back a few minutes later saying he had spoken to them and they had wanted some weed [herbal cannabis]. He was agitated and told his partner 'I ain't got no money and I don't know who these people are.'

While Primrose was having a bath with her daughter, she heard the doorbell ring. Ferguson was on the phone, but she heard him go to the front door. She closed the bathroom door but could still hear sounds from the hallway. There was a scuffling noise and Ferguson, raising his voice, shouted: 'I told you, I don't want anything from you. I don't have anything here!' Concerned at what was happening, Primrose got out of the bath, put on a dressing gown, and looked out of the door. First she saw the older man who had called earlier, and next to him Ferguson and another man holding each other at arm's length by each other's throats. She shouted out in alarm, 'What's going on?' and the second man she had seen earlier came out of her bedroom. Ferguson shouted:

'I told you I don't have fucking anything here,' and tried to push the man he was holding out of the door. But the man suddenly produced a gun. Primrose shouted, 'Oh, my God, please, no!' but he fired and Ferguson fell backwards to the floor, hit in the face. A neighbour heard a scream and saw the three attackers running towards him. The tallest of them appeared to be trying to put something down the front of his trousers. He heard another of them say, 'Oh fuck, I wonder will she recognise me?' He told police what he had seen.

Clearly the same gang was involved in all the attacks. Descriptions matched. They were all Jamaicans. They used electrical flex in three of their attacks, and their motive appeared to be robbery. But who were they and where were they going to strike next? The police needed help from the black communities in London, but that quarter was not inclined to cooperate, having suffered for years at police hands. There had been outrage about various deaths in custody, concerns about informers being allowed by their police handlers to commit violent crime, and most important, the death of black teenager, Stephen Lawrence.

However, the Metropolitan Police (Met) was beginning to show the first signs of wanting to change, owning up to mistakes, and it was about to admit to institutional racism. Some links had been forged before the murders and these now began to pay dividends. Black community leaders were just as worried as police about the dangers of further attacks by the murder gang on the loose. For the very first time in that part of London, they agreed to help a police operation aimed at fellow blacks. They joined the effort to catch the killers, urging people to cooperate with the police.

The level of cooperation achieved in south London was to have far-reaching, momentous effects. It marked the start of a change of attitude, not only in London but further afield in other areas of high gun crime such as Bristol, Manchester, and Birmingham. These cities and others all have their ruthless gangs, wielding prestige weapons such as Mac-10 machine guns, as well as shotguns, pistols, revolvers, reactivated weapons and converted air-pistols and gas guns. Many murders and shootings categorised as black-on-black, where the victim and perpetrator are black, are the result of turf wars over drugs. But some are 'diss' killings, where someone has shown disrespect to another.

This book lifts the lid on black gun crime. It traces the rise of the gun gangs, describing with first-hand accounts how they operate, and it has the inside story of how police across the country are tackling the problem. The background history of black gun violence is detailed in the first two chapters of this book, together with how the gang responsible for those horrific 1998 murders was tracked down and brought to justice.

'I was involved with guns from an early age. Guns were never a problem. They were easy to get in my days and now it's like buying a toothbrush.'

Gun crime barely registered in UK crime statistics in the 1950s, with firearms only used occasionally by professional criminals and in domestic murders or crimes of passion. The 1960s saw a slight rise, with guns being fired in gangland killings and armed robbery, most notably in the murder of three police officers shot in an unmarked car at Shepherd's Bush in west London. Significantly more guns were used in robberies during the 1970s, the increase becoming substantial in the 1980s. But that latter decade also saw the start of another trend – the use of firearms in the UK's black communities. Two interrelated factors lay behind the increase in these gun incidents in inner city areas – serious drugs and heavy violence, both imported from Jamaica.

Jamaicans had been coming to the UK since the 1950s, prepared to do the jobs left vacant by choosy whites. Most of these early immigrants were hardworking, but they also brought some of the negative aspects of their culture with them. Settling in Brixton in south London, Notting Hill in west London, Moss Side in Manchester, and St Paul's in Bristol, many smoked ganja. 'Jamaicans have a culture where they don't get married,' said one senior detective, describing the Moss Side scene in the 1960s and 70s. 'They have very loose relationships. They are all big strong lads, and they smoke cannabis. It's part of their culture. It was a mature population of immigrants who had come here. The problems occurred with the offspring of that generation.'

Barrington Foster was one of those offspring, ending up in 1982 with a 25-year sentence for murder and robbery. Now an articulate anti-gun-crime advocate, he spoke with passion as he told me his story. His grandparents came from Jamaica in the late 1950s, settling in Balham in south London, respectable and law abiding. Foster's short life of crime started when he was eighteen and made redundant from a garage job, paint-spraying and panel-beating. He tried to find other employment, but it was a difficult time, two years into Margaret Thatcher's government and a year after the Brixton riots. He told me he was up against racism: 'I was going for jobs which white youths were getting with far fewer qualifications. It was blatant. I know people will say, "Oh, he's just saying that," but it's true. It had a big impact on me. You have to remember that it wasn't all that long before then that there were signs saying, "No blacks or Irish".'

Foster started hanging out with British-born black friends at a youth centre. He said:

'They all had one thing in common – they were all carrying knives or guns, or machetes. Guns were fairly few and far between in those days. These were real ones, some of them used. Because guns were not as prevalent as now, you were reluctant to let anyone know you were carrying a gun, or let them see a gun, and there were people around who were grassing. I was getting dole money and money from uncles for odd-jobs, but it wasn't enough. I was smoking weed and going to clubs and I wanted to impress the girls and wear nice clothes. There was cocaine and speed available, but I didn't want any of that rubbish. I'd seen what damage it could do.

'One evening, coming home with a friend, we saw a man passing. My brethren said, "watch my back," and he ran at him. I just stood and watched. I felt fear and excitement at the same time. There was pushing and shoving and my friend got his wallet. We had about £200 off him, and he gave me fifty quid. From there it escalated. I had a choice and I chose to hang with them. The second time came. They knew someone who was carrying money and they needed a look-out – would you like to come along? Well, I got £50 the last time – money in my pocket – so I said yeah and we went down and robbed a shop, and ended up with a load of money. I was still in between. I knew the difference between right and wrong and I knew it wasn't right, so I was still going down the job centre. I didn't want to go and ask my grandparents for money.

'Then one of my mates said do you want a gun – there's one available. So I went round my friend's house and he lifted up his floorboards, and there was one underneath – a 32 snub-nose. So I had a gun too then. Then I was hanging more and more with this crew. Drinking with them, smoking with them, raving with these guys. It was like a family thing. Then one day we had a meeting and the talk was of licking a post office at Wandsworth. We went there and took about eight grand between four of us. All of us had guns. Sometimes when robbing, we never used to show the guns. We had knives, and we'd run in with them. Then we would show the guns as frighteners. Then more and more times when we were going out committing robberies, we were resorting to the gun because we realised people shake quicker with a gun than a knife. There were a couple of occasions when I fired the gun, at a couple of the post offices, but I fired it into the ceiling to frighten them. You say: "This is a robbery. Nobody move. Go on, find the keys for that." They'd say they ain't got the keys, then you'd put the gun over their heads and fire because you knew you'd get a response that way.

'It got to a stage where we were doing a combination of post office robberies and street robberies. Some of those street robberies were of people we knew in the sense that there'd be a briefcase with a handcuff round it and they'd keep the key in their shoe. We knew a lot of people who'd work in shops and so we had a lot of information. It got to a stage where my gun became my best friend. I remember going one night to Harlesden and having a beef with a crew at a party. My friend who had the beef didn't have his gun on him, but some of us did have one and we realised that if we hadn't had that, then there would have been trouble. They didn't roll us because we were carrying – we had the gun. We knew that if we didn't carry, they would have been on us. So I started carrying through fear of not being able to defend myself, because I thought if they know I'm carrying they won't sneak up and roll on me. But I didn't go out and bully people or deliberately shoot people.'

What Foster describes as six months of madness, during which he carried out sixteen robberies, ended in February 1982 when he was arrested and charged with the murder a week before of a store manager: an Asian man in his forties, who was carrying £500 in cash. Foster recalled:

'It was all terrible. Funnily enough, of all the nights, that was the night I wasn't carrying a gun. I had a knife. I had been to the youth centre and came out with a friend – my co-accused. We saw this Asian man, dressed impeccably. He showed that he had a lot of money because he went into a shop to buy something, and he didn't put his money back into his wallet until after he came out, so we saw he had a lot. It was crazy – a spur of the moment thing. My friend and I decided we were going to rob him. He was walking through an alley, and my friend went ahead of him and I walked behind. My friend then tried to stop him. He turned round and we showed him the knife and said we wanted the wallet. We said, "Hand it over and you won't get hurt." The man started to create – shouting and screaming. My friend took out his knife and there was a scuffle. He grabbed me as well, and in the end he got stabbed five times, and we ran off. I stabbed him twice, but I didn't mean to – I didn't go out with the intention of stabbing him. He died a week later on a life support machine.

'In that week the police arrested five or six guys I'd done robberies with. My friend got caught two days before me because he left his knife at the scene of the crime, and it was proven that he stabbed the man first. They caught him and the other five, and then I was walking down to the dole office. There were people who knew I'd done it. I put my dole card over the counter and the woman behind said, "wait a minute". I knew then that there was something wrong and the next minute there were about ten cops surrounding me, with armed back-up.'

Foster admitted to the murder and various robberies and, in September 1982, when nineteen years old, he was given a 25-year sentence. He served eighteen years of it. Now he is a reformed character, trying to save youngsters from the kind of mistakes he made as a youth.

While the early 1980s were marked by inner-city riots involving largely black, disaffected youths, unwilling to put up with exclusion and a life of unemployment and hopelessness, another group had started arriving in Britain – Jamaican gangsters. Problems in Jamaica in the 1970s led to criminals leaving the Caribbean island and spreading to the USA and then the UK, bringing with them violence and serious drugs. First it was cocaine, then crack.

Violence has marked Jamaican politics for years, particularly at election times. The two main parties, the People's National Party and the Jamaica Labour Party were always fairly evenly balanced. Each of them carved out territories in the capital, Kingston, and, in attempts to tip electoral advantage their way, each hired gunmen, members of gangs or posses, to enforce turn-out their way, taking on the gunmen in neighbouring districts and occasionally turning the city into a battleground. The PNP won the 1972 election with a socialist agenda. The rival JLP was a right-wing, freedom-loving party, and attacked the PNP as communistic. The parties' gun-toting supporters on the streets saw themselves as either PNP revolutionaries or JLP freedom fighters. The divisions extended down to the type of beer drunk by each side: red Stripe for the PNP because red stood for socialism, and Heineken for the other side, because its green bottle equated with the JLP's adopted colour. Woe betide anyone seen drinking the wrong kind in particular political strongholds.

The powerful links between senior Jamaican politicians and the posses were highlighted with photographic and documentary evidence by the FBI in New York. It reported that in 1976 the USA made $33m available to Jamaica in aid. The money was supposed to be for improving roads, but the FBI claimed that Jamaican government ministers handed it to posse leaders to ensure their support. The gangs 'agreed' that they would make local arrangements for the work to be carried out. However, years later little or nothing had been done to the roads. The money had disappeared.

A British police report summed up the Kingston gang breeding ground:

> 'The gangs are a loose knit set of geographic-political groupings who live in deprived and squalid slum areas, frequently no more than tin shelters. They have no hope of employment or improvement in their conditions and with no state welfare or relief, rely upon their wits to survive from an early age. Violent death, usually by the gun, is a normal event in the slums... It is said that almost every child has witnessed at least one shooting, or seen the body of a murder victim, by the age of ten years.
>
> 'The gangs align themselves to one of the two Jamaican political parties and a form of political tribalism dictates the activity of both criminals and the police, who are similarly divided. The influences can be traced back to before independence in 1962, when the PNP and JLP were formed. From that moment almost every aspect of Jamaican life has been divided on party political lines. Politics pervades the civil service, the police and business, with just the army, the Jamaican Defence

Force, retaining a reputation of freedom from bias...
Elections have been marked by murder and extreme
violence. Heavily armed gangs patrol the streets with
political leaders doing nothing to discourage the activity.
Whole areas of Kingston become electoral strongholds
for one party or the other. It therefore suits the purposes
of politicians to ensure their grip on a particular area is
retained by the street gangs, which have been known to
change their favour if a better offer is made from the
other side.'

One section of the report relating to the Jamaican police was
particularly damning, coming as it did from a senior Scotland Yard
officer. He did not mince his words: 'The police force is regarded
as thoroughly corrupt, brutal and inept by very influential people
on the island. They are regarded as the biggest and most powerful
posse. They are part of the problem.'

As the 1970s progressed, some gang members headed north
to US cities, especially Miami, the nearest to Jamaica. That Florida
city, followed by New York, acted as a gateway to the rest of the
States. What started as a steady movement north became a strong
flow after the 1980 general election, the island's most violent and
bloody. There were nearly nine hundred murders that year, the vast
majority of them during the election campaign. The police were
believed responsible for many of the deaths, more than double
the previous year's total. The JLP won the campaign, and in its
aftermath between three and four hundred members of one posse
alone are reckoned to have left for the USA.

Cannabis has always been around in Jamaica, with huge
shipments being sent to the UK. Annual seizures of the drug in
the UK were around 2,500 kilos in the mid-1970s, but this had
more than doubled by the end of the decade. Large amounts
were also exported to the USA which, to counter the threat to
its nation's youth, set up eradication programmes in Jamaica. But
a greater drugs menace was about to burst on the USA: cocaine
began showing up in the 1970s. Jamaican entrepreneurs, hit by

American anti-ganja programmes and seizures of the bulky drug, turned their attention to the new, more profitable and easily concealed cocaine. Jamaica and other Caribbean islands started to be used as staging posts between Venezuela and Florida. Where and when crack, cocaine's highly addictive smokable version, first surfaced is not known with any certainty. One authority says it was in the Bahamas in the early 1980s. It does not really matter. What is important is the impact it was to have not only in Jamaica, but in the USA, and later the UK.

By the mid-1980s, Jamaicans were 'cooking' (converting cocaine to crack) and dealing in the drug all over the US. They were quite unlike the gentle Rastafarians who sold ganja. These new guys on the block were hard, organised and violent, and they found it easy to obtain guns. More than 200 automatics were bought by the Shower posse in Miami and Ohio. Some of the guns from these two big purchases were sent to Jamaica, but others were used in drug-related shootings in New York, Washington, Detroit, Chicago and even as far away as Los Angeles on the west coast. One estimate is that more than 1,500 Jamaicans were murdered in drug turf wars on the east coast alone in the five years up to 1985. Detectives investigating one murder found the severed head of a black American drug dealer that had been wrapped in tape and used as a football. The dead man's crime was to attempt to steal three ounces of crack from a Jamaican gang. By 1987, Jamaican posses were linked to 625 drug murders and were branded by the Bureau of Alcohol, Tobacco and Firearms as probably the USA's most violent organised crime gangs. Raids across the country resulted in 124 arrests and seizures of guns and drugs in twelve cities. In addition to the cities above were Boston, Philadelphia, Cleveland, Dallas, Denver, Kansas City and Miami.

In the UK, Jamaican gangs were causing increasing problems by the mid-1980s, although on nothing like the USA scale. Known as 'Yardies', their trademarks were ganja dealing and robbery. Entry to Britain was fairly easy. Jamaican passport holders did not require visas. A short interview at the British High Commission resulted in entry clearance being given. It was only refused if a criminal background could be proved, and that was very difficult given Jamaican police record keeping. British passport holders, and there were many of them, were entitled to unrestricted entry. There was a huge black market in stolen passports and forged documents, and there was evidence that passports were lent to those who did not have them.

Barrington Foster remembers the Yardies coming in ones and twos, linking up with recent Jamaican arrivals, causing friction with his own British-born group. He told me:

'I mixed with them, but I didn't do crimes with them. They used to think they could come and bully the British-born. We'd say, "Don't come that shit with us." When they'd come to parties for instance, they'd come up to you and say buy me a drink. One time I was in the bathroom in a club in Balham, building a spliff when one of these Yardies came in with his mate, and he said, "You might as well get the rest out, because we're taking it off you, English boy!" I said, "OK, I'll go and get it," so I went into the cubicle, pulled out my gun and came back and said, "Who the fuck are you saying 'English boy'?" They started shitting themselves. I said: "This is England. It ain't Jamaica."

'We had that rivalry where that first wave of Yardies coming over, they thought they could bully us and tax us. A lot of the English or British-born did cave in – they found it quite difficult – but we weren't standing for it. So a lot of the times I had to draw my gun and I'll be quite honest, I would have used it because they were bullies, and they were trying to take from us. If they heard we'd been on a job, they tried to tax us.

'At that time, they didn't have the numbers so much as in the late '80s and 1990s. So you'd only have two together and they'd be frightened. I'd tell them: "I can go anywhere in south-west London and get you taken care of. I can go to east London and get you taken care of. These guns we've got, they come from white men in north London, so if you fuck about, people from another skin colour will hit you." These Yardies tried to scare you with fear of their mouth, but there were a few of us who'd say this is our country. We can get things you can't get. Because they weren't in those numbers – like if three of them were at a dance and wanted to take us on, they'd have to take on fifty of us. A lot of them did take people on, and they got hurt. They got shot. A lot of them got stabbed. A lot of them were walking around with cuts down their back and face from hatchets and all sorts. They weren't in the numbers and they didn't have the guns available at that time, as we did. They didn't know who to bully.'

One prominent man at that time was Robert Blackwood, senior gunman with the Shower posse in a JLP district of Kingston. After being linked to the murders of more than twenty PNP rivals and some policemen, Blackwood, known as Rankin Dread, came to Britain in the late 1970s. After finding initial fame through recording the hit reggae song 'Hey Fatty Boom Boom' he turned to serious crime – pimping, robbery and ganja smuggling.

Barrington Foster knew him and says he was told by Blackwood that British police were even then, at that early stage, trying to infiltrate the Jamaican gangs by using some members as informers. Whether he was right in his belief that the police at that time were so organised in their use of grasses is impossible to determine. Scotland Yard's 'corporate memory' extends back only a few years. However, in this area, maybe the facts are not so important. It is the perception that counts. And Foster is insistent that there were informers:

'Rankin Dread was one of the top members of the Shower posse. When you have someone like him here, the police were worried. You had a lot stabbings plus the odd shooting as well, most of them in north London, and the police wanted to break the mould before it developed more. So they brought a load of Yardies over, gave them a place, a different name, to infiltrate the gangs and grass people up. That's what was happening in the early 1980s.

'I was speaking to people like Rankin Dread and Stitchman, they told me a lot of the black guys coming here from Jamaica had to be checked – what they'd done in Jamaica, and what they were doing after they'd got here. Unless they knew them and what they were doing, they'd never be accepted. The police had been using informers way before. I know because I went to a court case in north London for a guy called Lance who used to bounce on a door. He was a British-born black but he knew a lot of the Yardies. He was an informer for about eleven years. It came out by accident at the case. The judge said he couldn't understand why this man's evidence was so unreliable because he was a police informer. That came out in court and they had to close the case down. Two weeks later he got shot dead. Everyone was shocked that he'd been an informer for so long. There were others running clubs who were believed to be informers. Clubs would get raided, but others would be able to keep running until seven in the morning. How come one club gets raided and nothing illegal's been found and this geezer, selling drugs to the community and doing all sorts, can stay open? It looked like the police were letting him do it to get information back.

'When you're in the criminal community, you pick up a lot of information. Out on the streets there's no law. Everyone talks, and everyone has a price. When you're in that world, everyone wants stripes so they want to big up themselves. They'll say, "I heard you done that job the other day." "Yeah," you'd say, "we got a couple of quid out it. Have a couple of drinks on me." That's the

way you get information. I've lived it. So, yes, I've seen a
lot of the early waves of the Shower posse take root in a
lot of places, a lot of clubs. The "houses" [crack houses]
and what they're doing now, I didn't see. But I see them
strapping – carrying guns. And in the clubs I used to go
to, they tried to bully even us, until we shoved the guns
in their faces and said, "you're not back in Jamaica now,
you're in England".'

By 1986 Barrington Foster had spent four years in prison and
Rankin Dread was into cocaine and allegedly involved in what has
been described as the first Yardie killing. It happened in March
of that year when five men burst into the north London flat of a
dealer who had ripped them off. He was thrown out of the window,
falling nine floors down to his death. Over the next twelve months
there were three other Jamaican murders in London. In May, a DJ
standing in a pub doorway in Stockwell, south London, was killed
with a shotgun blast to his head, fired by a man who had pulled up
in a Mercedes. A few days later in Brixton, a nightclub doorman
was shot in the head as he tried to prevent a gang of Jamaicans
entering. Then early in 1987 a cocaine dealer was blasted in the
head by a rival dealer at a party in Acton, west London.

Another cocaine dealer at that time was Tony Miller, who
– although then only twenty-one years old – had been involved
in crime for the previous eight years. He told me he was thirteen
when his mother threw him out of the family home. Now living
respectably as a pastor in south London, he recalls with vivid
detail a dramatic life which nearly came to a premature end with
him looking down the barrel of a Colt 45. In his second year at
secondary school, he had become violent to fellow pupils and
some teachers, and outside school hours had turned to burglary.
Exclusion followed and he was sent to a support school where his
rebellion continued. He told me:

'A teacher tried to help me there. I said look at you – how
much money do you earn? I said, I earn double your

money. What can you teach me? My shoes alone cost £300. They're made of crocodile skin, from Bond Street. My jacket cost the same. I was covered in gold, all over. I asked the teacher, what can you teach me? That was my concept of life. I got expelled from there as well. We got arrested on a school camping trip in Wales. We stole a car and reversed it into Curry's. My mum gave up on me and I got kicked out of my house. I went to live with some prostitutes in Brixton for three years of my life. I knew them through a pimp. I stayed with them, looked after their house and kids, and I was able during that time to do criminal activity – more burglaries, about three or four a week, sometimes every day. Walworth Road was where my crew were – the Walworth Road Boys, the Brixton Boys.

'The police were ruthless in those days. What they used to do was get you in a van or pull across you on the main road, and say, "drop your trousers". They'd look at your balls, your testicles. They'd say, "you either drop your trousers now or you go to the police station," and you knew if you went to the police station, a lot of the time they'd beat you up. I was taking mainly puff [ganja] in 1985 and '86. There was a code of practice on the street at that time. Back in the '80s if you were found taking cocaine or heroin, you would have got hurt, because everyone in the black community would say that it's a white man's drug and that it was going to destroy us. But it was weird. Guess what? Those that were saying it were also selling it. These were guys that used to get a big bag of weed and they would be up through the day and night selling it. It was too big and too slow to make a profit, and people wanted to get big cars. But with cocaine it was easier because it's in smaller parcels. You don't have to carry the dope. You can meet someone, do a deal and that was it. Crack was around but people were wary about it.'

With a street name of Younger T, and a smart red and white sports car, Miller remembers the impact of the Jamaican gang members.

'When the Yardies came over I had to learn a new way of culture, and a way of surviving on the street. They became the name brand and all the guys in Brixton started to try and speak like the Yardies. It used to sicken me, because we're British. Then there was like a war between the young British blacks and the Yardies. I was unfortunately involved in one incident on Railton Road and nearly lost my life because he tried to rob me, but I came back at him with my brother and battered him – a Jamaican. This guy tried to rob me. He asked for a cigarette. I said, "I ain't got one." He said he'd cut me all over. I went and found him later in a gambling club, went downstairs and battered him with a hammer. I didn't see myself as having an aggressive or violent nature, I saw myself as a thief.

'Eventually I started building relationships with some of the Yardie guys and I became close with them in terms of drugs, and I built up a career. From sixteen or seventeen I got into cocaine and became a dealer, and moved from burglaries and street crime and became a pick-pocketer. The money I got from pick-pocketing, I spent on cocaine, and it was a vicious circle. With the cocaine I was mixing with people all over London. I wasn't like some of the guys on the street. I had exclusive clients – not Brixtonians. They were businessmen in the city and in big corporate organisations. On a Friday I took all my parcels and went to their offices – "and how are you Mr Brown? That'll be £400. Thank you. See you next week".'

Tony Miller recalled how he and his friends loved film director Oliver Stone's 1983 gangster movie *Scarface* in which Al Pacino played the lead character, Tony Montana.

'Back in those days a lot of people of my age used to study *Scarface*. People were trying to find identities, someone to act as a role model, and they were all patterning themselves on Tony Montana. I remember what Tony Montana said: "If you are going to survive in this business, you have to be low key. If you get too big, you cause trouble to yourself and things start to go wrong. You don't want to have attention from police or from other people in the community knowing about you 'cos they'll come to your house and stick you for robbery." Anyway, my name was getting well known on the streets, with people I didn't want to associate with, like proper pipe-heads – which is the same as crack-heads nowadays. They would be free-basing – smoking cocaine, but still not crack. People would come and say, "are you selling drugs?" And I would get worried.'

When I asked him about guns, he replied:

'I was involved with guns from an early age. Guns were never a problem. They were easy to get in my days and now it's like buying a toothbrush. With guns then, you had to know someone who knows someone. You had to go through certain people. I had a gun, but I wouldn't use it unless I was in a life-threatening position or was going on a major robbery. I had someone's gun and was looking after it for him, but it was mine, if you understand. This person was mentoring me. He was an older guy. They'd see I was up and coming and I would live with their stuff – their guns. I'd keep it under my pillow. One day I met a friend who was planning an armed robbery. We used to work together and do burglaries and stuff. He was out of his head taking drugs. He pulled out a Colt 45, and he pulled the trigger three or four times, and pointed it at my head. Little did I realise that it had a bullet in it. His eyes were red and he was laughing. That guy was older than me. However, when I realised there was a bullet in it, I went crazy at him. I don't play silly games like that.

'Six hours afterwards he did the same thing to his girlfriend and blew her head off. The bullet went through her temple and through the window. Killed her stone-dead. This girl killed, she had a contract with Harrods to become a model the next day. I was sixteen at the time. My friend handed himself in to the police. He had a breakdown. He was young – nineteen – immature, and when he saw her brain splattered against the wall like mincemeat, he walked to Brixton police and handed himself in. His other friend took the gun and threw it into the Thames. My friend got eighteen months for manslaughter.

'There were guns on the street, but it was controlled. Guns had always been there, but no one would go and shoot someone unless it was something out of the norm – like if you attacked someone's mum, or violated someone by sexually assaulting someone's child, or if you killed someone – a brother, then I'm gonna kill you too. People would carry guns to do armed robberies – that was the big thing in the 1980s. Some people got shot, but it wasn't lots like now. These were the first guys getting whacked. People were surprised and shocked when they heard about someone getting shot. It's not like that now.'

Tony Miller was caught by police after a chase following a street robbery. He was seventeen and given twelve months in a detention centre, run on the lines of a 'boot camp' with strong discipline, a place where they were forced to march everywhere. Back outside he resumed his previous life, but disillusion gradually set in, and he saw at first hand the devastating effect crack can have.

'I got sick of crime, but didn't know how to come out of it. I had money but wasn't content. I'd go to clubs and look at these guys with clothes and money and I'd think, is this it? Where am I going. I saw guys up there falling rapidly and it was because of crack. I know a guy who had everything a man could want, and in a year, he lost everything, down to his carpet that he sold to go and get crack.'

In 1988, aged twenty-two, Tony Miller had a life-changing experience described later in this book.

Meanwhile, Scotland Yard responded to increasing gun crime with a new initiative called Operation Lucy, under the command of Detective Superintendent Roy Ramm, who later went on to head the Flying Squad. In 1987, working in the Yard's Intelligence branch, he put together a team which included five black officers and detectives skilled in handling informants. Their targets were the big-time drug dealers, those displaying their wealth and commanding 'respect' wherever they went in the black communities, particularly Brixton, Harlesden and Stoke Newington. All were from Jamaica rather than any of the other Caribbean islands and they had links to the main political parties there, either the PNP or the JLP. Kingston and Miami were believed to be the main sources of the cocaine they dealt with, the drug being brought into Heathrow by white female couriers. It was at that time that crack began to turn up.

As Ramm and his team planned the first raids on the Jamaicans who had set up shop in the black areas of London, they were conscious that they had to tread carefully because of racial sensitivities, as earlier over-aggressive policing and 'stop and search' tactics had caused major problems. The famous Brixton riot of 1981 was largely sparked off by Operation Swamp, an attempt to tackle street crime by flooding the area with huge numbers of officers. Black criminals were the targets then, and black criminals were to be the new targets. But Ramm tried to get round possible problems by enlisting the help of local officers rather than marching in mob-handed with his own men, leaving others to sort out any resulting mess. So local officers were used for arrests, acting on intelligence provided by the Lucy team.

One of the premises raided turned out to be a crack-factory, where cocaine was converted into its stronger cousin. During a long surveillance operation, up to fifty callers an hour were seen visiting a flat in Peckham, south-east London. When police raided, there were three Jamaicans inside. Two were from Kingston and the other was from New York. In another Lucy case, a crack dealer had taken massive security precautions to guard his flat. Edward Reynolds was operating from the nineteenth floor of a tower block in Deptford, south-east London. The flat's outer door was made of steel and protected by Chubb locks, and there was a steel-cased inner door with several strong steel bolts. Reynolds sold crack through a slit in the outer door, so that the buyers could not see inside. Raiding police had to cut their way in with oxyacetyline burners, finding Reynolds there with rocks of crack, cocaine and cash.

Crack was still new to the UK police in April 1989 when the Association of Chief Police Officers, ACPO, held its annual drugs conference. Invited over from the USA to speak about the new menace was Bob Stutman, the head of DEA, the Drug Enforcement Agency, New York. He shook the delegates with a devastating picture of how crack had spread across America to 49 of the 50 states in just three and a half years, accompanied by stabbings and shootings. Stutman said the highly addictive drug had started hitting New York in 1985, but warnings that it would strike elsewhere were discounted. He recalled that time: 'They said: "It's you crazy people who live in New York. You're all nuts. It can't happen anywhere else and it will certainly never leave the ghetto."' He then warned these senior British police officers that Britain would be next: 'The only thing I ask you is the following: learn from our mistakes. We have screwed up enough times, but I would hope all of you don't have to go through the same thing that we went through. Don't be like the people of Kansas and Texas and California who said "it can't happen here". I will make a prediction. I will personally guarantee you that two years from now, you will have a serious crack problem, because we are so saturated with cocaine in the United States, there ain't enough noses left to use the cocaine that's coming in.'

Stutman went on to say that the crack trade in the USA was controlled by two ethnic groups: Dominicans and Jamaicans. With a large number of Jamaicans in Britain, many of whom had friends and relatives in New York, it was obvious that Jamaicans would quickly accelerate the spread of crack here. 'These guys don't have to be geniuses to realise they don't need to import crack from the US,' he said. 'They can go out and buy a baby bottle at a department store and you certainly have water here and Bunsen burners. They can make their crack right here in Great Britain and increase their profits by something like three hundred per cent.'

However, Stutman's warnings were criticised in some quarters as being alarmist, and his linking of crack and its associated violence with Jamaicans did not go down well with some black activists. The latter group had also been critical of aspects of Operation Lucy, with the publicity accompanying some of the police raids being described as 'over the top', unfairly stigmatising the entire black community. The reality was that Lucy had indeed been investigating black crime and Jamaican involvement, in particular in violence and class-A drugs. The team had a database of more than three thousand records of drug-related crime involving Jamaicans, and claimed to have made or provided information resulting in about four hundred arrests. Nevertheless, it was decided to disband Lucy and draft some of its officers into a Crack Intelligence Coordinating Unit, a joint police and Customs effort. But its brief was to concentrate on the drug itself, researching its effects and looking at ways of limiting its spread. When big seizures failed to materialise by the summer of 1990, it too was closed down.

There was no let up, however, in drug-related shootings, murders and attempted killings in London. One confidential police report listed ten such crimes starting in November 1988 with shots being fired at a man. A senior official of the US embassy visa staff was stabbed to death in 1989 as she was about to inform on a colleague who was illegally providing visas to the USA for

Jamaican crack dealers. The next eight incidents all involved drug dealers seeking revenge. There were two gun murders in 1990, both believed to have been carried out by the same gunman, brought in from Jamaica especially for the hits. There were three attempted murders, two of them involving shots being fired at police. Both of these were thought to involve gunmen working on the orders of a major crack trafficker. The following year started with the ninth and tenth incidents: a murder and an attempted murder.

The next shooting led to the setting up of yet another major investigation into Jamaican criminality, Operation Dalehouse, concentrating on south London. It was in April 1991 that a gang of five black men robbed a jeweller's shop in a Brixton arcade. Faced with a sawn-off shotgun, the owner, Charles Fisher, cooperated by gathering up and handing over all the gold items on the display shelves. His reward for offering no resistance was to be blasted from two feet away. Amazingly, although very seriously injured, he survived. Detectives identified the five robbers as belonging to a group called The Syndicate. Some were British-born and some were from Jamaica. It emerged that one of the main suspects had been deported to Jamaica eight times in one year, returning to the UK each time using a different false passport.

Investigating The Syndicate's activities further, detectives were told that the group was responsible for a spate of robberies and shootings at nightclubs and dance halls. Yet none of these incidents had been reported to the police even though hundreds of people were sometimes on the receiving end of the violence. Fear of reprisals stopped people going to the police. In one case, three hundred young people were robbed by an armed gang at a disco. In another, in June 1991, a group fired handguns and shotguns at a Brixton community centre event attended by four hundred people.

Police were called to another incident that summer, which has become notorious for two reasons. First, it involved the shooting dead of a man at the Podium nightclub in Vauxhall, south London, for the most trivial of reasons. It appeared that the only 'crime' of the victim, Mark Burnett, had been to accidentally step on someone's foot on the dance floor. The episode was quoted repeatedly over the following years as a very good example of a pointless 'diss' shooting, where someone has shown disrespect to another. Second, when police arrived to investigate the murder they found uncooperative witnesses with a very marked reluctance to say anything at all. The Podium had been packed with two thousand people, but when police started to interview possible witnesses, the response was that people had either seen nothing, or they were in the lavatories. More than one hundred names and addresses were taken as potential witnesses, but ninety per cent of them turned out to be false. Only a handful answered any questions, the rest exercising their right to silence.

Shootings in south London were running at about six a month when police moved in on The Syndicate. They seized cocaine worth nearly £100,000, and an arsenal of weapons, mainly handguns, along with stolen cheque books, credit cards and passports. The frauds they ran also involved the gang's girlfriends or 'babymothers' (a woman who has a child. A man may have a current partner but still have girlfriends, past or present, who've borne him children. These women are referred to as babymothers.) In Operation Dalehouse's eighteen-month existence a total of 274 arrests were made for what was believed to be crack-related crimes, including murder, kidnap and armed robbery. The database taken over from its predecessor, the Crack Intelligence Coordinating Unit, had expanded to 3,500 names, and was made available to detectives throughout London. But the Met was still unsure about the best way to tackle problems caused by Jamaican gangs.

> *'The police had alienated the black community because they
> didn't have a strategy. They saw it as "them and us"… What
> they relied on was this broad swathe of unethical active
> criminal informants. And they had no real management of
> what was going on.'*

Early in 1993, a senior detective with Scotland Yard's Intelligence
branch was set a two-part task – reviewing what had been achieved
in combating Jamaican gangs, and recommending a strategy
for tackling a problem which, far from going away, was, in fact,
increasing. The introduction to Detective Chief Superintendent
Roy Clark's report in July 1993 makes stark reading. It describes
'an increasing threat to London by violent criminals who have
almost unlimited access to firearms and drugs, and an ability to
carry them across borders with apparent ease… There has been an
almost complete breakdown of a Met Police strategic response.'

Concern was growing about black gun crime and crack dealing,
not only in London, but in other major cities too, particularly
Manchester, Birmingham and Bristol. Three of the many cases in
1993 were significant. Big headlines followed the first, the murder
of an apparently totally innocent mixed-race youngster. Benji
Stanley had just turned fourteen when he was shot dead in Moss
Side, Manchester, as he queued for a take-away in Alvino's Pattie
and Dumplin Shop. A black gunman emerged from a car wearing
army-style combat gear with his face masked by a balaclava. He
fired his shotgun through the glass door, catching Benji in the leg.
The second blast tore into the boy's upper thigh and side, flinging
him to the floor. The gunman was not satisfied. He wanted to
make sure. He stood over the boy on the floor and, at point blank
range, blasted him in the chest. Benji Stanley died, almost certainly
the victim of mistaken identity. He bore a striking resemblance to
a youth who was mixed up with guns and drugs and was himself to
be accused of attempted murder.

The murders of police officers always attract headlines, and that of Police Constable Patrick Dunne in October 1993 was no exception. PC Dunne was a 41-year-old ex-teacher who had joined the police and become a community bobby in Clapham, south London. He stumbled into the aftermath of the gangland killing of William Danso, a drug dealer and nightclub bouncer. The officer was shot in the heart. Eleven years later, in 2004, a man was charged with the two murders.

The third case attracted much less publicity, but was a good illustration of the growing cost to society of crack addiction. A nineteen-year-old youth, Duane Daniels, on trial at the Old Bailey, reckoned that during an average day he got through twenty rocks of crack, half an ounce of cannabis, and two tabs of LSD as well as ten cans of strong lager. That lot cost him at least £300 a day, and to fund his addiction he committed crime after crime. Altogether he admitted 600 burglaries, 130 muggings and more than 200 car break-ins. He was given a ten-year prison sentence.

Detective Chief Superintendent Clark went to Jamaica himself and found the politicians' reliance on gunmen as bad as ever. Armed street gangs were seen at almost every polling station in Kingston during the general election in March 1993, and in some areas the vote was one hundred per cent in favour of one or other of the two main parties. Jamaicans working at the British High Commission were allowed home early to vote, but the next day reported that they were either not allowed near their polling stations or that someone had already voted using their name. Not one of them managed to cast a vote.

Clark's report used the 'Yardie' label to describe the Jamaican gang member, although he pointed out it was a term rarely used or recognised in the Caribbean or the USA, which he also visited. With traditional industries in Jamaica in permanent decline, he said the only hope for young men was through guns and crime, and moving abroad.

'A Yardie will not hesitate to commit acts of violence against police officers, members of the public or other

Yardies. Whilst many [ordinary] criminals will resort to violence as a last resort, a member of a Jamaican gang will use violence as a first step and without hesitation. To be seen in expensive clothes and jewellery, driving an expensive car and with the most powerful gun possible at his disposal will add to his status and afford him considerable kudos. He will finance his lifestyle from the sale of drugs or robbery. He will not hesitate to rip-off another Yardie of drugs or cash, but lives in constant fear of being so treated himself. They will lie and not hesitate to make allegations against police officers. A Yardie will constantly change his name and will use many stolen passports or similar documentation to support multiple identities. Whilst he will cling to his street name as far as possible, because it is around this name that his reputation is built, he will abandon or change it if necessary.'

Clark cited the case of a Yardie named 'Tuffie' Osborne who had been deported from the UK on at least two occasions. He arrived with a new identity at Birmingham airport in April 1993. He looked suspicious to an immigration officer who started to question him. But Osborne shoved him aside, jumped a barrier, and ran into the terminal. He was in the UK once again. However, a couple of weeks later he was shot dead in Brixton.

To tackle the problems presented by someone with several identities or street names, Clark recommended that Scotland Yard's fingerprint branch should exchange information with police in Jamaica and New York. He also wanted the British High Commission in Kingston to provide copies of photographs of those applying for entry clearance to the UK. But there were problems. The High Commission had to hold on to the originals, and photocopies would not be of sufficient clarity to be of any use for intelligence purposes. It was agreed that a high quality Polaroid camera would be fine, but Clark reported: 'Unfortunately the High Commission have no means of purchasing such a camera.' His solution was simple – Scotland Yard's Intelligence branch should buy a very good Polaroid camera and send it quickly and securely to Jamaica in the diplomatic bag.

The report said Yardies represented a two-fold threat to London and the UK. The Jamaican gangs saw the UK as a profitable, soft and easy option. They saw the police as less of a threat than elsewhere, court sentences as very lenient, drug dealing as more profitable and there was less danger from opposing gangs. They were also having a major impact on British-born blacks. 'They have become role models for young and impressionable black youths,' said the report. 'Young British boys are being lured into crime and possible imprisonment or death by the sight and word of the rich trappings with which Yardies surround themselves.'

Clark called for the police to work more closely with the Jamaican authorities, tighter entry and immigration controls, and a multi-agency strategy which would be intelligence-led. He said there was a vital need to develop new informants both in Jamaica and the UK. Because of the rapid exchange of information between gang members on both sides of the Atlantic, an informant in, say, Jamaica could come up with valuable intelligence about something that had happened, or was about to occur, in London. Tapping of trans-Atlantic telephone calls showed discussion of events taking place within hours of them happening in London. Clark quoted a district attorney in New York as having received a phone call from an informant in a US jail the day after the killing of Tuffie Osborne in Brixton, described earlier. Not only had the informant heard of the murder of this fellow Jamaican over three thousand miles away, he also suggested who was responsible, the motive and the background.

Clark said drugs liaison officers, DLOs, working from the British High Commission in Kingston used local informants for intelligence on drug smuggling, but had limited ability or funds to reward them. He said there were clearly considerable possibilities to develop a network of informants on the island who could gather information about crime and criminals in London, or on gangsters intending to travel to London. Payments would be made through the DLOs and it was thought a great deal of information would be forthcoming for little lay-out, because even sums as small as £50 or £100 were seen as considerable in the Kingston ghettos.

An existing informer Roy Clark had previously met in Jamaica was viewed by the Scotland Yard officer as having great potential. Apparently an ex-member of the Jamaican army, 'Andrew Gold' was born in Kingston and, although living there, he also regularly visited London. He had worked undercover for the US Drug Enforcement Agency, the DEA, and been registered to the Met in the past, being known to a detective in Brixton. 'Gold has expressed a willingness to travel to London where he knows he would be accepted by the Jamaican criminal gangs,' reported Clark. 'He is willing to act as an informant/agent and to be debriefed regularly. The cost to the Met would be that of the air ticket, accommodation and expenses. Any other payment would be on results or significant intelligence gained. I consider that after a period of time, perhaps four weeks at first, Gold should be returned to Kingston and continue to supply information from there. He would then continue to build upon his credibility and acceptance by the Jamaican gangs and be available for further deployment as and when required or desirable.'

Although Clark warned that more research was necessary on Gold's background, he recommended that the informer and other similar criminals in Kingston should be brought to London to infiltrate the gangs in an 'aggressive pursuit of intelligence'. Likewise, Jamaican informants in London should be paid to visit Kingston. All such informants should be handled by four or five expert detectives deployed as 'field intelligence officers', who would also visit Jamaican gang members in British prisons, in the hope that some of them could also be 'turned'. All of Detective Chief Superintendent Roy Clark's recommendations were to be acted on over the next few years, with some, such as the introduction of a visa system, taking longer than others. However, one of his solutions was to cause particular controversy.

The use of informants over major criminal activity had been criticised for years, going back to the early 1980s with attacks on the 'supergrass' system. Those were the days when violent robbers were given easy five-year sentences in special prison wings after agreeing to implicate others in what were serious and sometimes horrific crimes they had committed together. Informers have always been seen as a necessary evil. Their relationships with detectives form a very murky area. In extreme cases the informant could end up running his supposed detective handler. The more common danger was that a blind eye could be turned by the detective to criminal activity by the informant, supposedly to gather information about others' crimes. This could lead to the informant believing or acting as if he had carte blanche to go out and commit crimes. The rules and regulations governing informants' use were tightened in the late 1990s, but even in 1993, although looser, the Home Office guidelines were clear: 'The need to protect an informant does not justify granting him immunity from arrest or prosecution.' Those guidelines were to be breached with some Jamaican informants.

Clark's report said the Met should have formed 'a formal intelligence gathering and development structure' in London. Instead of this, there was only an informal network involving a very small group of detectives who exchanged information with immigration and Customs officers. Impressed by their dedication, Clark said that some members of this group had spent their own money and leave to study the problem, regularly meeting in a south London pub to discuss the issues. He named three of these officers, saying each of them had an excellent record of cultivating informants, but he warned that the tasking of informants should be more coordinated, as should the intelligence coming from them.

Just days after Clark wrote his report and recommendations, one of the Met's Jamaican informants was arrested by another force, plunging Scotland Yard into a controversy lasting well into the early 2000s. It damaged not only its anti-gun-crime efforts, but also its attempts to build bridges with the black community. The background to the eventual arrest of the Yardie gangster Eaton Green on 8th July, and the dramatic events that followed, were detailed in a joint investigation two years later by the *Guardian* newspaper and the ITV current affairs programme 'World in Action'.

Nottingham police had been after Eaton Green for five weeks, after more than a hundred people had been robbed at a party in an old warehouse in the East Midlands city. It was 3.30 in the morning when five armed men burst inside, fired guns into the ceiling, and then systematically robbed everyone there. Several were beaten up, with one of the robbers showing particular violence. Wearing a red bandana, he shot one of the partygoers in the leg and then stood over him gloating 'bleed, pussy, bleed'. The gunman was said to be a professional hitman from Kingston, and Nottingham detectives identified him as Eaton Green, aged twenty-seven, and that he and the other four raiders were all from London. The Nottingham officers contacted the Met and learned that Green was an informant. But they were to claim that they were given virtually no detail of the extent of his activities. That only came out when Green and the four others stood trial for the warehouse robbery.

What emerged at that later stage was that Eaton Green was no casual one-off grass. He had been a full-time registered informant for two years giving top-grade intelligence on Jamaican gangsters to the Met, the Home Office, Customs, the Jamaican authorities and the New York district attorney. *Guardian* reporter Nick Davies wrote: 'Green's apparently routine arrest was to trigger a chaotic chain reaction in which rules were broken, documents shredded, officers' sworn evidence was rejected, unspecified damage was inflicted on the war against international crime, while two police forces spat blood over each other's behaviour, and a thunderous row reached into the offices of the Attorney General and the Director of Public Prosecutions.'

Green, a gang leader in Kingston, had fled to Britain from Jamaica in February 1991 while on bail for shooting with intent to kill. In London, he fell in with crack-dealing former associates, carrying a gun to protect them. But then a couple of months later, arrested for a minor traffic offence in Brixton, he decided to turn informant. His handler was a Brixton detective, one of the trio of officers praised by Clark in his report for their skills in cultivating informants. Green was paid up to £1,000 a time for his assistance, and he was certainly prolific, supplying over the next two years 168 detailed intelligence reports with the names and activities of every

Jamaican he knew. But while informing he was himself dealing crack and using his gun. On one occasion he was arrested after being shot and discovered with two rocks of cocaine in his pocket. The case never got to court. Although arrested for at least two other drugs offences, he was not charged. A woman interviewed for *World in Action* said she saw Green smash his gun into an African dealer's mouth before stealing his cash and an ounce of cocaine. She says he was often to be seen sitting in a local gambling house with his gun in front of him, selling and stealing as he pleased.

Nottingham police were furious that such a notorious gunman and crack dealer had apparently been allowed such freedom, and to operate out of London in their area. They complained about the withholding of evidence by the Met. The trial judge agreed that Scotland Yard had failed to pass on key intelligence and, during the run-up to the trial, had misled the Nottingham officers, the Crown Prosecution Service (CPS) and also himself. Of the five defendants, one was jailed for fourteen years, another for eight, and two others, although acquitted, were deported to Jamaica. Eaton Green's role as informer was revealed in court and he was given a reduced sentence of six years.

Meanwhile, another similar case of a badly handled informant also hit the headlines. The same police team handling Eaton Green also recruited the new man, Delroy 'Epsy' Denton. But this time the informant carried out a far worse crime than robbery. He committed a frenzied murder. Delroy Denton was a posse leader in the Spanish Town district of Kingston, and had a history of extreme violence including an allegation that he had used an ice-pick to murder a prostitute. He jumped bail and fled to England, but was arrested in Brixton for possessing a gun and a small amount of drugs. He gave a false name, but under questioning his true identity and past emerged, and he was found to have entered the country illegally. Just like Eaton Green before him, Denton struck a deal. He would provide information on Jamaican gangsters if he was permitted to stay. The police and immigration agreed and he was allowed to remain while he tried to gain political asylum.

For several months he delivered the goods. But then he got

into trouble. Denton was arrested and charged with the rape of a fifteen-year-old schoolgirl. The case was dropped. Then came more disaster in April 1995 when Denton raped and stabbed a 24-year-old woman to death, slashing her throat eighteen times. Marcia Lawes was the mother of two children, and this time there was no escape for Denton. At his trial he was described as a 'sex-fuelled psychopath' and 'Premier League danger to the public', and he was jailed for life in 1996. Later it emerged that the police had known he was unstable and had boasted about killing no fewer than seven women in Kingston.

The two cases, Green and Denton, caused outrage in the black communities of London and further afield. In south London a campaign started for an inquiry into the Yard's handling of Denton and for compensation for Marcia Lawes's family, who also complained to the Police Complaints Authority. Police attempts to calm what was becoming a volatile situation only made things worse when they attended a public meeting in Brixton. It was organised by an umbrella group, the Lambeth Community-Police Consultative Group, and was chaired by Nicholas Long, who warned of escalated tension in the area with the possibility of rioting. Another member, Lee Jasper, the black chair of the civil rights group the 1990 Trust told me that a senior police officer had given a bizarre speech to those at the meeting, most of them black and very angry that Marcia Lawes had died at the hands of a serious Jamaican criminal specially imported by the Met: 'This officer said that recruiting Yardie informants was a public service and they were doing great work and were a valuable asset in the fight against crime. The audience went berserk. It was a fundamental mistake by the Met.'

Jasper and Long put pressure on the Met to change their system. Belatedly realising the seriousness of the situation, Scotland Yard set up a working party to review their handling of informants, with Jasper and Long the only two non-police officers on it. Jasper said:

'We delved deep into the informants issue and found the police recruited all kinds of characters. These guys were then going back into the black community and saying, "If anybody grasses me up, I'll find out and kill you. I'll do this because I'm working hand-in-hand with the police. I've got police backing – police protection." A whole fear was generated in the black community. People were saying, "Hold on, here's a complete psychopath – he's out on the road, claiming police protection. He's been arrested for crimes and he's been freed. It must be true." I gave an example to the police of how this worked. If you're a single mum living next to a crack house, and the dealer says, "If anyone reports me on this landing, I'll find out who it is," and when he is reported – whether to the police or Crimestoppers – he's taken into Brixton police station and he's back on the street in the afternoon selling crack, that has a most corrosive effect on the trust and confidence of the black community in the police. People were like frightened deer trapped in the headlights, between the criminals and the institutional racism of the police service. That was reflected in the police over-emphasis on using informers in the black community to counter what they saw as a wall of silence.

'The police had alienated the black community because they didn't have a strategy. They saw it as "them and us". They were incapable of engaging in any real trust with the community. What they relied on instead was this broad swathe of unethical active criminal informants. And they had no real management of what was going on. PCs were trying to stabilise gangs by arresting, not arresting, cutting deals, and playing games with petty low-life criminals. That led to reinforcement of the view well known in the black community that the police were not only racist but corrupt as well, particularly round drugs. There was a smell emanating from corruption cases that police were involved in high-level drug distribution. The institutional racism came when PCs on the street arrested black people for not showing due deference to the blue uniform. Then there were black deaths in custody. All that made a powerful cocktail of related issues that left the black community thinking these people [police] are not interested in justice at all. They're part of the problem, not the solution. People thought the police don't give a monkeys whether they kill us or whether we kill ourselves. That's how racist they are.'

Jasper's colleague, Nicholas Long, said confirmation of the view that the police were racist was coming from the way it was handling two separate cases. The first involved the stabbing to death of Rachel Nickell on Wimbledon Common. Although her murder had been in 1992, the investigation was still receiving a massive amount of publicity, and many in the black community said this was because she was young, attractive, and, most importantly, she was white. No one was too interested when young blacks were being gunned down. Further confirmation that the police were racist was coming from the Met itself over the murder of the black teenager Stephen Lawrence. Late in 1997, the Police Complaints Authority's inquiry reported, roundly condemning the Met for its murder investigation. The Macpherson inquiry, set up by the Home Secretary, had also started and it too was hearing evidence of police racism and corruption.

It was in this poisonous atmosphere in south London that the dreadful murder of Avril Johnson occurred, as described in this book's introduction. Her shooting, cowering on a mattress in front of her two children, shocked the black community, which demanded action from the police. When her sickening death was followed by two equally vicious murders in different parts of London, the Met grasped the opportunity to show people that it recognised its failings to ethnic minorities. They put extra resources into the hunt for the killers. However, they had a major problem. They did not have the faintest idea who was responsible.

The Met had been compiling information about black murders and shootings in south London through a secret intelligence cell which also used informants. But none of these regular, paid grasses came up with any names, which appeared to show the ineffectiveness of a policy relying on informants. Lee Jasper was in no doubt: 'Police intelligence at that time was no good. They were extremely naive, taking what they were told by informers as being true. They hadn't a clue what was going on. They couldn't see the wood from the trees.' Heading the investigation was DCI Steve Kupis who appealed for help from criminals. What was also needed was help from the local black community, and the police were to get that from the very same local activists who had previously been such severe critics. People such as Lee Jasper realised that a joint effort was the only way to confront the problems caused by crack and black gun gangs. He and the police had worked together on trying to resolve the informant problem and he knew and trusted DCI Kupis. 'We could see that the police appeared to be serious about catching these killers,' he said. 'But few among them said "we give our word that we want to do something". Steve Kupis did.'

Police and blacks started to work together. The wording of some police posters and leaflets was changed so they were made more appealing to the black community. Local leaders toured the area asking for help, standing shoulder to shoulder with those wearing police uniforms. In mid-July, local black activist Mike Franklin spoke at a public meeting in Brixton, calling on people to pass information to police. When someone in the audience shouted that this would mean acting as informers, and that 'they will come and kill us', Franklin replied that it was time to stand up and be counted. Lee Jasper, until then seen as the arch anti-police militant, appeared at a Scotland Yard news conference later in the month, after the third murder. He said: 'Three families were shattered and another couple left traumatised by this gang. It is time for the black community to stand up and be counted. This gang has committed wildcat robberies using lethal force. This level of callousness is not acceptable to the black community. We are witnessing a terror campaign.'

As well as featuring community involvement, the police investigation also highlighted other issues – the ease with which suspects could enter the UK under false names, and their use of mobile phones, a factor which was to play an important role in inquiries. What was not then publicly revealed by the police was that Avril Johnson's killers, as well as stealing cash and jewellery, had also taken a mobile phone. Also undisclosed was that police were linking the attack with a terrible rape and attempted murder ten days before in Clapham, during which another mobile phone was stolen. Another important clue came during the second in the murder series, when Michelle Carby was shot three times in the back of the head at her home in east London. Her house had been ransacked and jewellery stolen. One piece taken was a particularly distinctive bracelet with the name 'John' engraved on it. Police appealed for help in finding it. The next murder, that of Patrick Ferguson in Kingsbury, north-west London, was linked to the first two through ballistic evidence. The same gun had been used in all three killings.

Meanwhile, the police were making progress in tracking down the gang of three or four men thought responsible for the terror attacks, but they were hampered by the Met's then organisation. These were the days before the setting up of a London-wide Operation Trident, so although there was an overall head to the investigation, it was run from three separate incident rooms, one for each of the murders. Inevitably, there were communication and coordination problems. 'Holding that information together and dealing with it was a mammoth undertaking,' Kupis told me. 'If I get cancer of the ear, it was because of all the time I spent on the phone. We couldn't discount anything. It's the golden rule. But it was difficult, looking for people when we only had possible street names, and when we never really got the full truth out of anyone. We got there in the end and it was with a bit of luck too.'

The first good lead came from Kirk Johnson, who had survived being shot at by the attackers who murdered his wife, Avril. In a series of interviews, he said he thought he recognised two of the three men who had burst their way into his maisonette, having seen them with a Jamaican he knew only by his two street names, Junior and Lyrics. He said this man was being driven in a white Renault Clio by a cripple, whose name he did not know. The next time he saw the two men they were with the cripple and they told him that Lyrics had been arrested.

Armed with the information, vague as it was, the detective team searched their intelligence database and asked their informants if they knew either of the men described. They learned that there was some connection between the killers' gang and an earlier robbery at a Caribbean restaurant in Tottenham. There was also said to be a link between that robbery and Michelle Carby, the second murder victim, shot in the back of her head as she sat tied to a chair at her east London home while her three children slept upstairs. The suggestion was that the robbers had tried to get her to act as an alibi or witness for them, but she had refused. Confirmation of that angle came when a full search of her house turned up a letter from a solicitor raising the question of her appearing as a witness. Police also discovered a further possible connection. One of Michelle Carby's boyfriends apparently knew Avril Johnson. Further research resulted in the police obtaining the street names of four suspects, including Pepe, and a man known as Irone, a street name involving word-play on a punishment weapon – a hot iron used for branding victims.

The mobile phones stolen in the first two attacks provided crucial evidence. Checks with the telephone companies showed the one taken during Avril Johnson's murder had been used over the following few hours to make over thirty calls to Jamaica and the USA. Two of those numbers called matched numbers called by the phone stolen in the first attack, the rape and attempted murder. One call was to the girlfriend or babymother of a man who became one of the main suspects. Lee Jasper and Nicholas Long, members of the Lambeth Community-Police Consultative Group, were briefed on the progress of the investigation, and at their urging a detective went to Jamaica to liaise with the authorities. Inquiries there on the addresses attached to the numbers called, and work in the USA and England, gave fresh clues to the killers' identities.

In a follow-up raid in Clapham, a recently taken photograph of a man called Pepe was found. On one of his fingers was a large ring depicting Africa, identical to one stolen from Avril Johnson's husband Kirk. Pepe had at least two other street names, as did the other suspect, Irone. Earlier, police had identified the 'cripple' mentioned by Kirk Johnson. He was a paraplegic called Adrian Francis, aka Prento, wheelchair-bound since being shot in Notting Hill in west London. Francis had a specially designed car to carry him about. Detectives had been split over his significance, but after further interviews he admitted driving some of the suspects around London. Eventually he confessed to driving them to the Johnsons' home and then a few days later to Michelle Carby's. He claimed to have had no idea what was going to happen at the first address, and that they had forced him to go to the second address. He remembered driving them to other areas, but was vague about precise addresses. Driven around by police, he pointed out various places, amongst them a block of flats in Weir Road, Balham.

The net was closing in on the killers. But although the detectives had the names of the suspects, they did not know where they were and they had no solid evidence against them which would tie them to the terrible attacks. The key breakthrough came at the end of July after a late night review of all the evidence by DCI Kupis and Reg Field, the DI running the Intelligence unit, when they realised the possible significance of the Balham block. That general area was of interest to the detective team because, through cell-phone site checks, it had been identified as the probable area from which the mobile phones, stolen during the rape attack and Avril Johnson's murder, had been used. A surveillance team went there the following morning, and luck was with them. If they had gone a day later, they would have missed some devastating evidence.

The officers saw a woman leave the address and dump a black bin bag outside for collection by dustmen later that day. Searching it, the officers found the distinctive 'John' bracelet, stolen from the second murder victim, Michelle Carby, and the subject of well-publicised appeals by police. There was also a box for a pay-as-you-go mobile phone. Police interviewed the woman and searched her flat. They found that Pepe and Irone had both stayed there, and they picked up leads as to where they had gone.

Kupis learned that Irone was in Handsworth, Birmingham. He sent a description and details to West Midlands police, and then sent one of his own team of detectives there. DS Gary Richardson spotted their target in Handsworth. He decided not to tackle him on his own for fear that Irone would draw a gun and that some innocent passer-by would be injured. Instead, a firearms team was called in. A house in Junction Road was raided on 5th August, and Irone – 28-year-old Hyrone Hart – was arrested. A pair of training shoes was found in the house and forensic examination showed two microscopic spots of blood which matched that of the third murder victim, Patrick Ferguson. Nine addresses in London and the south-east were raided the following day. They included an address in Chingford, Essex, where Pepe, whose real name is Kurt Roberts, was arrested.

At the Old Bailey in December 1999, Hyrone Hart was found guilty of two murders, two attempted murders, two robberies and two charges of possessing firearms with intent. Roberts was convicted of one murder, two attempted murders, rape and two charges of possessing firearms. Sentencing them to life imprisonment, the judge, Neil Denison said: 'I will not waste words on you. Suffice to say your conduct was an affront to civilised society. You were part of what was in effect an execution squad.'

After the case, police said the pair were believed to be part of a nine-strong gang of Jamaicans who had all arrived in the UK at about the same time. One had been deported and the others were all behind bars. Hart and Roberts had little to show for their crimes, living what was described as a 'hand-to-mouth' existence. As to why they picked on their particular victims, police believe that they must have been tipped off that their targets were all involved in the lucrative drugs trade, and that there would be rich pickings at their homes. The killers were mistaken. Only Ferguson was a known dealer.

In July 2000, the paraplegic Adrian Francis, twenty-two, appeared at the Old Bailey admitting the manslaughter of Michelle

Carby, after denying her murder. He said two men had ordered him to drive them to Carby's home, threatening to kill him if he refused. Francis was given an eighteen-month jail sentence, suspended for two years, after the court was told of the help he had given to police investigators, and that, as a consequence, his life would be in danger.

The series of murders also highlighted another problem – the ease with which Jamaican gangsters could enter the UK. Both Hart and Roberts tricked their way into the country, using false passports which were easy and cheap to obtain in Jamaica. With convictions there for violence and escaping from custody, Hart flew into Gatwick using the name Anthony O'Neill Row-botham. Suspicious of him, immigration officers gave him permission to stay for twenty-four hours. However, once inside the country, he disappeared and a few weeks later carried out the first attack. Roberts arrived under the name Joseph Lee, and was given permission to stay for a six-month holiday. As a result of this case and others that followed, the UK was to introduce a much tougher visa system for Jamaican immigrants.

Meanwhile, the south London Lambeth Community-Police Consultative Group had success with their concerns about police informers. Major changes were being brought in to the way informants were recruited and handled. The review group set up following Marcia Lawes's murder and the exposure of the roles of the informants Eaton Green and Delroy Denton, made a report in mid-July 1998. Its report, *Informing the Community*, said there was inadequate training of detectives in dealing with informants, and the proper guidelines were not followed in Denton's case. There would be much stricter controls, including checks on any informant's mental stability. Informants would not be allowed to enter the UK illegally except under 'the most exceptional circumstances'.

However, paid informants were to continue to play a key role. Police said they were vital to countering the drug threat and black gang violence. Informant successes were outlined by the number three in the Met's hierarchy, Assistant Commissioner

Denis O'Connor. They had helped prevent eleven murders in the previous eighteen months, and over the past year they had also led to 1,600 arrests, the seizure of £40 million worth of drugs and seventy firearms. He went on to say that there were thousands of informants helping the Met, with about a quarter of the total being from the black community.

That report was quickly followed by another more far-reaching one from the Chief Constable of Hampshire, Sir John Hoddinott, who had investigated the matter for the Police Complaints Authority. His report slammed into the Met and the Immigration Service for hiring the two notorious gunmen, Green and Denton, and for allowing them such free rein. Sir John held that junior officers had breached laws and regulations, but the CPS decided that prosecutions were not in order. The Hoddinott report and European Human Rights Legislation led to Parliament passing two new laws – the Police Act and the Regulation of Investigatory Powers Act, known as RIPA, which covered surveillance and the use of informants. In came a whole new system governing the handling of the informants, to be known as 'covert human intelligence sources' or CHIS for short. Police forces throughout the country reviewed the informants on their books, ditching many of them, and grading the remainder according to their worth. Lee Jasper told me:

> 'We had two and a half years attacking over the informants situation. We realised that if we wanted to avoid full scale civil disturbances, we had to get into the institution and divert it from its course which would have ended in a murderous riotous situation. We decided that the only way to solve the problem was to intervene in the Met and create a partnership for tackling the issues. It would be a post-McPherson bridge-head to a new style of policing. By working together and emphasising that, the police got more resources, and started getting intelligence through normal channels. Crimestoppers was important here. People had to feel they had a duty

to call and give information. It needed someone to say "that's enough". We did that and then the community felt more comfortable.'

The cooperation in south London between the local community and police over the three murders and rape was to be repeated a short time later north of the Thames in what was becoming another black gun crime hotspot.

'I started selling drugs – everything. You name it, I sold it. You could make money out of it – up to three grand a day, profit. It's hard to tell someone don't do something like that when prior to that they've been struggling... Once you get into the drugs, you have to protect yourself, so you have to get a gun. You feel powerful with a gun.'

Another area hit by a series of murders and shootings was in north-west London – the Harlesden area of Brent. Over the years, incidents there became more serious as crack cocaine took hold. But things started spiralling out of control in 1999 with a shocking killing described as 'a wild-west shoot-out'. Guns blazed after a row over a badly parked car at a community centre that had been opened as a showpiece by the Prince of Wales.

A woman from Brixton had driven to the Brent Council-funded Bridge Park leisure centre but, instead of parking in one of the marked bays, she left her car outside the entrance to the complex. She was asked to park properly by one of the centre's staff, an argument developed and the woman, in a rage, smashed a bottle. Police were called and they escorted her away. However, she returned later, and this time she was with her husband, Dion Holmes, a 29-year-old. He was a member of a black gang, known as the Cartel Crew, and he brought some of them with him. However, word had spread of what had happened, and some of the Lock City Crew, a gang which used the centre, decided to defend their territory and exact revenge for what they saw as disrespect by a rival group from across the Thames.

They armed themselves with guns carried in a sports bag, and locked the doors to the centre, trapping people inside, including children, so they could pick off Holmes. But their plan went wrong when one of them accidentally fired a shotgun, spreading panic through the centre. Another gang member fired a shot, apparently trying to calm the situation down. But it only made things worse and more shots were fired from handguns. In the mayhem, Dion Holmes died, shot through the heart, and two others were injured. Seven people were later charged with murder and firearms offences. Two firearms were recovered. Four Jamaicans were later jailed for life for the murder. Members of the Lock City Crew, they were: Winston Harris, thirty-eight, aka Escobar; Stephen Murray, twenty-six, aka Beamer or Meima; Jermaine Hamilton, twenty-two, aka Mylord; and Leonard Cole, twenty-seven.

Police were shocked to discover the way the centre was run. It had been set up on the edge of the notorious Stonebridge Estate in the 1980s as a place for small businesses, leisure and study, and as somewhere, in particular, for jobless youngsters. Brent Council, the Government, the EU and the Business in the Community Partnership had all ploughed money into it, but there were problems and it went bankrupt in 1992. A community group then started running it, subcontracting security to an outside firm. This resulted in the centre's security being run by a 49-year-old man who had convictions for robbery, burglary and drugs. It appeared that the Lock City Crew kept arms, ammunition and drugs in a private room, and police were told that guns and bullets were regularly to be seen.

As police investigated and made arrests, a possible link was found with the double murder of a couple later in the same month, May. After having breakfast, Laverne Forbes, twenty-eight, was leaving her home in Kessock Close, Tottenham, with her seven-year-old daughter, when two young gunmen tried to get inside. Forbes pushed her daughter to one side and ran upstairs to escape them. But she was shot three times and fell. The gunmen then climbed the stairs and found her partner, Patrick Smith, aka Nookie and, forcing him to his knees, shot him in the head. The two men then ran to a car which screeched off. The seven-year-old girl ran into the street, screaming: 'My mummy and daddy have been shot.' Both parents were taken to hospital but Smith died later that same day, followed by Forbes nearly twenty-four hours later.

Police learned that one of the two gunmen could have been involved in the community centre shooting, and that there were two possible motives for the double murder. Smith owed money over a drug deal, and he was also being blamed for not returning a gun. His killer is thought to have lent the gun to him, but he lost it to rubbish collectors! The story picked up by detectives was that Smith had hidden the weapon in a rubbish bin for safekeeping when he went for a night out. But he had enjoyed himself so much that he did not return home until late the next morning, by which time the bin had been emptied by dustmen.

Two days after the double murder, there was another fatal shooting in Harlesden. Adrian Roberts, twenty-three, who had three street names – Buds, Blessed and Popeye2, was visiting a friend's flat at a bail hostel in Greenhill Road, close to Harlesden High Street. Four men entered the flat in the evening, intent on stealing drugs and money. Roberts was forced to lie face down on the bed and was then shot in the back. Police obtained the names of four suspects and, in follow-up searches, found two imitation firearms and a shotgun. A handgun was recovered from a vehicle at the dead man's funeral.

Just hours after Roberts's murder, one of the suspects, Clayton King, aka Loose, was himself shot dead in a revenge attack. Those responsible were thought to belong to the Kick Off Head Crew. King had gone to a Harrow Road nightclub, the Palm Beach, and left at 2.45 a.m. in his car with a friend, Marlon Abrams, aka Chuggie, along with a couple, a man and woman. With King at the wheel and Abrams in the front passenger seat, the couple were dropped off at an address close to the bail hostel. King and Abrams then drove on to Acton Lane, but they were ambushed as they stopped at traffic lights. King's car was sprayed with bullets fired from another vehicle, and he was hit five times. Although Abrams was also injured, he managed to drive the car to a nearby hospital, but King was already dead.

Information reaching police suggested that one of those responsible for King's death was a friend of the murdered Adrian Roberts. That suspect was also thought to be responsible for another Harlesden murder just over two weeks later. The victim was Henry Lawes, aka Erol Allen with a street name of John Joe. He was walking along St Mary's Road in the middle of the afternoon when a group of men started chasing him. Lawes tried to escape, but stumbled as he ran off. He fell to the ground and was shot in the head, neck and hand. Apart from one of the suspects being linked to King's murder, police could find no other connection or motive for Lawes's murder. He had not been suspected of involvement in the Roberts murder.

All these shootings and murders shocked the local community. The first in the series at the Bridge Park centre had particular ramifications for the local authority, Brent, because of the money and resources it had ploughed into the project. A public meeting was called in Harlesden by Brent Council and the police. Although fairly extensively advertised, no one had any idea how many people would turn up. There was concern that people might even be too frightened to show their faces at an affair aimed at putting a stop to the gun violence. As it was, the meeting was packed out, with council leaders reassuring the locals that they and the police were as one in dealing with the problem.

One of the meeting's organisers told me:

> 'It was heavy. People were coming in off the streets with lots of concerns and they were emotional, venting their spleen about the situation and the police. I can remember the parent of one gun victim complaining that their son had been treated like a drug dealer by the police. They were tarring everyone with the same brush, even when they were victims. There was also a march through Harlesden organised by the Nation of Islam, and to see the police escorting it, stopping traffic, and handing out leaflets of support was amazing. It showed excellent cooperation between opposite ends of the spectrum, and that whatever the differences, there was a need for people to work together.'

The growing cooperation between the black community and police in north-west London was matching what had been achieved south of the river. This new collaboration led to Brent being given special Home Office funding of around £1.5 million and the formation of the Not Another Drop campaign, of which more later.

Meanwhile, shootings continued in the area throughout 1999, with another gun murder in July. Although the victim, Dean Roberts, was unrelated to Adrian Roberts, he had convictions and was himself a suspect for murders two years before. It was about ten o'clock on a Monday night when the killers struck. Dean Roberts, aged twenty, was out and about in Harlesden dealing drugs from a hire car, a red Mercedes. As he drove up a slight hill in Furness Road a car came down towards him. Both cars stopped and while the two drivers chatted together, two men came down the hill on foot. They dragged Roberts from his car and he was shot four times in the face and abdomen.

At first, police treated the driver of the other car as a witness. He told them that he knew Roberts and had stopped to talk to him. Police wondered whether there was any connection between the murder and the killings two years before for which Roberts was a suspect, and they got their answer from more than one source. A nineteen-year-old, Ricky Sweeney, was named as one of the gunmen, and the motive was believed to be revenge. He and Roberts had been friends until two years earlier when Sweeney's brother, Rudi King, was shot dead, followed the next day by the murder of his best friend Marcus Charles. Both men were twenty-two. Although no one was prepared to give evidence against Sweeney for Roberts's murder, he was arrested. Predictably, he gave a 'no comment' interview and with insufficient evidence to charge him, he had to be released.

Detectives believed Sweeney was a leader of the Lock City Crew, the gang that had caused mayhem at the Bridge Park centre earlier in the year. They also knew he had a girlfriend called Sophie Lewis, but they made no approach to her to determine what she knew about the murder, if anything. That was to change, however, after they had a lucky break, and learned that the couple had split up acrimoniously. An off-duty police officer saw Sweeney trying to drag Lewis into his car in front of a parade of shops. The officer intervened, preventing what appeared to be an attempted abduction. He took names and ran them through police systems, discovering that Sweeney was 'flagged' to the murder investigation team. Told of what had happened, the murder detectives decided to approach Lewis, a bank clerk.

It was clear the young woman knew something about Sweeney and the murder, but she was very reluctant to help the police. However, her father, who was in prison for drugs offences, persuaded her to make a statement. What she told police provided devastating evidence against her former boyfriend. Lewis named two people and claimed the driver of the other car was also involved. Police started to tap their phones. Later the following month they found a pistol, silencer and ammunition. Describing what had happened after Dean Roberts's murder, Lewis said Sweeney arrived at her address with friends. He changed his clothes and then told her he had killed Roberts, but had made a mess of it. He was worried because he had left a McDonald's drink carton at the scene, and his fingerprints or DNA could be on it. In fact, police had retrieved a drink container at the murder scene, but had not released the information. The fact that Lewis knew about it convinced them she was telling the truth. The carton had already been to the forensics laboratory for testing, but it appeared that an officer had failed to submit a blood sample from Sweeney for comparison. That was discovered, misplaced, in a fridge. When further testing was carried out, Sweeney's DNA was found on the drinking straw. He was arrested and charged, and again made no comment.

There were other shootings and murders in the Harlesden area of Brent following Dean Roberts's murder, which are outlined later in this chapter. But the Sweeney case is important and worth a detailed look. As the case proceeded through the courts, it took a dangerous turn – one that led to the main police witness almost losing her life twice – provoking concern and embarrassment for the Met. The protection of witnesses was then, and continues to be, the main plank of its pitch to the black community to give information and evidence about gun crime – a guarantee that it would offer sufficient protection to witnesses, so that those they are giving evidence against are unable to get back at them, by intimidating them or their families to such an extent that they change their minds and withdraw from the case. What happened to Sophie Lewis should be recounted because it had such a dramatic effect on events. Although she was labelled 'the bravest woman in Britain', even five years later black people were continuing to quote her experience, putting it forward as being a reason for being wary of talking to the police.

After the murders of Dean Roberts and other gun crime victims, police received intelligence that Jamaican gangsters were sending gunmen to the UK to carry out reprisal shootings. Meanwhile, to protect her identity, Sophie Lewis was given a pseudonym by police. But as part of the legal process, her statement and other papers were disclosed to the defence, and they contained such an amount of detailed information that Sweeney was able to work out that it was his former girlfriend who would be the main prosecution witness against him at his trial, then just weeks away. He hatched a plot to silence her.

One of his associates, Shimie Youngsam, aged nineteen, had been to school with Lewis. Sweeney, held in prison on remand, got Youngsam to telephone her and she agreed to meet him. After getting into his car, Youngsam drove off with her and, after turning into a dark alley, he jumped from the car. Waiting in the shadows was a second man, Trevor Hamilton, aka Little T, one of Sweeney's closest associates. He approached with a 9 mm handgun and fired five shots. The defenceless Sophie Lewis, on the ground, was hit four times, in the head, face, shoulder and hand. But something was wrong with the gun, and Hamilton was himself hit in the arm. Taken to hospital, he was arrested and charged with attempted murder. Two days later Youngsam was also arrested and charged.

Amazingly, Sophie Lewis survived the attack and, far from silencing her, she seemed to police to be more determined than ever to give evidence against her former boyfriend. She did so and, in March 2001, Sweeney appeared at the Old Bailey and was found guilty of murdering Dean Roberts. Judge David Stokes described it as a 'cold-blooded assassination' and sentenced Sweeney to life imprisonment. By then Lewis had been given a new identity under the police witness protection scheme. But her ordeal was far from over.

Police picked up street talk that Sweeney had taken out a £20,000 'contract' to have her killed. Five months after Sweeney's jailing, still due to give evidence against the men who had tried to kill her, Youngsam and Hamilton, she went to Jamaica to see some of her family. And while there, another attempt was made on her life. As she was being driven to the airport for a flight back to the UK, five shots were fired from a car which drew alongside hers. She was hit by two bullets, one in the arm and the other in her chest. Another person in her car was hit in the neck. Once again, Lewis survived. Her attackers were never caught, so whether this was a revenge 'hit' on Sweeney's behalf, or an attempt to stop her giving evidence against Youngsam and Hamilton, is not known. If the latter, it failed.

Sophie Lewis appeared at their trial and both were convicted of attempted murder and each sentenced to eighteen years. Judge Martin Stephens said: 'This jury has convicted on overwhelming evidence in a truly appalling crime striking at the very heart of the proper administration of justice. A woman who showed exceptional courage appears to give evidence in a grave case of murder [Dean Roberts], so you two hatched your ruthless plot to do nothing less than execute her.' Describing Lewis as one of the bravest women in Britain, the detective in charge of the cases, DCI Julian Headon, said: 'This shows what can be done if people are prepared to stand up to these gunmen as Sophie Lewis has done. She has done more for the black communities of London than any of the well-publicised people we hear about.'

The next killing in the area was on 15th August. O'Neal Laylor, aka Chicken, was holding a pay party in a second floor flat in a block on the Kilburn estate. At 3.15 in the morning, with the party still in full swing, a masked gunman walked in brandishing a Glock pistol with a laser sight. He headed for Laylor who tried to escape over the flat's balcony. But he was shot twice, sending him over the balcony wall to the ground outside, two floors below. He was heard calling out for help, but the gunman showed no mercy. He went down the stairs and, finding Laylor still alive, made sure of his death by shooting him three times in the head. Finding no firm motive for the attack, detectives speculated that he may have been mistaken for the boyfriend of the girl he was standing next to at the party.

The same Glock pistol was used in another shooting three weeks later, on 7th September. This time the venue was Willesden High Street and it was the middle of the afternoon. A youth approached his target, a major drug dealer, Owen Clarke, aka Father Fowl. But as he pulled the Glock from the waistband of his trousers, the laser sight caught in his belt. This gave Clarke and his friends just enough time to jump on him. Although the youth managed to let off one shot, hitting Clarke in the hand, he was detained, and later arrested by police.

The man in overall charge of investigations into the spate of shootings in north-west London was Detective Chief Superintendent Dave Cox. Most of the incidents were linked, and two of them involved people from other areas of London – the Bridge Park community centre 'wild west' shooting and the double murder in Tottenham. But at that time there was no London-wide operation dealing with black or Jamaican gun crime, just the intelligence gathering unit being run out of south London. A bluff, hard-working officer, Dave Cox did not mince his words in a series of memos to his bosses at Scotland Yard, calling for more resources. The first was straightforward enough. Two days after the attack on Owen Clarke, Cox wrote:

'We have achieved some notable successes in recovering firearms, and in disrupting further murders and drug dealing. We have also established a number of new and very valuable sources of intelligence, which has been a major factor in the results achieved... The people we are dealing with are dangerous and violent criminals, the support we have received from armed units has been first class. Liaison and joint operations with Brent borough have been an outstanding success. Some risks remain. The killing may not be over. Certainly intelligence suggests that retaliatory murders are planned, and it is largely due to intense police activity that further offences have been disrupted... Much work remains to be done. The evidence chain is fragile, depending often on the word of informers, identification and co-accused who have turned for the prosecution.'

The memo went on to spell out that a huge amount of money had been spent investigating the series of murders, with staff putting in for massive amounts of overtime. In another report, Cox wrote:

'These investigations are characterised by a wealth of information. This has been forthcoming from the community, who are shocked by the violence, and from registered sources... The difficulty is in obtaining presentable evidence. None of the sources who are providing intelligence would consider committing to statements, nor could they be revealed without great danger in many instances. Our strategy has been to move forward by intelligence gathering and surveillance, to identify as many associates and addresses as possible for suspects, to maximise the chance of recovering firearms or forensic evidence from searches.'

Although the memos were written in the autumn of 1999, they could have summed up the position at any time over the next five years. The murders and shootings continued and by the end of the year Cox was complaining to bosses that his team had reached saturation point. The volume of work had resulted in so much tiredness and stress that staff were making mistakes, having arguments, and reporting domestic and health problems.

Looking back at those hectic early days, Cox, nearing retirement from the Met, has a rosier view: 'We were all shattered.

I worked a whole year without leave, every Saturday for six months. They still owe me eighty rest days from that time. But it was still great, because we were working flat out with the best people you could ever be with.' As for those he was targeting, he despairs: 'For them, killing someone is like a schoolyard game, almost like a badge. They tend to be just kids – sixteen to twenty years old. They just don't understand or have the same conception that ordinary people have of the damage caused to the families of those they've shot. They don't care. They have no fear. It's part of their persona. If they don't care, they're more powerful.'

With black gun crime an increasing problem in several different parts of London, the Metropolitan Police did the logical thing and, in July 2000, officially formed the group known as Operation Trident. In fact, Trident had been running for the previous two years – the group based in south London under DCI Steve Kupis. Interestingly, police use of the Operation Trident tag occurred at least a year before its adoption by the Met. Avon and Somerset police had a campaign against drugs called Operation Trident as far back as 1997. Kupis was surprised when I told him I had unearthed the information while researching this book. He said he was unaware of any predecessor and that he and others had thought long and hard about a name, coming up with Trident because it was to be three-pronged – intelligence led, with a separate proactive unit, and reactive teams which investigated shooting incidents. Kupis's unit had been gathering information on Yardies, the name still being used to describe the drug dealing, gun-toting Jamaican gangsters. A database of about two hundred largely Jamaican criminals had been built up and it was Kupis who made the big breakthrough in the Avril Johnson series of murders. But Trident then did not have the operational capability to deal with all black-on-black gun crime in the capital. Instead its role was largely to pass on information to police in other areas of London being plagued by a growing number of black shootings and murders.

The gun crime hotspots continued to be Brixton and its surrounding areas, Harlesden and, over in the north-east of

London, Haringey, with its sprawling Broadwater Farm estate. Next door was Hackney where many gangsters had congregated after arriving from Jamaica. Some reggae clubs there became associated with violence, but some incidents went unrecorded. Police were almost the last to learn of one shooting in which seven people were injured in crossfire. Two men with guns had fought it out at a crowded Orchids nightclub in Kingsland High Street, Hackney. But instead of alerting the authorities, the injured – four men and three women – were taken to hospital in private cars. Police were tipped off by a paramedic, but when they arrived at the club, it was empty – the usual story.

The Orchids incident appeared to have been unplanned, unlike others occurring during a two-month period in the first half of 1999. On 11th April a bouncer at a dance hall in Stratford, east London, was shot dead as people arrived for a show by the Jamaican reggae artist, Beanie Man. Two others were injured by ricochets. Two days later, at lunchtime, a couple of men walked casually into a music ticket agency in Lewisham, south-east London, and blasted the owner, Keith Balfour, in the chest with a sub-machine gun.

A month before, it was estimated that about fifty people had witnessed the fatal shooting of a Jamaican, Mervyn Sills, on a busy street in Brixton in the middle of the afternoon. Very few of the passers-by were prepared to tell the police what they saw. However, three months later, acting on information, police swooped on a car carrying one of the men suspected of murdering the 36-year-old Sills. Armed with machine guns and pistols, the police shot out the car's tyres and hauled out three men, spreadeagling them face down in the road in Kennington. The *Daily Mail* caught the scene in a dramatic photograph which was spread across its front page under the headline 'BRITAIN 1999 – Bronx-style swoop on Yardie murder suspects in a suburban London street'. The accompanying story said Sills' killing was one of thirteen suspected 'Yardie-style' murders, and thirty other shootings in London so far that year: the result of 'a battle for supremacy in the lucrative crack cocaine trade'.

The *Mail*'s use of the term 'Yardie' is interesting. The word derived from the Jamaican slang word for a home – 'yard' – and was much favoured by sub-editors because it summed up Jamaican gang crime in one short stark word. But the *Mail* story accompanying the picture talked of 'Yardie-style' murders, an acknowledgement that the gun-crime situation had changed. It was not just that people in the black community resented the 'Yardie' label. It was accepted that Jamaicans were responsible for many of the shootings and murders. But by 1999, when there was a violent incident, no one could be sure which black ethnic group was involved – Jamaican, British-born blacks or those of African origin. The reality was that British blacks were in the ascendancy – including people such as Wayne Rowe.

Rowe, a heavily built black man, was born in south London of Jamaican parents who arrived in England in the late 1950s. In 2000, two months before Operation Trident's official launch, he came out of prison having been inside for four years for possessing a Mac-10 machine-pistol. Softly spoken, he told me Jamaican and British-born blacks' cultures were different, but the two groups did not keep apart:

> 'I'm British but I grew up with Jamaican culture, and I get along with them fine. A lot of the youth now are not growing up with that Jamaican culture. They're growing up with British culture. I can walk into a room full of Jamaicans and you wouldn't know I was British. I can fit right in. British-born can't do that. A lot are not up with their culture. They're lost. They ain't got no culture. All they know is the street. I'm surprised with some of them – how uneducated they are about a lot of things. I don't mean education in the formal sense – I mean education about where they're coming from, their heritage. I will say that a lot of Jamaicans have come here and did things that got them a bad name and everyone labels them Yardies – the Yardies did this, the Yardies did that. Lots of times the Yardies weren't doing it, but they were still getting the blame for it. The English guys were doing it.'

Known as Fathead after a reggae musician, Rowe described growing up on the Stockwell Park estate close to the heart of Brixton. His experience was common to many of those being looked at by Trident:

'We little kids grew up together, and stuck together. You'd look after each other. You come out of the door and everyday you'd see the same people, and you hang about and start doing things together. We weren't necessarily the hardest, but we were hard. I grew up knowing most of the gangsters in my area and most of the gangsters knew my friends. When I was about thirteen, I started nicking things, sweets, going into shops, putting drinks into my pockets, silly things. Then I moved onto cars, nicked everything: stereos and the cars themselves. The older you get the greater your needs. Society puts a lot of pressure on you by the way things are portrayed. TV adverts tell you to get this, get that. Adidas trainers, but when you get to the shop, the trainers cost £125. If you're not working, how're you gonna get £125. Then there's peer pressure. If you're with a group of friends and they're all in designer clothes from head to toe, you're not going to be happy.

'Our crew had about fifty youths – about eighteen of them were white guys. You needed money. I started robbing people, pick-pocketing, mugging, robbing cars. But I had principles. I didn't trouble old ladies, or children. I'd be robbing members of other gangs. I'd sometimes be with others and sometimes on my own. I used to take anything. You'd see someone with a nice leather jacket and you'd take the jacket off them. I've seen guys lose their trainers. There are times I felt sorry for them, but I couldn't say anything 'cos if you do it's like you're being soft. You've gone so far in the gang that you can't say things like that. Sometimes you'd just get a fiver and sometimes five grand. You'd be surprised what people have in their pockets.

'Then people started selling drugs – cocaine came into the community. You saw guys driving big cars, having nice clothes, jewellery. I had no job. It's not that I hadn't tried. No one wants to know. I remember one time filling in eighteen or nineteen application forms and not even getting a reply. I started selling drugs – everything. You name it, I sold it. You could make money out of it – up to three grand a day, profit. It's hard to tell someone don't do something like that when prior to that they've been struggling. The bills don't stop coming through the door. It was a hectic life because you had to keep abreast of everything. But I made a lot of money. I could do what I wanted. I could buy what I wanted. I bought sports cars, jewellery, clothes. Some of my friends had Porsches, Mercedes. I got stopped by the police. They would talk about the cars. I'd basically say fuck off – you're only jealous because you're working and you can't buy it. It's a bit of bravado, innit? It's a game, only it's not a game. I didn't get caught because I had survival techniques. I wouldn't have anything [drugs] in the car – no way. Because of the way the estate is set up, I'd park my car up and do the business. I would only deal on the estate, not off it. Mobiles have been one of the greatest assets of drug dealers. This went on for four or five years.

'I was making up to three grand a day, but that's nothing to what these guys are making now. That's what's escalated all the gun violence. Back in those days you'd just get on with it. The guns weren't an issue. You didn't have to go there. Back in those days if you disrespected me, I'd knock you out, or if you had a row, you'd have a fight for the next couple of days and then somebody would stop it. But now no one's into that no more. The shootings started around then, and it just got gradually worse. Once you get into the drugs, you have to protect yourself, so you have to get a gun. You feel powerful with a gun. It goes throughout society. Guns are power. The guy from the street gets ridiculed for carrying guns and there's been a lot of shit with them, but George Bush and Tony Blair are using them under a legal guise. It's as simple as who's got the biggest gun has got the most talk. Who's got the most money has got the most talk.

'I've had many guns – sawn-offs, handguns, magnums – you name it. We had everything. We weren't swapping them around, but if the situation arose and you was my mate and you come to me for a gun, you'd get it. They were real proper guns. On a few occasions I've been close to being shot, but I was never actually hit. They've missed me by a few millimetres. I've seen other people shot. They were chaotic situations. Something's happened – then guns are being popped off. This is in clubs and on the streets, not when I was dealing. I never really encountered any problems when dealing because I wouldn't deal with just anyone. There's a greed for money that sometimes lures people to do business with people that they haven't done business with before, and they can't trust. That's when the problems start. I did business with people I'd known for years.

'It's basically like this. You're living in an environment where everyone's making crazy money. You're living on tenterhooks. The other gangsters know what you're doing so you're on your Ps and Qs all the time. You don't know who's gonna come through your door. You could be driving down the road and someone wants to cut you off in the road and rob you. A gun becomes part of your life. It's your protection. It would put people off who might want to take things off you. I was never robbed. I had a reputation because of where I grew up. But a lot of people round me got robbed.'

In 1999, out of the total of twenty-six gun murders in London, eighteen involved the black community. With no let up in black gun crime incidents in the early part of the following year, Operation Trident officially went London-wide in July 2000, with DCS Dave Cox in charge. Some of the community activists who had been advising and helping police in south London formed the nucleus of the Trident Independent Advisory Group (TIAG) covering the whole of the capital. Its chair was Lee Jasper, who by that stage was an adviser to the Mayor, Ken Livingstone.

'My friends and neighbours know I'm a cop but they simply cannot comprehend what we're dealing with. When I leave home for work, it's like I'm going to another planet.'

Operation Trident's declared brief was to tackle 'black-on-black drugs and gang related violence'. Gone was the word 'Yardie', which police now recognised was seen as a derogatory term for the wider black community. Trident's official launch date was 24th July, 2000. Five days later, there came another dramatic reminder of what the police were up against. Unusually, there was a warning of what was to come, but it was too vague for the police to take pre-emptive action. All that Brixton police were told in a telephone call just before midnight on 30th July was that 'Yardies' were preparing for a gunfight at around two to three a.m. that night. Then the caller rang off.

Shortly before two o'clock, two gunmen fired shots into a crowd outside Chicago's nightclub in Peckham High Street, south-east London. The club had been hired for the night and featured a Jamaican sound system. Eight black people were hit, five of them young women. One was hit in the arm and chest. A man had serious chest wounds. Stray bullets hit a passing all-night bus. No one was killed, but the injuries included bullet wounds to chests, arms, shoulders and legs. Passers-by described fleeing in terror from the nightspot. One eyewitness, who did not want to be named, said: 'I heard the gunshots and ran away to hide, and when I came out there were two women on the floor screaming. One of them had been shot through the arm and it looked like it had gone straight through and hit her side. The other woman had been shot in the leg.' Another witness was treated in hospital for shock after seeing the attack as he drove past.

It was an alien world for many of the detectives drafted in to Trident, and it remained so for many, even after a long time working there. One experienced sergeant burst out his frustration to me at the Old Bailey. He had calmly and confidently given his evidence against a man accused of gunning down a rival drug dealer one hot summer evening. But I saw this hardened detective flinch for a moment as he glanced across at the defendant while leaving the witness box. Still clearly agitated several minutes later, I asked him what had happened:

> 'I saw that bastard [the defendant] make the sign of a gun with his fingers. He mouthed 'mum' at me and then pretended to fire – he was threatening to kill my mother. I just can't understand the mentality. I'm white and live outside London in a nice area. My friends and neighbours know I'm a cop but they simply cannot comprehend what we're dealing with. When I leave home for work, it's like I'm going to another planet.'

Trident operates out of three anonymous-looking office buildings which look as though they were built in the 1960s or '70s. Its headquarters are in Putney in south-west London, behind entrance doors made of darkened glass. The building is shared with the Met's anti-corruption group, which tackles the endemic problem of bent coppers. No signs advertise its presence, and there's nothing to indicate the use of Trident's other bases. South London is covered from a building near Clapham Common. The north London base is in West Hendon, near the Brent Cross shopping centre, conveniently close to the junction of the M1 and the North Circular Road.

Inside, at first glance, they look like many other offices, untidiness surrounding the desks and computer screens. Detectives of inspector rank and above tend to have their own individual offices while most of the others are in open-plan areas. The walls show that these people are engaged in very serious business. Instead of the normal calendars and pictures, there are 'wanted for murder' posters as well as charts, diagrams and boards listing the murders and shootings being worked on, and the links between them. The personnel are different too. Women detectives are few and far between on Operation Trident, and the proportion of black officers in evidence is lower than expected, a level for which the Met has been criticised.

Intelligence continues to be the most important of Trident's three-pronged approach. The Intelligence team passes on information to the two other Trident groups. The information is used by proactive detectives as they target suspects, and by reactive officers investigating gun murders and shootings. But gathering that intelligence in the first place is difficult because Trident crime is seen as disorganised and chaotic, not only because of the lifestyle of those involved, but for other reasons too. Shootings can occur without any kind of planning or preparation. Even a perceived slight can provoke someone into producing a gun. Gang structures and areas are also fluid.

Some of the gang names have Jamaican origins. The Alligator Crew is based on Hannahtown in Kingston. Brixton is sometimes called Little Tivoli, after the Tivoli Gardens area of the Jamaican capital. In south London, most of the Peckham Boys are of African origin. Lewisham's Ghetto Boys come from a mix of African and Caribbean families. Covering Brixton and Lambeth is the PDC – the Peel Den Crew. Some split from the PDC to form the Muslim Boys. Most of the London gangs north of the Thames are British-born. There are the Hackney Boys and the Tottenham Man Dem (or TMD). Further out to the north-east are the Beaumont Boys and Chingford Hall Boys. Brent gangs are more likely to be Jamaican based, particularly the Lock City Crew and Luv'n'money.

Using Hackney as an example, one detective involved in gathering intelligence in north London said there are gangs on all the estates: Clapton, Pembury and London Fields and so on, and they break down into smaller groups, with the names changing all the time. He said:

> 'It's difficult trying to keep track of them, but at the end of the day they all belong to Hackney. They can pop

at one another, without it having any impact on us, the police. We don't necessarily know about these shooting incidents. Each small group does its own thing. If necessary, the hierarchy in each group can come together for a common purpose. The older ones do have an impact on us, with their higher level criminality. The younger ones are more low-level, the street-dealing type. When they get older there's more rank structure. They have the business on that estate. There's no direct conflict unless there's a beef, when they all work together. When you put people away [in prison] the groups re-form. If you take someone out, they change and adapt. Take one out and they all move up the pecking order.'

Gang disputes may be small-scale rivalries on an estate, but others are bigger and more longstanding, such as the one between the TMD and the Hackney Boys. The detective told me:

'Some hatreds remain for a long time. Nine-tenths of them forget what started it, but something did, and then it's tit-for-tat and there's no exit. They feel they have to do something about the cause. Take the TMD versus Hackney – they won't forget a dead man. They have to be seen not to be weak. If they roll over, it's open season on them. All groups, whether they're big or small, adopt the same tactics – trying to make money to maintain their lifestyle. If someone threatens them they have to do something about it. You get young kids growing up together and as they become older they get more trusted. There are no gang initiations, not like you get with some in the US. You don't have to slit a wrist and share blood or anything like that.'

There is no disagreement on black gang structures between the north and south London Intelligence teams. One of the south team told me at its Clapham base:

'The groups we're interested in tend to have ten to fifteen active members. There can be another fifteen to twenty in the background, providing safe houses, keeping a watch out for police or a strange car. Everyone knows everyone else on some of these streets. It makes it difficult for us if we want to watch someone from a nearby property. When we ask someone for help, whether we can use their house for observations, we don't give too much away. The worry is that people can agree, but they could be playing us and an hour later, trot down the corridor and tell the target. The common thread is that they'll have known each other since schooldays. Some of the larger group in the background can be older ones, brought up in Brixton and then moving further out. But they'll stay in contact with the area through relatives and friends, and still participate.

'It is fluid, people from one group linking up with those from another for a common cause, and then going their separate ways. It's summed up well with the one word "disorganised". White criminals are more organised, leading a more structured lifestyle. But these guys never sleep at the same time, they don't have the same girlfriend, and don't drive the same car. They go abroad. They use different phones with different SIM cards. They go to different hire companies for vehicles and give different addresses. They're eighty-five per cent disorganised, but they're very streetwise. You never know what they're doing at any one time. They can bump into someone at a nightclub, put in a call to a team, and then the guy gets shot. Hence their need for body armour. You can get it quite legally. Just put "body armour" into a computer search engine and see what comes up.'

I did just that later, using Google, and it showed 657,000 references to body armour. All those on the first few pages were advertising different qualities of stab and bullet-proof jackets.

One major problem facing Operation Trident Intelligence officers trying to keep track of suspects' movements concerns loose family relationships. Many of their targets have come from one-parent families, a factor that many believe may lead to children, usually boys, becoming involved in criminality, especially when, as is usually the case, it is the father who is the missing parent. There were, for instance, fifteen original suspects in the murder of Damilola Taylor, the black youngster stabbed to death by a gang in Peckham, south-east London. None of these fifteen had a father at home. With few male teachers at primary schools, this can mean no positive male role models for young children. At gun crime conferences, Operation Trident officers use slides to show how a couple who came to Britain from Jamaica in the 1950s, on board the SS *Windrush*, expanded their family over the decades, with many turning to crime. The couple had seven children. Six went on to have children themselves, some of them with more than one partner, making a total, by early 2004, of eighteen grandchildren to that original couple. However, their seventh child has had at least fifteen girlfriends or babymothers, resulting so far in a further twenty-two grandchildren. The expectation is that many of these grandchildren will also turn to crime. One detective said:

> 'It can all get very complicated. They may have four or five babymothers and each of these babymothers can have four or five partners, possibly belonging to different crews. I remember sitting with the wife of a victim in a room and she said the three other women on the other side of the room were her husband's babymothers. It was said as a matter of fact. It's a different way of life. It means that when someone gets shot, and there's talk of brothers and cousins and of it having been a revenge shooting, you have to work out the structure of the family and possible motives, and that can take a long time. South London gang members tend to have babymothers in north London, and they

go to music events in the north, where you tend to get
the second generation gangs, with the first generation
Jamaicans probably still pulling the strings.'

Street names also cause serious difficulties for Operation Trident.

'A Jamaican has a street name from birth, but if they're
in south London, they have a different name, and that
same person has a different name in north London, and
is known by another name in Birmingham. This helps
the target, but it obviously makes it difficult for us. We
can hit him hard in London, but he can still operate in
Birmingham under a different name. The active ones are
full-time criminals, running drugs, robbing, stealing from
other dealers. The British-born are trying to emulate the
Yardies. The only way they think they can gain respect
is by killing and shooting people. The Jamaican and
British-born groups tended to stay apart, but now they
sometimes come together. Even in prison, two groups
can unite and collude together to ensure that the outside
remains stable. When a major dealer is put away, it's like
a major Mafia boss has been put away, but they can still
run things from inside. You can get people from the same
gang all on the same landing. They corner the market
in phone cards and tobacco, so if a new person goes in
there, they can be drawn into the gang structure. Then,
when those foot-soldiers are released they have to do
favours in return outside.'

The confusion often arising over different street names was
illustrated by one senior detective who fished out a pocket organiser.
He told me that it contained 5,335 different street names, with
their real names alongside, when known. The vast majority were
from the Met file, with some from the West Midlands.

'One person can have three or four different street names,'
he said. 'Neighbouring gangs can have people with the same street

names, and the names can change all the time. One London group mimicked all the names of a gang in the West Midlands. I don't know whether this was done as a sign of flattery or to confuse the police.' I asked him about the street name Black. He looked at his machine and said there were sixty different variations on the name. These ranged from 'Black' to 'Blacks' and included 'Blacka', 'Blacker' and also many with other names attached ranging from 'Black Alan' to 'Black Willy' (not short for William).

Telling me about the unpredictability of neighbouring gangs, he said:

> 'They can be socialising one night, and the next night they fall out. It depends how they feel – just depends on their mindset. One day it can be guns out to kill. The next day they're sitting down together. It's gets more complicated because you have key people who can provide guns or drugs. And guns get rented out. Take the London Fields Boys. There's probably fifty to sixty of them, but they break into different groups. There's no leader. These are self-employed entrepreneurs out of one area on one day. Next day they could be with another group. You can have someone who's a member of two or three gangs.'

Generalising heavily, the senior detective went on to talk about the ethnicity of different gangs in London. 'Jamaicans and British-born don't do crime together, or shoot each other. Jamaicans shoot Jamaicans. British-born shoot British-born. In some areas of Jamaica, you have to be a member of a gang, having allegiance to a leader and a political group, and they have strong connections here. You've heard of the sunglasses feud?' He then described how the theft of a pair of sunglasses from one gang member in Kingston led to a series of tit-for-tat shootings there which spilled over to London with further shootings. One of them was the murder of a 23-year-old man who was said to have fled Kingston to avoid the dispute. He was shot dead, hit twice in the neck, in Coldharbour

Lane, Brixton, in December 2000. The Trident officer continued: 'Recently we've had a case where it's suggested that someone was lured back to Jamaica to be murdered. The father was deliberately killed there, because it was known the son here in the UK would return to Jamaica for the funeral. He did so and was killed.'

Another Trident detective working with an Intelligence team told me that as well as retaining links with Kingston, many of the older, more powerful Jamaicans had contacts with North America:

'In a recent search we found UK, US and Canadian passports all for the same person. These are big people with kudos, still having their fingers in class-A drugs, whereas the lower level have to rely on running the drugs themselves or on stealing from others. An organised Jamaican gang will recruit young British-born to return money to Jamaica, and then when they return here they act as mules. Then there are the poor Jamaicans, often women who are mules, the "swallowers". If you put six or seven on a plane with cocaine, you're making so much money that you can afford to lose two or three. We and Customs get tip-offs and it's not beyond possibility that two or three are deliberately sacrificed, informed on to Customs, to divert them from the others who are carrying. Over here they can live in squalor, but it's one hundred per cent better than in Jamaica. We looked at money transfers to the West Indies, amounts of £50. That's a lot of money there. People here were sending these small amounts from several different places, so as not to arouse too much suspicion. They're doing it to fund their families. Poverty is terrible there.

'The mules are often innocents, who don't know what they're getting into.

'Another gang may hijack a courier in a turf war, threaten them that if they don't shit it out, they'll have their insides ripped out. It may never happen, but the fear will induce them to deliver it up. Word then filters back to Jamaica about what happened and then someone says go and shoot the brother/mother or someone in the extended family in Jamaica, to get back at you. In one case there was a drug debt in Jamaica which was not settled. Then the baddies here said they wanted it settled here. It wasn't. So the brother of the man who owed the money was forced to phone his brother in Jamaica, and while he was on the phone to him, he was shot. His brother heard the sound of the shot and the debt was resolved. The injured person was found here – that's how we learned of it. Otherwise we would have heard nothing about it. Sometimes colleagues ask us [in intelligence] why we didn't know such and such. But it's like a big iceberg. You see just the tip. What's underneath, we never hear about.'

Operation Trident's Intelligence Section liaises with other government agencies and has a superintendent on permanent secondment in Jamaica. This officer can do checks there on what is known about those Jamaicans who have attracted Trident's attention here. It is useful, for instance, to know that someone is suspected of five murders in Kingston, because they represent more of a risk than a man who has fled the island out of fear of being killed. Information is also exchanged with Customs and the Immigration Service. Four immigration officers work with Trident, sometimes going on raids with them to gather information on suspected illegal entrants or 'over-stayers'. They also carry out research on anyone identified separately by Trident. This can mean that Met detectives get the option of either continuing with a prosecution or of simply having the arrested person deported.

MI5, MI6 and NCIS, the National Criminal Intelligence Service, also provide intelligence. To protect a source information is often so cleaned up that Trident officers do not know its origin, but they can gauge its strength from codes on their computer systems. Telephone tapping, or 'intercepts' as they are officially termed, can be productive and are more easily monitored than in the 1990s. Officers no longer have to visit NCIS which runs the taps. Instead, updates of a target's conversations are given the following day and, if necessary, 'live-time' information can be passed, virtually simultaneously, to a detective out on a job. Whatever the source, it is looked at to see if it is worth developing. If, for example, it is a tip that someone is supplying firearms, research would be done to find out if there was any supporting evidence. Has the person any previous conviction or a lifestyle suggesting an escalation to guns? Is he associating with Trident suspects or 'nominals' (i.e. number one targets)? Detectives on development teams work on the material, supported by civilian researchers and analysts. They are also looking at other wider long-term matters. Finding out why, for example, there is an increase in the number of crack-houses in an area, or disorder on particular estates. The resulting information is then reviewed and, if it is thought worth taking further action, it can be passed on to local police to deal with, or given to one of Trident's proactive teams who can pursue it in a number of ways. Sometimes urgent action is needed and that can lead to assessment problems.

For instance, information was received at a late stage that gunmen were going to have a shoot-out at the Prince's Trust 'Party in the Park' in 2004. One senior Trident detective told me:

> 'It would have had massive consequences if anything had happened and it turned out that we had been warned. It would have had massive consequences. This was an establishment event. Pop icons were there, supported by Trident and the Met, working for a safer London. It would have been a disaster, so we put in a number of strands. There were armed police at the event. We went to the addresses where many suspects lived. We had spotters on the way to the event and spotters at the venue. Up to the last eleventh hour we were asking whether we had enough people in place to avoid having to recommend that the event be cancelled.

'It's the same with nightclubs. A lot of intelligence is single strand but of such quality that you can't ignore it. Two individuals are said to be going to a club and if they see each other they're going to shoot one another. If you cancel the event, who bears the cost? You have to weigh it up. If you call it off, nothing happens, but you can't prove that something would have happened if it had gone ahead. And if you don't call it off and something happens, then you could be in trouble. You also have to question why people give information in the first place. It could be a jealous rival trying to close a place, or a producer who hasn't sold enough tickets and wants to get it cancelled. It's difficult to work it out.'

He recalled a case in a London borough where there was information that Trident suspects were going to cause trouble at a local nightclub.

'We couldn't ignore the intelligence. But we also knew that particular club was in difficulties. We could either close the club or let the event continue. In fact what we did was to give them free security. We put a vanload of police outside as a deterrent and an ARV [armed response vehicle] could be called in if necessary. Nothing happened. Was anything going to happen or was it that the gunmen were frightened off?'

Infiltration is another tactic which can be deployed by the proactive teams. Trident does not have its own permanent undercover officers, as the areas they would be working in are too risk-laden. They are generally limited in what they can do and the information they get is open to severe question in court cases. They can be so discredited and so much damage done to what was otherwise a good prosecution case, that acquittals can result of those the police strongly believe to be guilty. Instead, Trident uses Met undercover officers only occasionally rather than routinely, and only when thought absolutely necessary.

However, Trident continues to use registered informants, although far fewer than in the 1990s when the system came in for heavy criticism. There are now about twenty Covert Human Intelligence Sources [CHISs] although their number fluctuates. Some get arrested while others move away. They are given a dedicated police contact, a handler, who briefs the informant about an operation, and they are reminded that they are working to strict guidelines. 'CHISs can go to places that cops can't get to,' said the Trident Intelligence officer. 'They can ask questions that police can't. Some people wouldn't talk to cops. But a CHIS can ask "Where's Martin?" and be told, "He's at the coast". With the help of a CHIS we can follow a target's associates and go where he habitually goes.' The detective stressed the lengths to which they will go to protect the informant: 'When we arrest someone we have to be careful because we might expose an informant. If in questioning we told the man we'd arrested that we knew he was going someplace, the man might say to himself, "only one person knew I was going there", and he could take reprisals. We have a duty of care.'

Trident officers also have to be very careful when arresting suspects who could be armed. Trident detectives do not themselves carry guns, although there is an on-going debate about whether there should be a special armed unit within the section. Instead, risk assessments are carried out prior to raids or prolonged surveillance. If the target is believed to be habitually armed, then a Met firearms team with an ARV is called in to help. One senior detective said: 'Armed response teams are in great demand throughout the Met, but there's recognition that because we're involved in gun crime, the only things with greater priority are terrorism and kidnaps. ARVs can be with us for days. We've had jobs where we've had to cancel and then, when they're on again, the ARVs come back. It's completely unacceptable if there's surveillance and someone is shot because there's no response team.'

Armed officers have two options when arresting a known gunman in a property containing other people. They can burst their way in and hope to take the suspect by surprise. The drawback to that tactic is that it could result in police or other people inside the property being injured or even killed. The other option is for the police to do a 'call-out' – control the area, surround it, and then call for those inside to come out one at a time with their hands up. There are three disadvantages to the second option. Escape or throwing a gun from a window is obviously thwarted because the police have surrounded the property but, if there are drugs there, it gives those inside time to flush them down the lavatory. Secondly, a gunman could take one of these people with him as a hostage. The third possibility is 'suicide by cop' – the target bursts from the property firing his gun, knowing that police will open fire and shoot him dead. However, nearly always the preferred option is the 'call-out'.

Trident's intelligence database is made available across London, so that any Met detective can make basic checks on someone who has been arrested or who has become the subject of inquiries. However, about five per cent of the material is deemed too sensitive for general access, often because the information involves someone being worked on by a proactive unit. There are proactive Trident teams on both sides of the Thames investigating long-term suspects. Here again there are problems coping with unpredictability. A senior detective told me:

> 'These people can change their minds in seconds.
> It's difficult to deal with. You can have really good
> intelligence that someone is going to be kidnapped.
> You hear plans are being made – the meeting points,
> who's involved and even the place where the kidnap
> is to take place. You could bet your life savings on it
> being correct. But then you learn that instead of doing
> the kidnap, they're on a river cruise for some hours,
> and have no intention of carrying it through. You have
> to deploy on good intelligence. Only after a couple of
> hours, you learn it's not happening. Then you have
> to make a decision. Do you call it off, or do you stick

with it, because it could still happen soon? Making the wrong decision can cost us very dearly.

'We know they don't want to lose face by not going ahead. How they cope with explaining not doing something they've talked about and planned is something I don't know. You can get a violent person talking about specific incidents, and that represents good intelligence that there's a clear threat to someone's life. These are specific and timely, not hypothetical plans, and then we deploy. But then it can turn out that one of the individuals taking part clearly has no intention of doing the job. They can see a girl who's a more attractive option than going to kill someone. But then, as suddenly as it's switched off, it can be switched on again at short notice. Today's no show is tomorrow's hit.

'An intercept doesn't pick up someone's demeanour. Sitting in the bath talking of killing someone doesn't mean that you're actually going to do it. But if they're round the corner, then it probably means, yes, they're going to do it. Sometimes you can get false information, but it doesn't mean that it's deliberate. They could be building up their own reputation, their kudos. You need people who understand that talk's not the best intelligence. You need people who can look behind something and see what's really going on.'

The Intelligence teams develop and produce 'packages' for the proactive sections to work on. One such package pursued in 2000 turned out to be Trident's biggest, longest and most successful operation of its kind.

'There were only ten in the proactive unit and it was manic, very difficult, intense and exciting detective work. We managed to take out some major players.'

Mark Lambie, born in 1971, had a long history of violence, dating back many years. He first faced major allegations when he was just a fourteen-year-old and was charged with being part of the gang that hacked PC Keith Blakelock to death during the Broadwater Farm estate riots in north London. He was reported to have laughed as the case against him and two other juveniles collapsed. He then went on over the years to build up a fearsome reputation for shootings, robbery, kidnap, torture and drug-running. He flaunted gold jewellery, designer clothes and expensive cars, leading the TMD gang. But his influence extended far beyond that area of north London. He forged links and alliances with gangs all over the capital, and beyond.

By 2000, Lambie was viewed by many in the black community as an 'untouchable', and believed by some to possess 'ju-ju powers'. But then he became a Trident target. Several 'intelligence packages' had been given to Trident's newly formed north London proactive team. These outlined the backgrounds of a number of men believed to be sufficiently serious criminals in the black community to warrant major targeting. Foremost among them was Mark Lambie. He was labelled in police-speak 'prom. nom. one' – prominent nominal one. In other words, Trident's number one target. Heading the investigation aimed at finally nailing him was Detective Inspector Peter Lansdown.

Mark Lambie's first major conviction was in 1991 when he was convicted over a gang fight shooting in Holloway, north London. He pleaded guilty to assault causing bodily harm and was sentenced to three and a half years' imprisonment, later reduced by a year. By 1995, intelligence reports had him mixing with west London criminals in Brent and Notting Hill, and involved in a feud with a north London man, Jerome Maddix. There was a drive-by shooting at Maddix's home, and he was murdered the following year in Jamaica. That was followed by what appeared to be a series of tit-for-tat revenge shootings.

In 1996, police believed that Lambie and an associate, Clifford Angol, were behind the shooting and wounding of Kenneth Rowe in Willesden, west London. Rowe declined to help police. That was followed in April of the following year by a strange shooting and murder in what looked like a case of mistaken identity. Three gunmen walked into The Place To Be, a Caribbean restaurant in Kensal Rise, west London, and shouted out that they wanted 'Mark' to identify himself. Mark Lambie was believed to have been in the restaurant, but he kept quiet. Instead, at least two others identified themselves as Mark. One was Mark Spence, an unemployed painter and decorator, who was immediately shot dead. The other, Mark Verley, was shot in the spine and paralysed. He died some time later.

It is not known whether Kenneth Rowe, the Willesden shooting victim, was one of the gunmen at The Place To Be, but six weeks after the shooting there, he was himself shot dead in Mount Pleasant Lane, Upper Clapton, north London. Lambie and Angol, suspects in his earlier shooting, were arrested for his murder, but there was insufficient evidence to charge them. A few days later, Angol was shot dead as he sat in Lambie's BMW outside the Warwick Castle pub in the famous Portobello Road, Notting Hill, at closing time. The gunman pulled up beside him in a yellow car and calmly shot him six times.

During the late 1990s and into 2000 there was feuding between Mark Lambie's TMD boys and the Hackney Boys. Its origins were in the shooting dead of a sixteen-year-old schoolboy, Guydance Dacres, who was studying for his GCSEs. Members of the TMD were believed to have been behind his murder at a private party at Chimes nightclub in Hackney in January 1997. In a revenge attack a few weeks later a group of youths thought to be Hackney Boys hunted down another sixteen-year-old, Kingsley Iyasara, whose street name was Popcorn. He bled to death on the roof of a block of flats after being surrounded, kicked, punched and beaten with clubs and baseball bats, and then fatally shot in the stomach. Six young men, all under twenty, were given prison sentences at the Old Bailey of between four and six years each for conspiracy to cause him grievous bodily harm. 'This was lynch law of a kind that will not be tolerated on the streets of our cities,' they were told by the judge, Graham Boal. 'You all participated in a horrifying act of violence. A posse of a dozen or more hunted him down until he was cornered. Mob violence of this kind must be deterred.'

Two of those convicted were themselves shot dead in separate incidents, shortly after release from prison. In June 1999, Meneliek Robinson, by then twenty, was driving his red BMW convertible in Hackney when it was followed by two motorbikes, each carrying two black men. One pulled in front of the BMW, blocking its way, while the other stopped alongside. Its pillion rider dismounted, walked up to the side window and fired several shots. The two motorbikes then roared off, and Robinson staggered from the car, dying on the street from massive bleeding. The other convicted man, Corey Wright, aged twenty, who had received a five-and-a-half year sentence, was shot dead in a car in Hackney along with a friend, Wayne Henry, in April 2001.

Meanwhile, Mark Lambie's alleged involvement in shootings at nightclubs continued. There was another in November 1999 at the Coliseum nightclub in Vauxhall, south London. The victim named Lambie as the shooter and he was charged with attempted murder. However, the shot man later withdrew his evidence and Lambie was freed. There was also intelligence the same year that he and a man called Michael Thomas, aka Mallet, had fired shots at the EQ nightclub in Hackney Marsh in what police believe was an attempt at blackmail. In another incident at a Hackney nightclub the following year, Stephen Grant was shot dead in what Trident detectives believed was a dispute between the TMD and Hackney Boys. Lambie was said to have been there. Six handguns were found in the boot of a car abandoned at the scene. Two days later in Southgate, near Tottenham, TMD members shot at a Hackney youth, missing him but hitting his girlfriend. The gun used in the attack was found later the same day when a car driven by men thought to belong to the TMD was stopped in the City of London. The men ran from the police, who chased after them, eventually catching and arresting them for driving a stolen vehicle. A gun was found during the chase, which had been used in the Southgate shooting, but it could not be forensically linked to the arrested men.

By this stage, police knew that Mark Lambie was a major criminal, but they had never gathered enough evidence to nail him for a serious crime. There was, however, sufficient to prosecute two of his main associates, other men capable of great violence. The first of these, Michael 'Mallet' Thomas, was convicted for an attempted murder. The second associate, Ricky Sweeney, was convicted for one of a series of tit-for-tat killings, outlined in the previous chapter. With those two men behind bars, Trident set about tackling the elusive Mark Lambie.

The proactive operation against him started with detectives studying his Intelligence files. It was claimed at a later stage that police were out to get Lambie as revenge for PC Keith Blakelock's savage murder in 1990. Since his acquittal, said his lawyer, he had been subjected to a relentless police pursuit: 'The murder of PC Blakelock is an event every Met police officer will never forget, and never let go.' But this version of events was disputed by DI Peter Lansdown, the officer in charge: 'When we took him on, the decision was made on recent, current intelligence. He had a reputation for violence and there was a fear of intimidation if anyone gave evidence against him. We didn't know of his alleged involvement in the Blakelock murder. The names of the juveniles were never made public, and because he was acquitted it didn't show in his criminal record.'

But, surprisingly, Lambie's whereabouts were unknown in 2000, which made any attempt at determined surveillance impossible. Put simply, if his home address was not known, no bug could be planted, no intercept put on his phone, and no tracking device put on his car. 'Despite all that intelligence, we didn't know where he lived,' recalled DI Peter Lansdown. 'I can remember one meeting and saying, where is he? Is he an enigma?

We couldn't put conventional tactics in place. He had no known home and no regular lifestyle pattern, so we started hunting down his associates, to take them out and to gather further intelligence on him.' He said Trident took the same approach as adopted by the US authorities against Al Capone, the Chicago gangster who had escaped arrest for so many years. If they could not get him for serious crime, they would get him for something – anything. Capone was eventually locked away for income tax offences and died in prison. Lansdown recalled: 'We found that Lambie was living in south London, which was a surprise, because we expected him to be somewhere in north London. Normally they stay geographically near their homes.'

Trident traced his new home by putting out an arrest alert across the Met. But it was not only under his real name. Trident reckoned that he had avoided being picked up by using false names in police checks. Looking back they found that he had used the name 'Paul Gordon' and variations on it in the past. So the alert went out for him under a number of names. Trident did not have long to wait. A suspected stolen car was stopped by police. Two of the occupants gave their correct names – one of them was Lambie's brother, Wesley. The third man said his name was Paul Gordon. Trident was informed, and a quick check established that 'Gordon' was indeed Mark Lambie. Eighteen wraps of heroin were found in the car, but police had difficulty in prosecuting because the owner of the vehicle refused to substantiate that it was indeed stolen, and the drugs could not be linked to any of the occupants. The three men were released on bail, and although 'Gordon' gave his mother's address, Trident managed to establish that Lambie was in fact living in Streatham. It meant that serious surveillance was now possible.

Police caught Mark Lambie 'at it' on 19th April, 2001. The day started uneventfully, with Lambie followed from Streatham north to Tottenham. He met up with friends and associates, and then things began to look interesting when they all moved off together in a convoy of three cars, one of which was a large Mercedes, with Lambie driving a VW Golf. But the police following them drove into difficulties fairly quickly. The convoy went into the Broadwater Farm estate, but police decided it was too risky to stick too close, because they were mostly white and stood out on the predominantly black estate. Instead they waited outside the estate, hoping to see Lambie drive off. He was seen leaving in the Golf, together with a blue sports car, which had not been in the original convoy. There was no sign of the other two cars. The significance of this was to become apparent a few hours later.

After a few minutes, the blue sports car was abandoned, and the driver got into Lambie's car. The two then drove to south Tottenham, parking in Turner Avenue, where the pair went on foot to a party at a house on a nearby estate. The surveillance team kept watch on the car, with Lansdown and other Trident detectives on hand nearby. By 11.15 p.m., with all the signs indicating that the party was still warming up, and Lambie set to be enjoying himself there for some time, Lansdown decided to call it a day. There had been twelve hours of surveillance, and it looked like nothing was now going to happen. To continue would be expensive in terms of overtime and it could also prove risky.

'We had to draw the line somewhere,' said Lansdown. 'Surveillance on these people is particularly difficult, as they don't lead conventional lives. You never know when they are going to get up or where they are going. I was also worried about having too much surveillance. If you follow someone for a long time, eventually you are going to be compromised.' So he and his team of detectives went to Tottenham police station for a debriefing. But while they talked through the day's events in an upstairs room, something happened below which was to set off further hours of exciting activity.

A Jamaican, frightened and injured, dashed into the police station with an amazing story of kidnap and terrible torture by Mark Lambie. It emerged that it had happened right under the noses of the surveillance team. Lansdown went downstairs and a very distressed Gregory Smith told him that he and his fellow Jamaican friend, Towayne Morris, had been lured to the Broadwater Farm estate by an associate of Lambie, Anthony 'Blue' Bourne, the head of an Edmonton gang known as The Firm, who said he wanted a meeting so they could discuss a mutual girlfriend. The two Jamaicans went to the estate, driving there in their blue sports car – the same car spotted by police being driven away later, with Lambie's VW. But instead of having a meeting on the estate, the two Jamaicans had been attacked. They were pistol-whipped and bundled into the boots of two cars – the same cars the police had observed going to the estate in convoy with Lambie. Smith said he and Morris were then driven to Turner Avenue, to the same house which police had seen Lambie visit for what appeared to be a party.

Bourne and others had bullied their way into the house, said Smith, telling the woman who answered the door to mind her own business. The two Jamaicans were taken to an upstairs room, where they were partly stripped and tied with strong tape to two chairs. They were then attacked with a hammer and a kettle of hot water was thrown over them. At some stage Lambie arrived and joined in the assault. The pair were threatened with burning by an iron unless they agreed to pay the gang £20,000 in drugs and cash. To avoid further torture Smith identified a house used for hairdressing, telling his assailants that was where money was kept. Some of the gang then took him to the premises in Wakefield Road, leaving the rest holding Towayne Morris.

Two women, with children, were at the hairdressing house when the gang burst in, attacking and robbing them of money and jewellery. As they scoured the house, a man arrived at the front door and was dragged inside. This man described later how they fell on him 'like a pack of hyenas'. He was pistol-whipped to the floor and held there. The women were tied up. Somehow, in the commotion, Smith managed to escape, and ran to the police station.

DI Lansdown was confronted with not one but two very serious situations involving hostages being held at separate addresses. He resurrected the surveillance team, put out an alert for the three cars used by the gang, and called for armed officers. Meanwhile, however, events were moving on fast outside. The detectives' main concern was for the two women and man in Wakefield Road who had been robbed and held by the gang. Some of the Trident team went there with armed police, prepared for a hostage situation. But when they arrived, they found the three had managed to free themselves and had dialled 999. Piecing together what happened, the police believed that, after Gregory Smith's escape from the house, Lambie's gang had fled the scene, apparently warning the rest of the gang holding the other Jamaican, Towayne Morris, of what had happened. Taking the struggling Morris with them, that group then left the Turner Avenue estate house and headed towards their car, one of the three seen in convoy by the surveillance team earlier in the evening. However, by sheer chance, and luckily for Morris, a passing police car saw the group, and his captors, realising they had been spotted, ran off. A relieved Morris, covered in blood, flung himself across the bonnet of the police car, pleading for help from the startled officers inside.

Other officers saw the Mercedes, the third car from the convoy, and began following in their unmarked vehicle. But they were spotted and the Mercedes accelerated away, followed by the police. A chase developed through the streets, only ending when the Mercedes crashed and rolled over on to its roof, with a bag containing a quarter of a kilo of heroin falling out onto the road. The driver, Francis Appiah, escaped major injury and was arrested.

But what of Trident's main target, Mark Lambie? Where was he? When Trident officers returned to Turner Avenue they were surprised to see his VW Golf still parked in the same place. They reckoned it unlikely that he had remained at the nearby party which, from the sounds coming from inside the house, was still very much in progress. They decided to wait and see what happened. They also needed to gather evidence from the party premises but were not going to raid it and endanger the lives of possibly innocent people, who may have known nothing of what had happened at the house earlier. It was not until 4.00 in the morning that the party started to break up. One of the party-goers, a woman, went up to Lambie's car, unlocked it, and drove off. Police let her go.

It was time for Lansdown's team to review the situation, to work out what had happened, and what they should do. They concluded that Lambie had probably left the party after learning of the escape of the two Jamaicans. Fearing that his car was being watched by police, he must have been driven off in another vehicle. Although no one was known to Trident as now being held by the gang, at least five and possibly as many as ten very violent men, including Lambie, were still on the loose, and only one man, Appiah, was in custody. What should be done with him? It looked to Lansdown as if the investigation and hunt for Lambie was going to take a long time. He doubted that the gang had any idea of the scale of the operation against them, or that the two Jamaicans were in police hands and prepared to give evidence in court. It was better to keep things that way. However, the problem was that if Appiah was charged, the police, under legal regulations, would have to disclose at least some of their operation to him, and word would then soon get back to Lambie and the rest of the gang. The danger was that there could then be attempts to intimidate the two Jamaicans, to frighten them out of giving evidence. Lansdown also reviewed the evidence against Appiah. At that stage, he had not been positively identified as being one of the gang which had kidnapped the two Jamaicans, and there was no forensic link between him and the heroin found when the Mercedes crashed. He could also say that he had been driving the car for a friend and had no idea there were drugs inside. Lansdown decided to give him police bail with the hope that the criminal would simply think himself lucky.

With the two Jamaicans in the Met's witness protection programme and prepared to pick out their attackers at identity parades, Trident again went on the offensive, making various arrests. Two days after the kidnapping, their main target, Mark Lambie, was arrested along with one of his lieutenants, Adrian Crawford, aka Buckhead, as they visited an associate in Wormwood Scrubs prison. Lambie was identified as one of the attackers. But Crawford was not picked out by the Jamaicans as one of their assailants and he was freed. Five days later he was again arrested after another dramatic car chase.

It began when another of the suspects, Clint Ponton, was spotted in a VW Golf. He was seen talking to other men in a Peugeot 406 coupé. A police car moved in on him, but he drove off at high speed, ramming the police car aside. Other police cars joined the chase, during which a gun and a bag of powder were thrown from the Golf's windows. The pursuit lasted for five minutes, ending when the Golf crashed into another police car. Ponton, Crawford, and a third man were all arrested. Police continued chasing the Peugeot for half an hour before they burst its tyres, forcing it to stop. Inside, there were gun parts, and a shotgun was found at the address of one of the occupants. The three arrested in the Golf were all charged with gun offences, but were acquitted because police could not prove which of them had thrown the gun from the window.

Months later, Clint Ponton was arrested for other alleged offences. Adrian Crawford, described by newspapers as a prominent Tottenham gangster, was murdered in December 2002, shot down in a hail of bullets in front of his pregnant girlfriend as he left a north London restaurant. Working with Crawford's family, who appealed for witnesses to come forward, Trident obtained enough evidence to prosecute a leader of the rival Hackney Boys, Daniel Cummings, aged twenty-three. Cummings was said by police to have assumed that 'his reputation for violence would shield him from prosecution'. He was jailed for life at the Old Bailey in 2003.

Police arrested another suspect, Curtis Davis, who had been with Mark Lambie throughout the day of the original police surveillance. But he was not picked out by the Jamaicans at an identity parade. Later he was charged with shooting a doorman in Birmingham, but was acquitted. Back in London, he was chased in King's Cross by police who claimed he had pulled a gun out and threatened them. He tried to escape by shooting his way through the glass door at the entrance to a block of flats, but he was rammed by a police car before he could get inside. He was convicted for various firearms offences. Francis Appiah, the man in the crashed Mercedes, went to ground, but he too was arrested later for other offences.

Mark Lambie's arrest over the brutal attack on the two Jamaicans was only half the battle for the police in bringing him and the others involved to justice. A campaign of intimidation started against the two main witnesses against them, the Jamaicans. One of them, Towayne Morris, reported to detectives that the day following the incidents he had received a call on his mobile from Mark Lambie who was apparently unaware that Morris had agreed to become a protected witness. The Jamaican claimed that Lambie told him Appiah had been arrested with £5,000 worth of drugs, and that Morris should reimburse him. If he refused, he would lose his car, and possibly his life. Lambie also threatened that all of his family would die if he – Lambie – was arrested. Morris said another of the attackers, Lambie's lieutenant, Anthony Bourne, made similar threats over the phone.

Four weeks later, despite these threats to his life, and the fact that Lambie had by then been arrested, Towayne Morris opted out of the witness protection scheme, and returned to his old haunts in Tottenham. Within twenty-four hours he was hit by gunfire. Two men wearing balaclavas walked into an address in Park Lane, Tottenham, and fired guns at him and the two men with him. Morris was hit three times while the other two received only minor injuries. In hospital, Morris named Bourne as one of the gunmen. Realising he was lucky to have survived, Morris again became a protected witness. But there was no let up of the intimidation against the two Jamaicans. Threats continued to be relayed to them via their friends and families. This culminated in the two men making statements withdrawing their evidence.

Prepared by defence lawyers, they were presented to a shocked DI Lansdown. Without the Jamaicans' evidence there was little against Lambie and Bourne, who had by then also been arrested. 'I immediately went to see the witnesses and they told me they had succumbed to severe intimidation on them and their families,' said Lansdown. 'They said they had followed instructions and gone to see solicitors and withdrawn their evidence. They went on and told me that they still wanted to give evidence although they were convinced their lives would still be in jeopardy if they did so.' Faced with a difficult life or death situation, the police then decided on an unusual tactic. They would go along with a pretence that the pair had indeed pulled out. 'We agreed that while the gang thought the two had withdrawn their evidence, they'd be safer than if we let the defence know that they were still wanting to give evidence,' said Lansdown. The officer took further statements from the Jamaicans about what had happened and gave them to the judge who was to be in charge of the trial. Although the defence lawyers tried to find out what was happening, the judge agreed that the new statements should not be disclosed to them until just before the start of the trial in 2002.

Towayne Morris, aged twenty-four, and Gregory Smith, aged twenty-two, did give evidence against Lambie, Bourne and two others at the Old Bailey. Prosecuting counsel Nicholas Hilliard said the gangsters believed Morris and Smith were drug dealers with access to large amounts of cash. He called the defendants a 'malign and corrosive influence on the black community'. Lambie, thirty-one, and Bourne, twenty-one, were convicted of kidnapping and blackmail and jailed for twelve years. Gang members Warren Leader, twenty-one, and Francis Appiah, twenty, were given sentences of eleven and nine years respectively for the same offences. Bourne was cleared of attempted murder.

The judge, Martin Stephens, told them: 'The sentence must reflect the public outrage at the use of firearms and violence by men who appear to consider themselves above the law. These offences are all too prevalent and are blighting the lives of whole communities. The evidence during this eleven-week trial must have shocked and disturbed all who heard it. The offences you committed demonstrated an outright disregard for the rules of society and the rights of your fellow citizens, not least those who lived in the communities where you lived.' He also praised the two Jamaicans for their bravery in coming forward. They and their immediate families are understood to be still in the Met's witness protection programme.

After clearing up the case on Mark Lambie, Operation Trident's proactive team in north London turned its attention to the TMD gang's rivals, the Hackney Boys, some of whom had linked up with Turkish gangsters to deal in heroin. An attempted murder in 2002 provided a first for Trident. It sparked two full investigations running in parallel with one another, the first time this had been attempted in Trident's short history. The first investigation was into the attempted murder and the other was a financial inquiry into the suspect group's assets and money laundering activities.

It was a very frightened and badly injured Christian Robinson who dialled 999 on 7th May, telling police that some men had tried to kidnap him and then, when he had escaped, shot him twice. Robinson's story was that they attacked him because they believed he had information about the whereabouts of a man they were after. He said that three hours after collecting his children from school, he gave two men who had turned up at his house a lift to Amhurst Road in Hackney and turned off into a cul-de-sac in order to turn his Astra car around. As he dropped off his two passengers, he noticed that a silver Ford Focus had followed him into the small tree-lined street. Inside it were two men he had known for about ten years, Marvyn Campbell and Fabian Brissett, from a large, well-known family with its roots in Hackney. Robinson claimed that Campbell drove up directly behind his Astra, blocked him in and told him: 'You are stupid. Where is he?' Then another car drew up, blocking the entrance to the road. Four men jumped out of it, according to Robinson, and two of them had guns.

Robinson said he was surrounded and one of the men, Dwayne Brissett, shouted: 'Where the fuck is he?' He heard someone shout, 'Get him in the car', and he was then grabbed and felt a rain of blows on his head. It appeared that his attackers were trying to get him into the boot of one of the cars, but he fell down on the road. One of the men shouted, 'shoot him', but he somehow managed to break free and run off. He heard another shout of 'shoot him' and then felt a stinging pain in his back. He had been hit. He stumbled and fell to the ground and two of the men grabbed him again, one firing a gun at close range, hitting him in the face. He managed to start running again, and seeing two people leaving a house, forced his way inside, ran upstairs and called the police. Robinson was taken to the Royal London Hospital where he was treated for the two bullet wounds.

Dwayne Brissett, of Bethnal Green, was arrested three days later. His brother Fabian Brissett, of Finsbury Park, and Marvyn Campbell, of Barking, were arrested separately a month later. All three appeared at the Old Bailey in 2003, each denying charges of attempted murder and kidnap, wounding with intent to cause grievous bodily harm and possessing firearms. They were all found not guilty.

'We knew from the beginning that it was going to be a difficult case, because it depended on the witness, Mr Robinson, and we were never sure that we had got the full story from him,' said Peter Lansdown, the same DI who was in charge of the Lambie investigation. 'However, when we arrested one man we found some expensive items from Selfridges in the boot of his BMW. That led us on to a financial investigation, Operation Keyhaven, which went on alongside the main inquiry.'

With help from Scotland Yard's fraud squad, the Trident team traced several safety deposit boxes. One of them, at Selfridges, contained twenty-four Rolex watches worth £283,000. It seemed they had been purchased downstairs in the store and then taken upstairs to be deposited. Also found were wads of cash, which had been folded and thrown into carrier bags. A total of £443,000 in cash was recovered, much of it contaminated by traces of heroin. There were also six vehicles valued at £143,000, found at various places as well as £228,000 worth of jewellery. Altogether police seized cash and property worth more than £1,200,000. Eleven men were arrested for money laundering. Three of them pleaded guilty, three were found unfit to stand trial and five eventually appeared at the Old Bailey. The prosecution case went on for several weeks, but then the defence lawyers made legal submissions and the five were acquitted.

'It was on a legal technicality, but all was not lost,' claimed

Lansdown. 'We managed to retain all that we had seized as the proceeds of crime!' He said wider lessons had been learned from both the financial investigation and the attempted murder case.

> 'The attack case confirmed the view that we should not have to rely too much on the evidence of victims, because they can easily be distracted in court. Much better is to use professional witnesses – police, bank evidence, mobile phone evidence and so on. We also learned that asset recovery can be an enormously powerful tool. Until Keyhaven we hadn't seen the gangs show this level of organisation over their money. Usually it would be squandered within a few days, but these people were banking for the future. Keyhaven's success led on to a Met-wide initiative against criminals, Operation Payback.'

Peter Lansdown was promoted to Detective Chief Inspector, and he went to the Met's crime academy at Hendon in north London, where he lectures on investigative skills. Recalling his Trident days, particularly the proactive team's investigation into Mark Lambie, he said: 'There were only ten in the proactive unit and it was manic, very difficult, intense and exciting detective work. We managed to take out some major players.' He distinguished between Trident's two different areas. The north team was generally up against British-born gangs in conflict with other groups. These gangs had formed at school-age, making penetration of them more difficult, and because they were well known in their localities, the fear of repercussions remained strong for anyone wanting to help the police. He said the south team dealt with more open drugs violence, often involving Jamaicans. Because these people were largely unknown in their local communities, it was easier for people to give evidence against them.

Lansdown's team was so busy from 2000 to 2003 dealing with Lambie, his TMD gang and the Hackney Boys, that he could not undertake another major proactive operation in his north London patch. Another big job had to be handled by his counterparts south of the river. The target, like Lambie, had been known to the police and other agencies for many years. The investigation into the man known as Father Fowl was to be equally intriguing.

'We had taken enough of his people out. He was running out of couriers, his chief financiers had bitten the dust, and we knew that the opportunity to get him was never going to be as good again.'

It was an ignominious end for one of the Mr Bigs of drugs – wedged in a window, trying to escape from police who were battering their way into the third floor flat. A huge, long-running Trident operation had gradually whittled down the cocaine and crack empire built up by Owen Clarke, aka Father Fowl. His trusted lieutenants and couriers had been picked off one by one, forcing the main man to adopt a more 'hands-on' role. When finally cornered, Clarke was just starting the cooking process on a batch of cocaine, turning it into crack. His arrest was the culmination of three years of hard work by a Trident team. They had succeeded where others had failed.

Owen Roger Clarke had been in the authorities' sights for several years before being targeted by Trident. Born in Kingston, Jamaica, in 1957, and regarded there as one of the country's most notorious criminals, Clarke moved to the UK in 1990, marrying a British-based Jamaican woman. They lived together in the outer suburbs of north-west London, at Greenford. Although their two-bedroomed bungalow in Rugby Avenue was unassuming, Clarke's lifestyle was anything but modest. He travelled all over the world, especially to and from Jamaica, and was suspected of running a network of international drug traffickers spanning North and South America and Africa. Amongst the agencies looking for and tracking him in the 1990s were MI6, Customs and NCIS, the National Criminal Intelligence Service. But they had never managed to turn suspicions into sufficient hard evidence to put him behind bars with any long sentence. It was partly a question of resources. Any kind of surveillance, let alone the full-time kind, is time-consuming and expensive, and involves international cooperation when the target travels so extensively. That situation changed with Trident's formation.

In 2000, it was decided that Trident should attempt to tackle one of the main causes of black gun crime – the crack cocaine trade. The idea was that taking out the big crack dealers would stem the supply of the drug and the violence associated with its distribution would be reduced. Trident was given the resources to mount the long-term operations needed to hit the big-time dealers. Proactive teams were created, which worked secretly using Intelligence reports, and cooperated with the various agencies both here and abroad. One of the first targets was Owen Clarke, listed by NCIS as being one of the top three Jamaican dealers in the UK. The investigation into his activities, code-named Operation Jasle, was to be Trident's biggest.

Clarke was ostensibly a music promoter, using the name 'Father Fowl' or 'The Father'. He headed the 'British Link-Up Crew', a notorious Jamaican-UK drugs gang, as well as fronting and hosting raves and lavish parties in the UK and Jamaica. On the Caribbean island, he flaunted his wealth, having influential political and sporting contacts. He had at least three houses and a club that would easily hold 3,000 people. In London, he held riverboat cruises on the Thames and up to a thousand went to his events in Harlesden in north-west London. He exported several luxury cars to Kingston, including top of the range Jaguars with personalised number plates including WH1P and 007. Police believed the parties and the music business were a front for laundering money and raising funds for financing large-scale drug trafficking. He and his trusted lieutenants would organise couriers and mules, who brought cocaine into the UK in a variety of ways, from false-bottomed bags to carrying condoms stuffed with the drugs in their stomachs or pushed up their bottoms. They came by plane, and to avoid detection at British airports, they increasingly flew to the Continent first, sometimes then taking the Eurostar to Kent or London. Once here, couriers would distribute the drugs around the country to local wholesalers, who would then sell on to the retailers, the street dealers.

It is a dangerous world largely because of the huge profits that can be made from dealing in the highly addictive crack, and because the user can be irrationally violent. Police say converting cocaine into crack is a fairly easy process, but the profits to be obtained from selling the drug can be three times more than with simple cocaine. In 2001 alone, crack dealers from south London were arrested all over south and south-east England, from Hastings and Canterbury in the far south-east to Portsmouth and Bournemouth in the south-west. 'It's wherever you can get to and from in a day,' one Trident Intelligence officer told me. 'The danger for the big dealers is that if you send a boy to, say, Brighton, to deliver some crack and he brings back payment of £10,000, although he gets a cut of it, he's tempted to start dealing himself. If he does that, then the gang is going to be upset and they'll hit back. That guy has shown disrespect.'

Owen Clarke was himself the victim of at least one shooting. In 1999 a youth approached him in Willesden High Street in north-west London, fired a gun and hit him in the hand before being overpowered. The incident was recorded in a huge file of around 2,000 separate pieces of intelligence amassed on him over a thirteen-year period. Looking through these and liaising with NCIS and MI6 over continued intelligence was the job of Detective Inspector Peter South. Under him was Detective Sergeant Steve Waller, in day-to-day charge of the proactive operation against Clarke.

Waller told me:

> 'Clarke had been the target of several unsuccessful attempts by various organisations, ranging from local borough crime squads to NCIS itself, but like all Mr Bigs, he didn't drive round dealing drugs himself. He didn't get his own hands dirty – he had others do the work for him. And because he was out of the country for long periods, he was difficult to keep tabs on. If we had targeted him alone, we would have got nothing. We would just have seen him driving around going from one party to another and from one airport to another. You can know lots about

someone, but not have the evidence to charge him. It's a bit like Al Capone. You couldn't get to him. We had to develop a long-term strategy. So, rather than targeting him as an individual, you target the organisation. We identified who his main associates were and attempted to disable the organisation. Only by making inroads into his business – bringing it down, could we expect to get him and his associates round the world.'

The first of his lieutenants to be targeted was an attractive woman, Nadia Codner, who lived in Hackney. She worked for Owen Clarke, who had originally set her up. But she also ran her own sub-organisation, like a franchise, giving her mentor a cut. Like Clarke, she tried to keep some distance from those making the actual drug runs from the Caribbean to Britain, supervising the smugglers through middlemen. However, it was her habit to take a more hands-on role when new couriers were employed. One of these occasions was to lead to her downfall. Her phone was tapped and she was kept under intermittent surveillance. On one day she was seen driving her brand new Volkswagen Beetle and meeting a man in Hackney to whom she passed two large, apparently empty, Adidas sports bags. The man was followed, and hours later he was seen giving the bags to a young Portuguese couple at a hotel in Golders Green in north London. It looked to the watching police as though a drugs run was in the offing, with the sports bags probably fitted with secret compartments. The hotel was staked out, as was Codner's home.

Early the following morning, a cab collected the couple who were carrying the sports bags, which now looked quite full. It was followed to Gatwick where the couple waited in line for a flight that would take them to Antigua, the most northerly of a string of islands stretching from the cocaine-exporting Venezuela in South America. Nadia Codner was also on the move. She left her home in Pickering Court, Cassland Road, went to Gatwick, and joined the same flight, ignoring the Portuguese couple. None of the watching detectives was able to travel with the trio. As they had learned of the trip only that day, they could not obtain the prior permission necessary to carry out police work in another country. Instead they learned more about the trio's travel plans from Customs and Special Branch. The couple, posing as holidaymakers, were due to return to the UK a week later. Codner had a more flexible ticket, and she flew back after three days. It appeared that she had completed the arrangements in Antigua and did not want to run the risk of returning on the same flight as the couple. Customs would have tipped off Trident if the Portuguese pair had also changed their travel plans, but it was not necessary. The couple arrived back on their arranged flight, with the sports bags, and that meant decision time for Trident and DS Steve Waller, who told me:

> 'We had to decide whether to arrest the couple at the airport or to follow them through and arrest them when they met up with someone else. The problem with the first option is that the couple might have failed, for some reason. Something had gone wrong and they didn't have the gear. The chances were that they would be carrying it, but if we arrested them there, we wouldn't have enough evidence to do Codner. Sure, we would have caused her disruption. She'd owe money for the coke, for which she'd have paid up-front, and that would have put her in a difficult position. But there's always another time, and we knew she was planning another one. Normally we would want to see them through to the conclusion, but the downside to that is that they can go to a hotel and not be contacted for a few days. To keep a watch on them for that length of time is resource wasting, and they still might not have the gear!'

The Trident detectives decided to keep their options open and on this occasion they were in luck. The pair were met in the arrivals hall on 29th May 2001 by the same cab driver who had taken them to Gatwick. The surveillance team followed them to the short-term car park. The officers were conscious that another woman seemed to be taking an interest in the trio pushing the luggage trolley, looking around as though she was trying to pick out anyone observing the scene. It was only when they all got to the short-term car park that the mystery woman was recognised as Nadia Codner. They were all arrested and eleven kilos of cocaine were found hidden in the bags' false bottoms.

The cab driver, Antonio Ferreira, aged thirty-five, of Colindale, and the Portuguese couple, Damasio Dos Santos, twenty-four, and Angela Pena, twenty-three, all pleaded guilty to their parts in the smuggling operation and were each sentenced to nine years imprisonment. Codner fought the case, blaming the man who had taken the sports bags from her. Conveniently, he had disappeared to Nigeria. She maintained she had been on holiday in Antigua and had returned because she had fallen ill. It had simply been coincidence that she was at Gatwick at the same time as the couple, who she professed not to know. By the time of her trial at Lewes Crown Court, Trident had amassed further evidence against her. She had stayed at the same hotel as the couple and computerised phone records for their rooms showed contact between them. The jury spent only a few minutes before declaring Codner guilty. She was given a fifteen-year jail sentence.

Next on Trident's target list were two highly trusted members of Clarke's team, fellow Jamaicans Paul Hamilton, forty, aka Pepsi and Vander Anderson, twenty-nine, aka Luddy who lived in one of Clarke's houses in Northolt Road, Harrow. After being kept under surveillance, they were suspected of playing two roles in Clarke's organisation. First, they supervised the mules arriving with ingested cocaine, keeping them in a safe house until the drugs had passed through their bodies, a process which could sometimes take several days. The cocaine used to be put in condoms, but the favoured method now is to put it in the fingers of surgical gloves; because of their greater strength, it is less likely that they will split in the mule's stomach, which could not only endanger the carrier's life, but also cut into the profits of the smuggling operation. The surveillance also showed Hamilton and Anderson regularly visiting a house in Luton, Bedfordshire, and after staying a short time inside, leaving with a large envelope for another Luton address before returning to north London. Trident detectives suspected that the first Luton house was being run as a crack factory, with Hamilton and Anderson taking the raw cocaine there, and picking up rocks of crack for distribution from the other Luton address.

It was decided to arrest them in December 2001. One day they were seen visiting a house in Willesden in north-west London, leaving with a parcel which they took to the first Luton house. As they left it, police moved in. Hamilton ran off and tried to hide a bag in a neighbour's garden. He was caught and it was found that the house was indeed being used to store cocaine and to turn it into crack. A kilo of the raw drug was found, along with evidence that about fifty kilos, worth around £10 million, had passed through the house, being converted to crack and sold on. In a simultaneous raid on the Willesden address, police found two 'mules', both poor Jamaican farmers, as well as more than half a kilo of cocaine, and another man, Tentroy Gordon, who was trying to throw smelly pellets of the drug over a balcony wall. At Luton Crown Court, Hamilton, who had served an earlier five-year sentence for drug offences, was imprisoned for thirteen years. Anderson was given a discounted sentence of nine years after pleading guilty, and Gordon was sentenced to seven years. The farmers were found not guilty, having convinced the jury that they had been forced to take part in the smuggling operation against their wishes.

After the arrests, there was further assessment of Operation Jasle by Trident. Although there were clear links between Owen Clarke and those so far imprisoned – Nadia Codner, Hamilton and Anderson – Trident decided not to arrest Clarke at that stage, believing that the most cocaine or crack he would be carrying at any one time would be just a few grams. Instead they played a watching game, hoping to catch him with several kilos, having been forced by police action into becoming more actively involved in moving drug consignments around. At the same time, information was given by the Met to other agencies and police forces in areas known to be supplied by Clarke, amongst them Birmingham, Bristol and Leeds. There were more arrests of the minor players, making it more difficult for Clarke to operate, and more likely that he would make a mistake.

Meanwhile, two other people were put in place to fill the void left by Hamilton and Anderson. Trident surveillance on this new pair, James McDaniel and Maureen Findlay, immediately bore fruit. Owen Clarke had never been seen with Hamilton and Anderson. But an indication that he was beginning to feel the squeeze came when a surveillance team spotted him visiting the replacements' home in Tintern Way, Harrow. However, Clarke was not with the pair when Trident decided to move against them. DS Waller was at a case conference over Hamilton's pending trial when he was contacted by the two detectives watching McDaniel and Findlay. Detective Constables Ian Titterell and Trevor Gardner saw the pair on the move with a parcel and they wanted their sergeant's go-ahead. 'I told them to do it – arrest them – take them out while they were in the process of making deliveries,' Waller told me. 'It was the right time because they had a parcel with them. If the DCs had waited until the pair had met up with contacts, they could have been in trouble. You never know how many people are going to be receiving the drugs. There could be five of them and some of them could be armed. And anyway, arresting more than two wasn't all that important as far as the big plan was concerned. The main reason for doing them was for it to have an adverse effect on the Clarke organisation.'

When arrested, James McDaniel and Maureen Findlay were carrying half a kilo of crack on their way to a delivery address. At their home, police found another kilo waiting to be turned into crack. It was hidden in a washing machine in a shed, along with a large quantity of money. McDaniel and Findlay pleaded guilty and received sentences of six and four years respectively. 'It turned out that the reason Clarke had visited the address was because he was adept at cooking the coke,' said DS Waller. 'It's not a particularly difficult job, but there are different ways of doing it. He wouldn't bother too much for ordinary customers, but some like it done a certain way, like you get with any kind of cooking. He'd get involved in the cooking if it was an important customer, and we think it was in this case, though we never did find out who it was.'

The next significant move against the organisation came in 2002 with surveillance on a man viewed as Clarke's chief lieutenant, Michael Sutherland. He operated out of south London, working closely with his brother Gifford, who had a legitimate job, earning more than £50,000 a year with a telecommunications company. The Sutherland brothers were thought responsible for arranging many importations of cocaine from South America, particularly through Panama and Caracas in Venezuela. At one stage Michael Sutherland had been arrested in Panama following a seizure of cocaine, but he is believed to have bribed his way out of prison there before managing to return to the UK. The two brothers varied the couriers' travel routes from South America and the Caribbean, reckoning that if they travelled from a Dutch or French-linked country in the area to Amsterdam or Paris then the border restrictions would be more lenient. The Sutherlands also hired many couriers themselves, selecting people they had learned from associates were in need of money, and the older the person the better, as they were less likely to arouse suspicion. One such recruit was Phoebe Doran, a Zambian with an Irish passport. She had tribal scars on her face and wanted money to pay for surgery to remove them.

In March 2003, after months of surveillance, the Trident team closed in on the Sutherlands. Phoebe Doran was arrested at the Eurostar station in Waterloo, having travelled from Ireland to London to Paris to Guadeloupe, where she had picked up ten kilos of cocaine, concealing it in her luggage. She then took a plane back to Paris and the train to London. When arrested she only had one kilo of cocaine on her, having offloaded the other nine in Paris. She was charged on the basis that she had made at least five trips to the Caribbean bringing back ten kilos of cocaine on each occasion. Evidence came from airline records which showed that her luggage always weighed 10 kilos more on her return to Europe than when she left. But a more important arrest was made at Waterloo at the same time – that of Michael Sutherland.

It was the first time any of the Sutherlands' couriers had used Eurostar to bring cocaine into Britain. In that sense it was a test run, and Michael Sutherland was at the Eurostar terminal to meet Phoebe Doran, to make sure that all had gone to plan. The evidence Trident had amassed against Sutherland and his brother was so compelling that both took the unusual step of pleading guilty to drug smuggling. Phoebe Doran fought the case, as did a middleman, Christopher Syrus, who had helped Doran as she passed through France on each of her trips. They were found guilty after a fifteen-week trial at Kingston Crown Court. All four defendants were given sentences of nine years.

The operation against the Sutherlands had also provided useful evidence against Owen Clarke. In the run up to Doran's arrival at Waterloo, the brothers were in phone contact with Clarke who was also anxious to know whether the new route worked. Police intercepted the phone calls, and while the law prohibited their content being used in any court case, they provided proof to the Trident detectives that Clarke was becoming increasingly desperate, with his supply routes being closed down one by one. 'We had taken enough of his people out,' said Waller. 'He was running out of couriers, his chief financiers had bitten the dust, and we knew that the opportunity to get him was never going to be as good again.'

Conventional as well as electronic surveillance started in earnest against Clarke at the beginning of April 2003, on his return from Jamaica where he had hosted a lavish event known as the British Link Up in the La Rousse nightclub outside Kingston. According to Trident, this was a party held for British-based Jamaican criminals, most of whom displayed signs of their wealth and opulence. Some wore designer clothes with price tags still on, drank expensive champagne and even showed off by burning £50 notes. Within days of being back in London, Clarke was beginning to get his hands dirty.

Followed to King's Cross station he was seen meeting a Jamaican, known as Cleveland Dunbar, who had travelled from the north of England. Clarke drove him to an address in north

London where Dunbar bought a kilo of cocaine. However, Clarke then drove off, leaving an associate to take Dunbar back to Kings Cross. Trident followed Dunbar on to the train back north and arrested him at Leeds. Minutes afterwards, Clarke phoned Dunbar, presumably trying to find out if there had been any problems on the journey. Police let the phone ring unanswered. There were further calls from Clarke later in the evening, his mobile number registering on Dunbar's phone. 'The evidence against him was good,' said Waller, 'but not good enough to do him. It would have been only a 50-50 chance at trial as he could have come up with a number of stories to explain things away.'

Forced into becoming less choosy about who he worked with, Clarke's next lieutenant was Jason Sadler, aka Jazzy P, a crack addict living in a bedsit in Harlesden. Sadler acted as go-between, and was seen supplying Clarke's drugs to a man who was arrested in Islington. Sadler was not arrested at that stage. During their surveillance, police had identified what appeared to be another safe house, a flat in a block in Colindale, north London. Both Sadler and Clarke were seen visiting the flat. The police believed that Clarke was now taking the direct hands-on approach they were waiting for – that the flat was being used either to store drugs, or even better, as a place to convert cocaine to crack. 'We anticipated he'd go to that flat again, so we got a key to the communal entrance, preparing for that day,' said Waller.

That day came on 26th June 2003. Clarke and Sadler were observed in Harlesden being given a large bulky envelope by a Nigerian, Napoleon Eronini. Clarke handed the package to Sadler and then they split up, each getting into separate cars, but both setting off northwards. Guessing that one or both men were heading for the Colindale flat, Trident detectives, led by Steve Waller, raced ahead, letting themselves into the block and hiding in the ground-floor stairwell. With them they had a ram for battering down doors. Seconds later, Clarke arrived in his Mercedes and went up to flat number 5 on the third floor. Five minutes later, Sadler arrived with the envelope and also entered the flat.

There was no time for the Trident officers to call for armed back-up, and anyway, a number of factors made the use of police shooters inappropriate. Although Clarke and Sadler would have access to guns, they were not known to regularly carry them. It was also the police firearms unit tactics to surround a property and, if necessary, play a waiting game in order to tackle the criminals outside in the open, rather than bursting inside, and running greater risks of injury by not knowing the lay-out. But such tactics, known as 'call-outs', in cases like this could also result in drugs being flushed away down the lavatory.

'We suspected that they were either cooking up the coke or were cutting it up,' said Waller. 'This was as good an opportunity to get Clarke as we were ever going to get. So we waited a reasonable amount of time, letting them get down to whatever it was they were doing. Then we bashed at the door and took our chances. We got to the kitchen and saw Clarke was wedged in the window, trying to get out. We dragged him back.' The Trident team had timed their entry well. On the kitchen table was a bowl containing a slowly solidifying substance that turned out to be 263 grams of crack. The paraphernalia of crack production were also there – bicarbonate of soda, clingfilm and a microwave oven. Next to Clarke's wallet on the table was 274 grams of previously prepared crack. Nearly £1,000 was found inside the flat, and there was another £1,000 outside in Clarke's Mercedes.

On trial in 2004 at Snaresbrook Crown Court, Clarke tried different lines of defence. He claimed police had fabricated evidence against him, portraying himself as a poor unfortunate with no knowledge of drugs until 1999, when, after being shot, he was forced into small-time drug dealing. In the mass of documents supplied under disclosure rules by the CPS, there was one fragment of evidence that he used to support his case that he had acted under duress. Although someone had been convicted for shooting him, an intelligence document named the notorious Mark Lambie as possibly being behind the man who pulled the trigger. This allowed Clarke to claim, as other drug dealers had done before him, that he had been so frightened of Lambie that he had no alternative but to carry out his orders, acting as a low-level courier for him and running other chores. When Clarke was caught out lying and evidence of his great wealth emerged, he tried to claim that he had made his money by being a big-time music promoter. But he paid no tax and was unable to produce any other supporting paperwork. The jury rejected it all, finding him guilty.

Judge William Kennedy told him: 'Your own arrogance made you believe you were untouchable. Suppliers like you shatter the lives of so many. Crack cocaine is a pitiless and vile trade and when the courts are confronted with it, it is their duty to sing out.' He gave Clarke a sentence of thirteen years. Sadler, aged twenty-four, of Chadwick Road, Harlesden, admitted manufacturing and supplying crack cocaine. Eronini was acquitted. In all, sixteen people connected to Clarke's network were convicted in UK courts. A similar number have been convicted in other parts of the world, and at the time of writing further attempts were being made to identify and seize Clarke's assets in Jamaica.

'Bound and gagged, a hot iron was held to his face and scalding water poured over him, taking off some of his skin. At some stage, his tongue was slit. Eventually a bag was put over his head and he suffocated.'

After Trident had been fully operational for a year and a half, there was a blast against the media for failing to report black-on-black murders and shootings. It came at the end of 2001 from Sir Ian Blair, then Metropolitan Police Deputy Commissioner. He complained that sixteen fatal shootings of black men and seventy-four attempted murders in London over the previous eight months had gone largely unreported. But they were having an incredibly destructive effect on parts of the black community who were in fear. He told *The Independent*: 'If this was white young women being murdered at the rate black men are being murdered, it would be headlines everywhere. I think there's something really wrong. To me, it is pretty close to institutional racism within the media. It seems extraordinary that this level of violence is not reported. I think there's a sense of "these people are black drug dealers, and so what". I think it is quite shaming.'

National newspaper crime correspondents agree with Sir Ian that there is little coverage of black murders and shootings, but disagree on the reasons. It is because they have become so commonplace, one Trident murder being pretty much the same as the other, and, as for court cases, there were no fewer than eleven separate Trident trials going on at the Old Bailey at the same time in 2002. A tabloid crime reporter told me: 'It's very frustrating because there are often very good stories behind these incidents, but my news desk is just not interested. To stand a chance of getting into the paper, unless it's a very quiet day, these murders and court cases have to involve either two people being shot, a child, or an innocent passer-by, who's preferably white.'

Confirmation of this view comes from a trawl through newspaper cuttings and the broadcast media over the three years

up to publication of this book. Only three fatal black shootings
made big headlines during that time. The first was in January 2003
when two teenage girls were gunned down during a New Year's
party in Birmingham. Seventeen-year-old Letisha Shakespeare
and Charlene Ellis, eighteen, died after being shot as they stood
outside the venue with other friends. They were shown together,
happy and smiling, in a photograph taken shortly before they met
their death. The next fatal shooting incident to hit the headlines
was nine months later when seven-year-old Toni-Ann Byfield
was shot dead along with her drug-dealing 'father' in north-west
London. A year later fourteen-year-old Danielle Beccan was shot
dead in Nottingham. She had been enjoying herself at the city's
Goose Fair, and was making her way home with a group of friends
when she was the victim of a drive-by shooting. There is more on
the circumstances surrounding these deaths in a later chapter.

They represented a vivid reminder that the problem of
serious black-on-black violence had spread far beyond London, a
fact officially recognised by the police as a national issue in 2002.
It was then that ACPO, the Association of Chief Police Officers,
set up a Caribbean Gun Crime Group aiming 'to coordinate police
policy and assess the effect for the police service and other agencies
in tackling the occurrence and impact of gun and drug related
crime, predominately influenced and orchestrated by Caribbean
organised crime groups.' The police group's first meeting was in
March of that year and attending were officers from London, the
West Midlands, West Yorkshire, NCIS, the National Crime Squad
(NCS) and Customs. Three months later, the ACPO sub-group
produced a report, *Strategic Assessment of the Impact of Caribbean
Gun Crime in the UK*. I have obtained a copy, each of its 32 pages
marked 'confidential', and it makes interesting reading.

Of the two main groups involved in gun crime, the report
says British-born blacks of Caribbean origin and those from
Jamaica itself share mobility and gang structure, and had spread
throughout England and Wales, and were now developing links
to Scottish cities, particularly Edinburgh, Glasgow and Aberdeen.
According to the report:

'Whilst the major metropolitan areas – London, Manchester, Bristol and Birmingham – have their own Caribbean gangs that tend to be territorial, have been established for some time and engage in their own feuds over territory, drugs and issues of "respect", it is clear that since 1998, Jamaican crime groups have spread rapidly throughout the country, driving the use of crack cocaine in hitherto established heroin markets...the distribution of Jamaican groups throughout the UK has spread at an alarming rate. Their influence is now being felt throughout the entire south of England, a greater part of the Midlands and Wales, and increasingly in the North.

'The spread of Jamaican groups has coincided with the growth of the crack cocaine market as the drug appears to be their core criminal business. They are also heavily involved in illegal immigration, prostitution and money laundering, usually in support of their drug dealing activities. Caribbean groups of both ilk will associate with each other and criminal groups of other ethnicity where it assists their criminal enterprises. There are numerous examples of Caribbean groups working with both white and Asian gangs, particularly in the supply of drugs, and there is increasing evidence of their association with Turkish groups. Caribbean groups as a whole are more willing to resort to the use of firearms than any other established crime group in the UK. In areas where they are established, the number of shootings, typically black-on-black, rise significantly. These shootings are frequently over minor arguments, termed as "respect" shootings.'

Continuing to deal with Jamaican groups, the report says they are adept at recognising and acting on a business opportunity, usually being introduced to an area by a contact with local knowledge. One of their favoured methods is to use local prostitutes to set up crack houses and to break into the existing heroin market.

With a foothold established, other dealers or rival gangs will be targeted through intimidation, kidnap and the use of firearms. The report observes that a tremendous amount of law enforcement is aimed at the gangs, but it tends to lack central coordination and direction, which frustrates the sharing of intelligence, along with incompatible systems. Practical difficulties were also caused by the fact that many Jamaicans were known only by their street names.

The ACPO sub-group asked each police force to state whether it had a problem with either of the two black groups. In addition to the conurbations already listed, the following forces replied that they had a 'developing' problem: Surrey, Kent, Lancashire, Humberside, Gloucestershire, South Yorkshire, Bedfordshire, Derbyshire, Devon and Cornwall, Northamptonshire, Wiltshire, South Wales, Dorset, Hertfordshire, Cleveland, Sussex, Thames Valley, Warwickshire, Hampshire, Merseyside, Norfolk, Suffolk, and Gwent and Dyfed-Powys in Wales.

Manchester's gangs have grown over the previous two decades, says the report, with four acknowledged groups – the Gooch, Doddington, Longsight Crew (LSC) and the Pitt Bull Crew. The latter was said to have been largely dismantled because of police operations while the LSC was breaking up due to internal differences. The Gooch were dominant in terms of numbers and activity, and where its 'business areas' overlapped with other gangs, shootings and murders occurred. The report says:

> 'Whilst these gangs are undoubtedly engaged in the supply of drugs and control particular areas, they also appear to display a degree of cohesion fostered by long associations and the shared threat posed by opposing gangs. Anniversaries of earlier murders frequently prompt retaliation or shows of force or respect. Gang heads are readily identifiable but whilst some members are more respected than others, no formal structure exists. Members will pursue their own activities but come together when there is a war in progress or for specific objectives.'

Gooch members also travel to pursue drug dealing, according to the report, its members coming to police attention in London, Bedfordshire, West Midlands and Avon and Somerset.

In Birmingham, the ACPO report says there were Jamaican gangs as well as British-born groups sometimes referred to as 'Home Boys'. These form three main gangs – the Burger Bar Boys, the Johnson Crew and the Black Rose Posse. The ten most prominent members of each gang were targeted by West Midlands Police, but their membership was fluid and without a rigid structure. The Burger Bar gang were the only ones sufficiently conscious of their identity to wear red bandanas, representing their membership of the group. 'This appears to be a trait only demonstrated in Birmingham,' says the report. It continues:

> 'The Jamaican elements in Birmingham have links with the Home Boys, but these appear to be of a temporary, expedient nature, and often end in conflict. Despite the size of the West Midland gangs, there appears to be a reluctance to take on the Jamaicans because of their reputation for extreme violence. Operation Ventara [Birmingham's equivalent to Operation Trident] recognise the possibility that Home Boys may increasingly be displaced, or at least be in regular conflict with Jamaican groups.'

Bristol is another city with Jamaican gangs – about twenty-five in 2002. They were thought to be smaller and more fluid in structure than other places, having between six and ten young men in each. Policing such groups was reported to be difficult because of their transient nature, a lack of police intelligence and because many gang members were known only by their initials or street names, for example T, Crazy, Yardie Tony, Bigga… The Bristol gangs were spreading out, according to the ACPO report, supplying drugs to Plymouth along with dealers from London, and coming into conflict with suppliers from Liverpool who traditionally controlled the Plymouth market. West Midlands police reported regularly encountering American-based Jamaicans. It was also becoming increasingly common for Jamaicans to be brought to the UK for specific tasks. In Derby, for instance, a Jamaican dealer who had been shot brought in two other Jamaicans to exact revenge on his behalf. Kidnapping was also an increasing problem, according to the report, with Hertfordshire, Bedfordshire and South Yorkshire police all facing a spate of them in early 2002.

The report says Immigration Service action was able to disrupt Jamaican groups, forcing them to move to other places – a positive result for the current host city but causing new problems for wherever they ended up. West Yorkshire police said Operation Trident successes in London had forced some Jamaicans to Leeds, which at that time had an open drugs market. Having established a foothold in the city's Chapeltown district, others then joined them. For a time they co-existed with local black dealers, but then started to oust them at gun point. However, they were in turn being disrupted by police, and West Yorkshire was one of a few English forces saying that some of the main gangs were spreading to Scotland. Jamaican dealers were moving from Leeds to Edinburgh and Glasgow, while some Jamaicans in Wolverhampton were travelling to and from Aberdeen, exploiting the city's oil-generated wealth. Their chosen method was to move prostitutes with drug addictions to the area who then supplied cocaine to the oil workers. Profits were much higher than in Wolverhampton.

One man wanted in London for a particularly gruesome double murder in 2001 was found to have moved to Birmingham. It was in the middle of summer that Anneta Johnson had arrived at Heathrow airport from Jamaica. Inside her stomach were condoms filled with cocaine. With the drugs estimated to be worth £20,000, she was a valuable prize for the Jamaicans supposed to be welcoming her, all in their early thirties. Unfortunately, they had a falling out which ended in the death of two of them and the jailing of three, including a Birmingham man, Bryan McLeish. The story of what happened was later pieced together by Operation Trident detectives led by DCI Julian Headon.

After managing to get through Customs and immigration, the

21-year-old Johnson, from Kingston, met Kirk 'Bonnie' Ambersley who took her to an address in north London. As the drugs started to pass through her system, two other Jamaican men arrived, Ray Samuels and Godfrey Scott. Anneta was driven off by Scott in one car, with Ambersley and Samuels in convoy in a second car. Scott told the driver of his car to 'lose' the following vehicle, and drove Anneta to his flat in Stoke Newington. Ambersley reported his loss to another of the gang, Bryan McLeish, who travelled to and from his new home in Birmingham. Ambersley still had Samuels and took him to McLeish's old flat in Clapton. There McLeish was amongst those who tortured Samuels into revealing Scott's address. Bound and gagged, a hot iron was held to his face and scalding water poured over him, taking off some of his skin. At some stage, his tongue was slit. Eventually a bag was put over his head and he suffocated.

Ambersley then went to Scott's home, lured him outside and shot him in the neck in a nearby road. When police arrived, they found him dead, lying in a pool of blood. Anneta Johnson was also found. Having been a valuable prize for the Jamaican drugs gang, she then became a valuable witness for the Trident officers called in to investigate. However, the police intervention came too late to save Samuels. His mutilated body was dumped overnight and discovered the next day by a woman walking her dog near Rangers Road, which runs through Epping Forest.

At the Old Bailey in June 2002, McLeish, aged thirty-one, of Winson Green, Birmingham, was jailed for life for both murders with a ten-year sentence for falsely imprisoning Samuels, three years for perverting the course of justice by disposing of his body, and eight years for conspiracy to possess cocaine. Ambersley, thirty, was sentenced to eight years for Scott's manslaughter. Anneta Johnson was jailed for thirty months after admitting importing the cocaine.

UK crack consumption was estimated by the Home Office to be eighteen tonnes in 2001. ACPO reckoned that in addition to the much larger amount of cocaine coming direct from South America, more than twenty tonnes of the drug leaves Jamaica each year for Europe, much of it ending up in the UK. The favoured methods of smuggling were by couriers, the 'swallowers' and 'stuffers', inside whom up to one kilo of the drug can be hidden. The number of Jamaicans caught with drugs at Heathrow had shot up. In 1994, of the non-UK nationals importing illegal drugs, only one per cent were Jamaican. By 2001, 530 Jamaicans were caught, representing seventy-six per cent of the total. West Midlands police reported that locally based Jamaicans rely on 'the little and often' mule method, whilst their Home Boys, British-born blacks, have access to larger shipments of cocaine from continental Europe. Customs said large quantities of the drug had been brought to the UK on two cruise ships. The crew disembarked taking small packages ashore, meeting Jamaicans who they were able to recognise because they were wearing white baseball caps.

The high cost of using crack means users need more money to fund their habit. A Home Office research paper from 2001 suggests regular heroin users spend £16,000 a year on drugs, while the equivalent for a crack user is £21,000. To get that kind of money, the user turns to what the police term 'acquisitive' crime. Avon and Somerset police figures showed a five per cent decrease for this kind of crime between 1999 and 2000. But the following year, corresponding with the spread of crack, it had shot up by just under thirty per cent, with street robberies in Bristol up by seventy-seven per cent for the same period.

The ACPO report also noted increased collaboration between different ethnic groups in the supply of class-A drugs. In Gloucester, Jamaicans had teams of local white 'runners'. Gangs in Birmingham were working with local Asians to supply heroin. In Sheffield, local Asian drug dealers had joined forces with black gang members from Manchester to target rival Asian groups. An NCIS intelligence assessment highlighted Turkish organised crime groups as clashing with black gangs over drug deals. The report said:

'The collaboration of such groups has clear implications
for the supply of class-A drugs in the UK, but also offers

the potential for criminal disputes leading to firearms incidents. With Turkish gangs apparently becoming less discriminating in their possession and use of firearms and also using ethnic Albanians and Jamaicans as enforcers, the potential exists for Caribbean groups to extend their victim base from the currently most common black-on-black shootings. The situation may deteriorate further as it is anticipated that the supply and quality of Afghan heroin will decrease, increasing possible tensions over the market share for heroin distribution and increasing the significance of the cocaine market.'

Illegal immigration forms another large section in the report, with Jamaicans said to be engaged on a massive scale, facilitating entry through forged documents, bogus sponsors and abuse of the rules allowing foreign students to study in the country. In just one month in 2001, of Jamaican arrivals at Heathrow, 36 had forged documents, 279 were refused entry, 62 were prosecuted for drug offences and 56 failed to comply with temporary admission conditions. One of the many scams identified was false marriage to gain UK residence. Another tactic was the abuse of the student entry system with three colleges named as being involved. One was in London, one in Bristol and the third, in Manchester, went under a number of different names. It came to police attention when large numbers of its 'students' were arrested for drug-related offences. Police said: 'The college is housed in a large dilapidated detached house which would appear unsuitable for its purported purpose both in terms of its size, condition and lack of facilities.' A problem repeatedly highlighted by many forces was that when illegal immigrants were deported or refused entry, they could often make a quick return, using different documentation. One Jamaican criminal 'responsible for firearms offences and rape' had been removed from the UK on four separate occasions by West Yorkshire police and the Immigration Service, only to return each time.

Jamaican gangs were skilled at identifying drug market

opportunities, usually in places with no significant controlling interest, says the report. A majority of police forces said a frequently used method was for a gang to choose an area with an existing heroin or cocaine market, and then target a single vulnerable female there, usually someone with a drug habit herself. The woman would be supplied with crack and then used to supply that area. Prostitutes were often used in this way.

The tactic was illustrated with two case studies. In Camberley, Surrey, a lone woman in her own property was targeted by two Jamaican men. Known only as C and T, they used the woman's home to sell heroin and crack. Police learned that a large number of low-level criminals and dealers were visiting the address and mounted a surveillance operation. C was arrested and deported to Jamaica. The police activity forced T into moving to another woman's home nearby. Selling drugs from that second address was estimated by Surrey police to be earning him about £10,000 a week. T was eventually arrested and, although he was believed to be an illegal Jamaican immigrant, his true identity remained unknown. In the second example, Lancashire police blame a prostitute for the introduction of Jamaican criminals and crack to Preston. Originally from Preston, the woman spent several years working as a prostitute in Northampton. She returned to Preston, introducing several gang members to the area. They saw it as a lucrative market for crack distribution and so decided to stay, targeting other prostitutes and taking over their addresses to use as crack houses.

Another case study shows how quickly an outside gang can take over a city's class-A drug market. A Hampshire police report described what happened in April 2001 when six Jamaicans arrived and started dealing crack and heroin in Southampton, a city with an existing African-Caribbean community and a serious drugs problem.

'The males purported to be Yardies and boasted that they were wanted for serious offences in Jamaica and the USA. Intelligence reports suggested they were using extreme violence to take over local drug dealing networks. Whilst there was no evident structure to the groups, which appeared small and fluid in their associations, the overall numbers involved began to spiral. Operation Trojan, which is targeting the problem, currently has 260 subjects and has made 154 related arrests.

'The local dealers have been intimidated out of competition and the majority of crack and heroin supplied in Southampton is controlled by these gangs. Initially the Yardies came from London, but increasingly they now come direct from Jamaica. Whilst heroin is still predominately sourced from London, Southampton now has its own courier network, using local prostitutes to bring cocaine from Jamaica via the London airports. There have been numerous violent incidents attributed to these groups including one murder and two shootings. There has also been an increase in criminal vendetta kidnappings. Revolvers and semi-automatic pistols have been recovered whilst intelligence reports suggest that groups have possession of numerous firearms, including sawn-off shotguns and Heckler and Koch 5s.'

The ACPO report observes that many gang offences are not reported to police. These include intimidation, beatings, 'taxings'(one criminal forcing another to hand over cash, drugs or other goods – this can be done as 'protection' or simply stealing) and some shootings and kidnapping. Because of this, it stresses the need for police to develop an active flow of intelligence in order to respond effectively to gang activity, and suggests a number of intelligence-gathering methods. Infiltration of gangs using undercover detectives poses difficulties, however, because of the necessary 'referencing'. The 'legends' or false backgrounds carefully built up for an undercover officer in the world of conventional organised criminals will not work when dealing with young black gangs because British-born members have usually known each other from their schooldays, and such is the Jamaican network that checks can easily be made on people claiming to be from Kingston. Instead of using undercover officers, ACPO recommends the use of CHIS (covert human intelligence sources) informants reporting that police forces have found no greater problem in recruiting and running them in the black criminal community than in other criminal areas.

Conventional surveillance also poses problems. Because the black gangs tend to operate in largely black areas, surveillance teams comprising mostly white officers stand out. The gangs' mobility causes police further difficulties. Greater Manchester and West Midlands police report their targets' use of mountain bikes on urban estates has frustrated surveillance whether it is on foot or mobile. The same applies when some gang members use 'team' or 'pool' cars rather than sticking to the same vehicle. The problems with conventional surveillance 'can be exacerbated when subjects are believed to be carrying firearms as tactical options for dealing with them are extremely limited.' This is especially true when some gangs use 'blocking cars'. If one team member is carrying a gun in one vehicle, others will drive with him in a convoy, with those behind acting as decoys or obstructing any unmarked police vehicles following them. However, the report recommends technical surveillance, a term which includes bugging, phone intercepts and tracking devices on cars. It says there is 'little evidence of the targets being more aware of these tactics than other criminal groups.'

One tactic recommended by ACPO for dealing with gun crime came from an anti-terrorist measure in London. A machine which automatically reads car number plates is able to flag up suspect vehicles within seconds, alerting officers nearby at roadblocks who can then halt them to question the occupants. The scanning machines have been adapted and fed with vehicle registration details of cars which are believed to be used by gang members. At least three of London's gun crime hotspot areas were targeted in this way during 2004 with armed police manning the roadblocks. The Met claimed each was successful and that local people supported the action.

A year after delivering the sub-group report, its author, Greater Manchester Police Deputy Chief Constable Alan Green, spoke at ACPO's annual conference, telling police bosses that they were burying their heads in the sand if they thought firearms crime in their area was not a problem. 'Gun crime, impacting particularly on our black communities, has spread across this country like a cancer. If you compare the situation five years ago with today, it's frightening. If you think you have not got a problem, you will get one quickly. It's coming your way, believe me.' Delegates were told that gun crime had spiralled out of control in Nottinghamshire, leading to the launch of a campaign code-named Operation Stealth, which had resulted in 352 arrests. A large slice of the increase in fatal shootings came from 'straightforward assassinations that twelve months ago were unheard of in Nottinghamshire,' said Detective Chief Superintendent Phillip Davies.

Another ACPO member, West Midlands Assistant Chief Constable Nick Tofiluk, wrote a few months later that the rise in gun offences from 2001 to 2003 in his area was related to increased friction between drug gangs. Extreme violence and guns were being used to maintain drug supply lines and markets. He said there was now an additional complicating factor: 'Firearms themselves have become a symbol of power, lifestyle and "respect" with a sub-culture that has little in common with the traditional use of firearms as a specialised and rare business enforcer.' While he said that African-Caribbean networks were responsible for much of the gun crime in the West Midlands, intelligence indicated the emergence of similar networks amongst British Asians and people of white backgrounds. To think of the drugs–gun link as being solely a black issue was erroneous in his area, he said, and likely to 'inappropriately label' African-Caribbean communities. The same theme was to come to the fore in London during 2004.

The spread from cities to towns of hard drugs such as crack cocaine and heroin, with their accompanying gun crime, causes major policing difficulties for the smaller forces. Bedfordshire police had a particular problem in dealing with a gun carrying gang controlling heroin distribution in Luton. A huge amount of police time and money was spent gathering evidence against the gang, prosecuting them and then gaining convictions. Investigation of other 'normal' crimes was neglected. After the arrests, Luton was fairly free of hard drugs. But being clean lasted for only a week before other groups moved in causing more problems for the police. Tracking and trying to control several groups was much more difficult than dealing with just one gang.

In London, Operation Trident recognises that its actions have displaced some gang members. Gunmen, wanted for shootings and murders in London, have fled to other cities, lying low with friends or relatives. Drug dealers have been forced to seek markets elsewhere, either moving permanently to other towns or making day-trips to deliver their goods. Trident detectives travel to other places in the country chasing their targets and helping cash-strapped provincial forces with joint investigations. One Trident officer told me: 'We liaise with other forces, but it's easier to investigate here in London if the subject is travelling to other places. We can do searches here, and can keep it up day after day, whereas the county forces are on limited budgets. Much to the annoyance of these investigators, their bosses pull the plug on continuing operations because of their cost. So we can get involved in joint operations.'

London's gun hotspots are still seen as a world apart from the more affluent suburbs, but the picture is changing, taking by surprise even those in charge of dealing with the capital's gun crime. That was brought home at an Infolog gun-crime conference in 2004, with a speech to delegates from around the country by Lord Toby Harris, then chair of the Metropolitan Police Authority, the MPA, which controls the Met. He said gun crime hotspots such as Lambeth, Harlesden and Hackney were very different from the leafy suburbs of outer London, such as Kingston-upon-Thames, where nothing much happened. He was immediately corrected by the next speaker, Operation Trident's head, Detective Chief Superintendent John Coles, who told him there had been a major incident in Kingston that very morning. A car had been ambushed there and a gunman had killed one of the occupants. Later that same day it was back to one of the usual places. In a totally separate incident that evening in Brixton – the original hotspot – shots were fired at a man and his girlfriend as they left a shop. The man died and the woman was injured.

Another fatal shooting in September that year also caused surprise because it took place in High Wycombe in Buckinghamshire, a quiet, conservative town in the beautiful countryside in the Chilterns, and not a place readily associated with gun crime. But a young woman died there from a gunshot wound during a special reggae night at the local community centre. Natasha Derby, aged twenty-three, who lived locally, was one of about one hundred people on the dance floor when the sound of a gun being fired was heard above the music. She slumped to the floor with a bullet wound to her head. After a two-month long investigation, a 29-year-old man was arrested and charged with her murder.

'Guns have been recovered disguised as screwdrivers, cigarette packets and lighters, pens, and belt buckles. Most have limited range and accuracy and have only a one- or two-shot capability, but one disguised as a mobile phone could fire four bullets.'

Wayne Rowe was caught by police with a Mac-10 machine pistol in a car. He served four years of a seven-year prison sentence and is now working with young people, trying to steer them away from crime. Although having turned his life around, he still has a vivid memory of firing the fearsome weapon, which can empty a thirty-round ammunition clip in two seconds. Rowe told me he went to a graveyard to test it before handing over the £3,000 purchase price:

'It was fantastic. I'd become a superman. It's like an adrenalin buzz, the same buzz as when I was a little boy and used to play with guns – bang bang – only it was like a hundred times more. Not because it was firing real bullets, but because of what it was doing – the action of it. It wasn't that I was thinking I could kill ten people with this. It was the simple fact that I had a machine gun and I was firing it. I could feel the gun shaking in my hands – that's what it was.

'If anyone tried to threaten me, I would think to myself "if you only knew what I had tucked away". I felt invincible and I know that's the case for most of the guys carrying guns. There are youths out there with £100,000 stuck underneath their beds and enough fire power to start a small war. It's the same the whole world over – the person with the most money and the biggest gun is the one with the power. The Mac-10 was brand new. It never shot anyone. It cost me three grand and you get what you pay for. You can get any gun that you want on the street, and when I say any gun, I mean any

gun – AK47s, M16s – they're all out there. You could
even get a bazooka. Northern Ireland is just a stone's
throw away. It's that easy. Anything they've got over
there, we've got over here.'

Wayne Rowe's gun was real and in the right hands packs lethal
power. But not for nothing is its firing action referred to as 'spray
and pray'. The same shaking action Rowe referred to makes it
an inaccurate weapon for the inexperienced. Many of the other
guns seized by Trident officers are converted air or gas guns or
replicas. They lack fire power and because it can be difficult to get
real ammunition, bullets are often handmade. A gunman without
training will also fail to take into account the firing 'kick', which
jerks the weapon, destroying the aim. It is because of these factors
that so many gunmen's victims survive shootings. To overcome the
various problems, the more experienced gunmen know that without
a real gun they have to get close to their intended victims to cause
serious injury or death. But that can give detectives extra clues.

One senior officer at Operation Trident's headquarters
pointed at a large screen about twenty feet away on the opposite
wall. Forming his hand and fingers into an imaginary gun, he told
me that a typical young gunman would miss even such a big target.
'Because of the poor quality of ammo and guns, to hit someone and
injure or kill, you've got to get close up to the victim – and that's
useful for us, because you can then get good forensics – powder
residue, blood etc. on hands and clothes. It's difficult to get off
and you can match it with what's been found on the victim.'

The main Government agency dealing with gun crime is the
National Criminal Intelligence Service (NCIS). Its annual 'threat
assessment' has a section on black-on-black firearms crime which
sums up why such criminals use guns:

'They appear quick to resort to firearms to settle
disputes over territory or drugs markets, or in clashes
with members of rival gangs. A number of factors
encourage this behaviour. These include the existence of

a gun culture in which possession of firearms is related to image and machismo, meaning that members at all levels of a criminal group or gang are likely to possess a firearm. There is also an apparent lack of concern about drawing themselves to the attention of the police by the use of firearms, and a tendency to use firearms, rather than merely threaten with them, when enforcing drugs debts, even when the sums concerned are small. In addition, firearms are used to punish perceived "diss" (disrespect) to the criminal, his associates or family members, which in turn can lead to vendettas and further firearms incidents.'

Well under half of the firearms seized each year are genuine weapons such as sub-machine guns and larger calibre handguns. Such guns represent under twenty per cent of firearms recovered in London according to 2004 figures from Scotland Yard. These real guns tend to be used in planned shootings or turf wars where reliability is needed. They are usually held at safe-houses or buried at strategic locations for easy access. Many thousands of handguns were held legally and illegally before a change in firearms legislation in 1997. Those in criminal hands stayed in circulation, added to by illegally imported weapons, some of them finding their way to the UK from the old Eastern European countries. Other genuine guns were deactivated and were sold quite legally. One estimate is that there could be as many as 120,000 such guns in existence. These deactivated weapons can be reactivated quite easily with a minimum of equipment, turning them once again into lethal weapons. A father and son in Derbyshire did just that – running a huge business operation, providing thousands of guns to criminals.

Although the gun was never found that killed Avril Johnson and two other people in the series of murders described at the beginning of this book, forensic and ballistic evidence showed that it was one of a batch of guns that passed through the hands of William Greenwood, aged seventy-six, of South Wingfield in

Derbyshire. Weapons used in other murders and shootings have been linked to Greenwood and his son Mitchell, forty-two, who were described in court as 'quartermasters to the underworld'. At least three thousand weapons sold by the pair are thought still to be in circulation.

Police were first alerted to their evil trade in the mid-1990s. It was then that their previous home in Long Eaton was raided and a variety of weaponry found. There were Uzi sub-machine guns, AK47 automatic rifles, automatic pistols, and propped against a fridge was a bazooka. Father and son were given suspended jail sentences for illegal firearms possession and they were ordered to dispose of their guns or decommission them. Instead of doing that they tried to get round the law. They advertised and sold deactivated weapons which had their barrels blocked and vital parts removed. But along with the guns, they also sold missing parts, equipment and instructions on how to reactivate the weapons. During another long police inquiry involving NCIS, an undercover detective posing as a buyer was offered a 9 mm Browning pistol and a pen and paper to take down instructions on how to reactivate it. The Greenwoods were again arrested and in March 2004 were each given a seven-year prison sentence after being found guilty at Derby Crown Court of conspiracy to convert deactivated guns to live weapons.

One of the pair's customers was Arthur Shaw, who was jailed for ten years after buying one hundred semi-automatic weapons and then reactivating them. Anthony 'Machine Gun' Mitchell was another big customer. He bought more than a hundred guns from the Greenwoods, including Uzis, AK47s and PPK handguns. Mitchell, a former special constable, drilled out or replaced the barrels and fitted new parts, some of which he had engineered himself in his workshop in Brighton. Mac-10s were his specialty. Through middlemen, they were sold to notorious criminals such as Paul Ferris, who acted as an enforcer in Glasgow. Police learned that Ferris was travelling to London to buy guns which Mitchell had supplied to a man called John Ackerman who lived in Islington. Ackerman's home was staked out and Ferris was seen arriving. Police moved in and found three Mac-10s and 360 rounds of ammunition. Ferris was jailed for seven years, Ackerman for six, and Mitchell, who admitted several weapons offences, was given an eight-year sentence.

Undercover and surveillance officers often come up against a particular problem during long proactive operations. What do they do if they witness a crime while out on the street? Moving in and arresting those responsible could jeopardise months, and sometimes years, of careful work against a larger group of criminals. Such a dilemma faced Operation Trident detectives targeting gun dealers and converters in south London in what was to be a series of successful proactive operations.

It started in February 2002 when police received intelligence from Customs that a Stockwell man called John Robbins was supplying guns. Robbins was white, and Trident would not normally have dealt with him. But because it was believed his weapons were being sold on to black gunmen, Trident was called in. Through surveillance and phone-tapping, they learned that Robbins was about to sell some guns. But unknown at that stage was where the weaponry was coming from.

Trident learned that Robbins planned to meet and sell guns to two men travelling down to London from Liverpool. The venue for the meeting was to be the Cock and Monkey pub in Rotherhithe, south-east London, and Trident officers staked it out. They saw Robbins meet three men, the two Liverpudlians and a third man, another Londoner acting as the middleman in the transaction. Guns were handed over, and then, to the consternation of the watching officers, the buyers took them to the pub's car park and, in broad daylight, at around 4.30, it was guns in the afternoon. The weapons were fired at a wall. The men were testing them, making sure they worked. Satisfied, the buyers handed over money. Arrests could have been made at that stage. Certainly there was enough evidence as the police had filmed the transaction. 'That test-firing caused us a few grey hairs,' said Graham Wiseman, the detective sergeant heading the Trident proactive team. 'But we let it continue because we believed more guns were going to be sold.'

While Trident kept watching Robbins, the two buyers and the middleman drove off with guns and ammunition in a BMW. Armed police moved in on them well away from the pub so as not to alert Robbins. Marked police cars from Scotland Yard's firearms unit blocked in the BMW on the Old Kent Road and arrested the three men inside, the two from Liverpool, David Turner, forty-three and Peter Bennett, forty-one, and the middleman, Richard Boyd, forty-four. Also in the car were forty-eight bullets and eight replica Italian police Walther PKKs which had been converted to fire live rounds. Meanwhile, Robbins had travelled to a pub in Bermondsey. It looked as though his day's business was over, and because he would eventually learn of the arrests and possibly go to ground, Trident officers moved in, arresting him as he waited for a mini-cab. Robbins and the other three all pleaded guilty and in January 2003, at Inner London Crown Court, they were given sentences of either eight or nine years.

After the arrests, but before the court case, the Trident team started to investigate the guns' origins. Intelligence reaching police suggested that a Bermondsey man, Stephen Herbert, could have been the man who converted and supplied them. Checking their surveillance records, the detectives found that an associate of Robbins had visited Herbert's flat before the handover of guns to the Liverpool men. Crucially, they also discovered that, unknown to them, Herbert had been arrested previously in May 2002 after being seen to have thrown away two guns. Trident had not been informed because Herbert was white and the arresting officers did not know of the covert operation and of a possible link. Herbert had been charged, but the case was thrown out at the committal stage because of a legal technicality. Later, however, on learning of the case, the Trident team examined the two guns and found that both were of the same type as those bought by the Liverpudlians. It looked like Trident had discovered the source, but they needed evidence. A second big surveillance operation started in October 2002, focusing this time on Stephen Herbert and his associates.

On the very first day, Herbert was seen leaving his home in Bermondsey and driving in his black Mondeo to a shop selling blank-firing guns, replica and deactivated weapons, airguns and other types of militaria. He then drove home and was next seen talking to a black male, before driving to the flat of a girlfriend. The next day, he again visited the shop. This time a surveillance officer followed him inside and overheard him complaining to the owner that something 'didn't fit'. Because surveillance is expensive in terms of time and manpower, Herbert was only watched for two or three days in each of the following weeks. During November and December he was observed visiting the gun shop and meeting various young men, black and white, and handing them packages. 'We had opportunities to arrest him, but we wanted everyone else involved, the whole organisation,' said DS Wiseman, the officer in charge of the Trident operation. 'Herbert was very surveillance conscious. He'd drive down a cul-de-sac and see if anyone followed him, or go into a pub car park and see who else arrived.' I asked Wiseman if he was surprised that his target should apparently be dealing in guns so soon after having been arrested by other police. 'No, I'm not,' replied the detective. 'It's his job, his trade, and he was making good money out of it.'

In phone conversations Herbert was heard referring to a 'shed' where police believed he was storing the replica or deactivated guns. He was then seen visiting a shed next to a block of flats close to the Old Kent Road, on one occasion leaving a large box inside which he had picked up at the gun shop. Police were careful not to enter it themselves. If they had done so and found guns, they would have had to arrest Herbert and that would have blown their wider investigation. Instead they installed a video camera in a 'hide' covering the shed, and Herbert was seen going inside it on several occasions, sometimes with another man.

A criminal called Gary Beard was identified as the man helping Herbert in converting and supplying the guns. Surveillance started on him at the end of January 2003. Over the following few days he was seen leaving his home in Kidbrooke, south-east London, and buying equipment which could be used for gun conversion, including tubing from B&Q to form barrels. He also went to the same gun shop visited by Herbert, sometimes leaving with packages, but making deliveries there as well. Beard and Herbert were also seen going together to a flat in Mountacre Close, near Crystal Palace, taking in boxes and packages, spending time there and then leaving, carrying plastic bags weighed down with what appeared to be heavy items. The watching detectives reckoned that they had found the gun factory, the place where the conversion work was done, turning replicas into lethal weapons.

From phone taps, Trident learned that Herbert and Beard had converted about forty weapons and were preparing another ten PPK handguns. 'We knew the guns were about to be moved,' said Wiseman. 'We didn't know where or to whom, but if we let them go ahead, we would lose control of the situation. So we scrambled a team together to arrest them.' Gary Beard was arrested outside another gun shop and Stephen Herbert at his home. Police found several unconverted blank-firing guns and deactivated weapons in the flat the pair both used, along with tools for the conversion work. Some of these guns had been broken down into parts, ready to be converted. In a lock-up shed attached to the block of flats was a bag containing sixteen converted PPKs. More guns and ammunition were discovered in the shed used by Herbert.

Then came discussions with Crown Prosecution Service lawyers which proved to be frustrating for the Trident team, and doubly so the following year when the case came up at the Old Bailey. The detectives believed the evidence against Beard and Herbert was overwhelming and that, given the number of weapons recovered, the pair would receive heavy prison sentences. But that could only be achieved, according to the CPS lawyers, if every single gun was 'proved' to be potentially lethal. Without such proof, they could only be charged with conspiracy to convert replica or deactivated weapons, which would attract lesser sentences. And, they argued, it was not enough to prove that only a sample few were lethal because that would mean the more serious charge could only relate to those guns. It was the difference between possessing one or two lethal guns and forty or fifty. The seizures were a record for Trident and the team were determined that the sentences should reflect that. So all the weaponry had to be taken to a laboratory for a detailed examination of every single gun. That exercise alone took up many weeks of police and lab time and is understood to have cost close to a million pounds.

In 2004, on 11th September, Herbert and Beard appeared at the Old Bailey for sentencing, having admitted conspiracy to manufacture and supply prohibited weapons and conspiracy to supply firearms with intent to cause fear of violence over a ten-month period. Mark Gadsen, prosecuting, said it was thought the pair had bought nearly 600 replica and blank-firing guns, converted them into deadly weapons and then sold them on to gangsters, both black and white, at the rate of one a day. Bearing in mind the earlier sentences of eight and nine years given to the Liverpudlians, Trident officers were amazed when the judge, David Paget, said that he was taking into account the pair's guilty pleas and was sentencing them to only six years in prison. The detectives' surprise was shared by the two defendants. As he was led away, Herbert called out to the judge: 'That's lovely. Thank you. Got away with that.' The CPS took the unusual step of referring the sentences to the Attorney General for undue leniency. A few months later the case went to the Appeal Court, and Beard and Herbert were each given an extra three years.

Meanwhile the Trident proactive team's investigations into gun-dealing in south London had continued. Surveillance was mounted against some of the other customers visiting the same gun shop as Beard and Herbert. These included a young black man, Eli Powell, who worked with another man, identified as Abdul Motileb, known as Bush. Motileb converted the weapons and Powell's role was to find and sell to buyers. On 15th October, 2003, three men were seen arriving by car at Powell's home in Bow, east London, leaving with a package. Police decided to arrest them but, so Powell would not be alerted, the car was allowed to leave. Armed officers pulled it over a few minutes later in City Road, finding a converted gun in a carrier bag on the back seat. One of the three men eventually pleaded guilty to possession and was given a two-year sentence.

Surveillance continued on Powell and on 10th December he was seen meeting two men at garages near his home. Powell handed a bag to one of them, Nazim Uddin. Plainclothes officers approached and Uddin ran off. Powell dropped the bag near some old tyres in front of the garages. Both men were arrested and the bag was found to contain a black handgun with ten rounds of ammunition. Powell's mobile phone rang while at the scene, displaying Motileb's street name Bush. Uddin was carrying £340 in cash. Various types of ammunition were found in searches of Powell's home and garage. Abdul Motileb was arrested the next day for conspiracy to supply firearms. A search of his home in Nettledon House, Chelsea, turned up ammunition, gun parts, gunpowder and tools to make bullets and firearms. He admitted working on conversions in his kitchen, agreeing that he supplied the finished product to Eli Powell. In June 2004, Powell, Motileb and Uddin were all found guilty of conspiracy to convert firearms. Powell was given an eight-year sentence, Motileb seven, and Uddin was sentenced to five years. At the time of writing, others caught in the Trident proactive operation were due to stand trial on gun charges.

In another Trident proactive operation in 2004, a man was caught with a powerful sub-machine gun, capable of firing 750 bullets a minute. Mark Lee, aged twenty-two, had been under surveillance for some time and in March, Trident acted. Supported by the Met's firearms team, they raided his fourth floor flat in a block in Wenlock Street, Shoreditch, in north-east London. The door was reinforced and as police started to smash their way inside, a bare-chested Lee appeared on the balcony and threw a carrier bag to the ground. It contained a Croatian Agram 2000 sub-machine gun, a silencer and sixteen rounds of 9 mm ammunition. Lee admitted possession and was given a five-year sentence at Southwark Crown Court.

The same prison term was given to another man arrested by Operation Trident officers in February 2004. Brian Matthews had been given a five-year sentence in 1999 for drug dealing, and when Trident detectives raided his flat in Wynton Gardens, south Norwood, in 2004, they had a search warrant to look for drugs. They found only a small amount of cannabis, but there was body armour in a cupboard and more than £3,000 in a kitchen drawer. Underneath the floorboards, in a plastic bag, was a machine pistol and twenty bullets which fitted it. Matthews admitted possession and was sentenced at Croydon Crown Court five months later.

Those found guilty of gun crime after pleading not guilty receive bigger sentences than those admitting the same offence at an earlier stage. Mark Smith found that out the hard way in 2004. Smith, thirty-one, was an unlikely character to become a gun-runner. He came from a respectable black family, and was a regular church-goer. One brother was a surveyor and another was a trainee lawyer. He himself worked as a social worker for a Youth Offending Team in Oxford Gardens off Ladbroke Grove in Notting Hill, west London. His job, looking after fifteen- to eighteen-year-olds in trouble with the police, provided the perfect cover for his criminal activities, and whenever he was out transporting guns around London, he made sure he was wearing the big badge identifying him as a social worker. He reckoned it would make police less inclined to stop him, and if, by some chance, he was stopped, he could answer questions plausibly without using the street slang or patois associated with young black criminals. In addition, he had a lisp, another factor making him appear an unlikely candidate to be involved in gun crime.

The exposure of Smith's secret side-line came from very good intelligence on another gun courier Peter Mattheou, also thirty-one, a club bouncer, who had a string of convictions stretching back ten years. These were for assault, criminal damage and possession of offensive weapons, including a knuckleduster, a telescopic baton and a stun gun. Police learned that he was to receive some guns on 24th March, 2003, but they did not know who else was involved.

A team of ten officers, some armed, kept watch on Mattheou's car, a green Corsa, parked near his home in Streatham Hill, south London. They were in position for only an hour when Mattheou arrived with another man, who turned out to be Mark Smith. Mattheou went to his home, leaving Smith standing by the Corsa. The social worker kept looking around anxiously, but he failed to spot any of the police surveillance team. Mattheou returned to the car and the pair drove off, followed by police. The car pulled up behind a pick-up truck near the South Circular and then followed behind it to Penge. Mattheou was then seen to get out of the car and join the pick-up driver in his cab. After a few minutes he returned to the car and the pick-up left, only to return a short time later, pulling alongside the Corsa. It then drove off. To the watching police it looked as though the exchange had been made, that Mattheou had paid over money when in the pick-up's cab, and the driver had returned with guns and passed them over. If the police were right, there was little point in following the pick-up, and, anyway, there were not enough of them to divide into two effective teams. The decision was made to stick with the Corsa.

Police followed it for a short time and then, in a quiet road, moved in and stopped it, shooting out its tyres. Smith and Mattheou were dragged from the car out on to the pavement and handcuffed. Inside the front passenger footwell, where Smith had been sitting, was a small hold-all containing what looked like two tool-kits. However, inside each of the dark grey boxes was a replica Glock pistol which had been converted into a lethal weapon. There was also a small box containing twenty-five rounds of ammunition. Another 'killer's kit' was found in a Sainsbury's plastic bag under the driver's seat. Later that evening, under arrest at a police station, Smith's mobile phone rang twice. The caller's number was the same on each occasion, and had been listed in Smith's mobile as belonging to 'Ricky'. Mattheou's phone had the same number stored under the name 'Yardie'. Police believed that the 'Ricky/Yardie' character had organised the gun delivery and had been expecting Smith to contact him, and that he was ringing him to find out what had happened.

Confronted with all the evidence, Smith stuck to the story he gave when first questioned by DC Gail Lilly – that he had been with Mattheou because the doorman was going to give him reduced price concessionary tickets for nightclubs, and that the pick-up driver had handed over what Mattheou had told him were tool-kits to repair the Corsa. He claimed 'Ricky' was a woman involved with a ticket agency. A different, more truthful story came from Mattheou, who confessed that he and Smith knew exactly what the 'tool-kits' contained.

Mattheou refused to give 'Yardie's' real name, but said he was a well-connected member of an organised criminal gang who was paying him £300 to collect and deliver guns. 'Yardie' had introduced him to Mark Smith at Wembley Park in north-west London, saying he used him to transport guns because his social worker's position did not arouse suspicion. He was also able to gather intelligence from the council's computer system which was linked to police information. Mattheou said that on the train journey south to Streatham Hill, Smith told him that he enjoyed dealing with criminals – that he got a buzz out of it.

Mattheou pleaded guilty to possessing firearms and conspiracy to sell or transfer them. He agreed to give evidence against Smith and did so at Middlesex Crown Court. Despite his compelling evidence, the jury failed to reach a verdict on Smith and a retrial was ordered. However, when that eventually took place at the Old Bailey in August 2004, Mattheou, held on remand in prison awaiting sentencing, declined to enter the witness box. He told police that he had been threatened, and while he believed he could look after himself in prison, he could not protect his family outside, which included his eight-year-old daughter.

At his trial, Smith stuck to his story that he had no idea the tool-kits contained guns. He was ridiculed by the prosecuting barrister, Mark Gadsden. His outline of the case included Mattheou's role in it, but the jury were not told why he was not appearing. In fact, they asked the judge, David Farrer, if Mattheou was backing up Smith's story, but were left none the wiser, being told that they must decide the case on the evidence presented to them. They found Smith guilty of possessing the guns and of conspiracy with Mattheou and others unknown to supply or transfer them.

The jury was called back to court later in the day for the sentencing of both Smith and Mattheou, who they were seeing for the first time. The judge told the guilty men, separated in the dock by a security guard, that the guns they had received and were going to hand to others could have been used instantly as lethal weapons. He went on: 'The people of London have had enough of those who trade and use guns. I have no doubt whatever that they were intended for criminals who would use them. Those prepared to pass on guns are little better than those using them.' Credit was given to Mattheou for his guilty plea and he was given a sentence of five and a half years. The judge called Smith two-faced. He had deceived the Youth Offending Team managers who had provided testimonials for him. He had a challenging and responsible job, dealing with young people predisposed to crime. The possibility that the guns could have ended up in their hands was a very disturbing consideration, said the judge. He gave Smith an eight-year sentence. As the social worker left the dock, he smiled and waved to his family in the public gallery.

Detectives never did find out the identity of the Ricky/Yardie figure, to whom the guns collected by Smith were to be given. But evidence from the case helped convict another armourer. There had been a separate investigation by another Scotland Yard unit into Paul Packham, a 36-year-old from south-east London. Although unemployed, he appeared to be a wealthy man. He drove a Mercedes and kept a boat worth £46,000 at a marina in Chichester, west Sussex. He also went on a £5,000 cruise to the Canary Islands with his girlfriend, who sported a gift from him – a £3,000 ring. Police suspected his money came from converting blank-firing replica guns into lethal weapons.

When detectives raided Packham's home in Plumstead and went into his garden shed, they found an array of weaponry and sophisticated equipment and machinery for carrying out conversion work and making bullets. A full search revealed more than eighty Beretta handguns bought via the internet from companies in continental Europe. Converted into lethal weapons, they would have been worth more than £1,000 each on the street. There were also twenty-five stun guns, seventeen CS gas canisters and nearly 2,000 bullets. As a side-line, he was also growing cannabis plants and selling the drug.

Although caught red-handed, Packham tried to play down

his guilt, claiming he had been pressurised into doing the work. He said a month before his arrest, he had agreed to convert a couple of guns, and had then been forced into doing more. Police suspected him of lying as two murders had already been linked to the bullets he sold, and proof came from the Smith/Mattheou case. Fingerprints had been found on the packing surrounding the three guns. They had been fed into the records system, but no match was found for them. Then came the arrest of Packham. He had no criminal record so his fingerprints had not been stored. However, after his arrest, when they were entered into the system, it was found they matched those found on the packing. But Smith and Mattheou had been arrested two months before Packham. This meant that his story did not stand up. It proved that he had been handling weapons for at least a month before he claimed to have been forced into the conversion work. In February 2004, Packham pleaded guilty at Woolwich Crown Court to possessing firearms and was given an eight-year sentence, with another year for producing and supplying cannabis.

The majority of guns seized by Met police pack less power and accuracy than the genuine or reactivated weapon, and are much cheaper and easier to obtain. Sometimes referred to as 'entry level firearms', they are blank-firing or air weapons converted to fire live rounds. Most common amongst these are the blank-firing Remington Derringer and the Brocock air pistol. Until the early 1990s, air-powered handguns had to be reloaded each time a pellet was fired. But the Brocock company then produced a pistol allowing the user to fire six shots, one after the other, without having to reload. It was soon realised, however, that the pistol's cartridge system was about the same size as .22 bullets, and that adding a 'sleeve' to the chamber was all that was required to let it fire real ammunition.

It is almost as easy to convert blank firers into lethal guns. A normal gun works by exploding a small charge behind a bullet in an enclosed chamber. The bullet is then projected along the barrel, with the expanding gas trapped behind it, giving it more power and speed. To prevent this process, blank-firers have two main features. The barrel is blocked and there is a vent hole which allows the hot gas to escape instead of pushing the bullet down the barrel. Turning them into lethal weapons is simply a question of hollowing or drilling out the barrel and blocking the vent hole.

Such conversions are not very accurate as the 'normal' conversion will not have a rifled barrel. But there is a more serious problem for someone wanting to use them. Blank-firers are made from lower grade metal than that of their genuine counterparts, so they degrade quickly because of the physical force and heat produced when firing live bullets. This makes the cheapest only good for a few shots. A blank-firing revolver can be bought for £20 and converting it to fire a live .22 calibre round requires little more than drilling out the barrel blockage. Such cheap weapons are 'use once' guns. Revolvers are easier to convert, but semi-automatics are viewed as being more desirable because they look more professional. Blank-firing copies of police issue handguns, such as the Glock 17, cost under £100. A Berretta mini-automatic costs around £50 and is easy to conceal as it is only slightly bigger than a packet of cigarettes. Even a large weapon like the Desert Eagle costs under £100 and its heavier construction means it can be used several times after conversion.

Just under half the guns used in Operation Trident cases in 2003 were replicas or converted airguns or blank-firers. Of the last two categories, the most frequently seized, according to NCIS, is the Brocock-type cartridge airgun. Then there are ball-bearing weapons, known as BB guns, which can cost under £20. Although firing either plastic pellets or ball-bearings which usually inflict only bruising, these 'air-soft' guns also look very realistic. When police put on anti-gun-crime shows or visit schools, they often ask people to try to distinguish between the genuine gun and the replica, BB gun or even the water pistol, and to put themselves in the position of an armed officer with a gun being pointed at him or some other person.

Similarly realistic, but in a different way, are the so-called disguised guns, most commonly seen in James Bond-type films. Amongst those recovered in the UK, according to NCIS, are guns disguised as screwdrivers, cigarette packets and lighters, pens, and belt buckles. Most have limited range and accuracy and have only a one- or two-shot capability, but one disguised as a mobile phone could fire four bullets. The manufacture of disguised weapons was previously limited to central and Eastern Europe, for example Bulgaria, Croatia and Slovenia, but intelligence now suggests they are made throughout Europe.

A gun disguised as a key fob was featured in a Manchester Crown Court case in November 2004. Police stopped and searched Junior Collins, twenty-seven, after a high speed car chase through the city's Moss Side area. The three-inch double-barrelled fob gun on his keyring was loaded with two bullets. It could be cocked by pulling a metal ring on the back and then fired by pressing buttons on its face. Although of limited range, police said it could be lethal close up. The judge did not believe Collins' claim that he was simply transporting it for a friend and did not know it was a gun. He was given a six-and-a-half-year prison sentence. Later, police said that thirteen such key fob guns had been recovered in the previous few weeks in Manchester and London. It is believed that they came from a batch of 100 smuggled into Britain.

An NCIS report says that real guns, either seized by Customs at ports or by police at shooting scenes or from gang members, originate from all over the world, including Argentina, Australia, China, Croatia, Israel, South Africa, Switzerland and the USA. Some are brought into the country by military personnel as 'trophies' from places such as Iraq and Afghanistan. Firearms or component parts arriving by post or by parcel courier are an increasing worry. That method of importation is not only cheaper but it seems there is less risk of discovery due to the large amounts of post arriving in the UK each day. It is simply impossible to X-ray everything that arrives. Even so, between five and ten packages are detected each day containing either suspect firearms or gun parts.

The internet has also opened up new import possibilities for criminals. NCIS tracked purchases of weaponry by people in the UK via the website of a French company, hosted by a US server. In June 2004, police across the country swooped on 270 addresses of people who had received goods from the French company. They found shotguns, rifles, ammunition, explosives, a rocket launcher, forty-eight stun guns, CS gas and 198 blank-firers, a quarter of which had already been converted into lethal weapons. More than one hundred people were arrested for firearm and drug offences. The exercise was repeated a few months later in November with similar success.

Whichever way criminals get their hands on guns, they have a continuing problem in finding the correct kind of ammunition. Real bullets of the correct calibre can be difficult to find, so the armourers and gunmen often make their own. They can use old cartridge cases, stuff them with a new primer and gunpowder and then fit a bullet at the end. If the bullet is too small, the cartridge case can be crimped to hold it in place. Such a used-cartridge case was found next to the body of the BBC TV personality Jill Dando, who died from a bullet wound to her head. Clingfilm can also be wrapped round the bullet so that it will fit. Blank-firing cartridge cases can be used and the bullets themselves can be made from molten lead poured into moulds.

Early in 2004 new laws were introduced in order to tackle gun crime. A five-year mandatory minimum prison sentence was brought in for illegally possessing a gun or ammunition. Tighter controls also came in for air weapons. The manufacture, sale and import of gas-guns – those with a self-contained gas cartridge system – was banned, and it became an offence to possess replica guns or air weapons in public places 'without legal authority or reasonable excuse'. The age when young people are allowed to buy air weapons was also raised from fourteen to seventeen. How successful the new deterrent laws will be remains to be seen. At the end of the year, some were suggesting that young people were turning to carrying knives rather than guns, and there were calls on the government to bring in stronger penalties for knife possession in public places as well.

Meanwhile, another important feature of gun crime investigation was reorganised and streamlined. Forensic examination of guns and bullets has always been a key element of shooting cases. Fingerprints and DNA can be found on weapons while markings on bullets recovered at shootings can be matched to particular guns. It is not worth testing all bullets and every part of a weapon. The softer metal of some home-made bullets means that they often squash or distort on impact. A gun with a hatched handle is not good for fingerprints, but would go for DNA testing because the rougher surface is more likely to have skin debris. Similarly, the magazine from a pistol is smooth, so there is more chance of finding fingerprints. However, testing of everything could take several weeks as ballistic results have to be checked manually on a card index, and there were two centres doing the same work, one in London and one in the north. This meant staff sometimes shuttling between the two places. In addition there was little liaison or coordination over laboratory results between the country's 43 different police forces.

During 2004 the Forensic Science Service introduced a new system, the National Firearms Forensic Intelligence Database (NFFID) comprising of two separate computer databases. The first gathers information on gun case files, such as the type of weapon used in an incident, its make, model and calibre, and details of any conversions made to it. The second is the Integrated Ballistics Identification System (IBIS). It can compare ammunition found at crime scenes or inside weapons recovered. IBIS suggests a list of possible matches, linking, for example, a gun found at one place with a bullet or cartridge case found in another. The two computer databases operating together can make matches across the country within hours instead of days or even weeks, and because IBIS operates in most EU countries, it means that cross-border checks are also possible.

Forensic intelligence obtained from weapons and ammunition is a very important tool for the police in clearing up murders and shootings, as can be seen in the next chapters dealing with some major Operation Trident investigations in recent years. Some are gruesome, involving torture. Others are more straightforward cases of gangland execution, sometimes for apparently trivial reasons.

'Carrying a gun does not demonstrate power. It demonstrates that you are both despicable cowards... We don't want people like you here to roam free in our society, whether citizens from here, or whether you came here from another country.'

Operation Trident forms the section with the second largest number of detectives in the Metropolitan Police. Most of these officers are engaged in 'reactive' investigations into black-on-black murders or shootings. These were running at about four a week in London when Detective Chief Superintendent Dave Cox took command of the recently formed Trident team in July 2000. Six months later, in a confidential review for his bosses, Cox wrote of the unique combination of problems faced by Trident, quite unlike those encountered by any other of the Met's investigation teams.

> *'Every job* [his emphasis] passed to Trident is a complex inquiry, involving gang culture, firearms usage, witness protection and reluctance to supply basic evidence. The criminals responsible are experienced and wise to police methods and forensic evidence. The shootings generally take place in black clubs or their environs, or in isolated places conducive to drugs transactions. They are solved largely through the use of CHIS [informants] or surveillance. Surveillance must be armed. Issues of officer and public safety feature in all arrest operations. Whilst other serious crime group teams face similar problems in a small proportion of their jobs, they at least have the other inquiries that are more clear cut, for example the occasional domestic, or reliable independent witnesses who are not in fear of retaliation etc.'

Four years on, the officer who took over from Cox gave a very similar assessment. Detective Chief Superintendent John Coles is a bright, active, plain-speaking officer who moved into the Trident hot seat after a punishing time with the Met's anti-corruption group, followed by a spell in charge of the Flying Squad. He told me that there had been important changes. The number of incidents was down. Relations with the black community had improved. Witnesses were more likely to give evidence. More on these aspects later in the book, but Coles agrees that the challenges facing his detectives remain largely the same.

'It's very hard relentless work, but most of the officers who come here absolutely love it. You're working in one of the most complex investigation environments that there is. You need to preserve the scene of a shooting, you need detailed forensic examination, determined seeking of witnesses and so on. If it's a non-Trident murder where someone's stabbed, or it's a domestic murder, it's fairly straightforward what you've got to do, but if you get a shooting in a nightclub in south London, you've got two hundred witnesses you have to find. You've got all the problems of identifying who those witnesses are. Nine times out of ten a shooting is linked to another shooting – a reprisal – and sometimes we're talking about five, six, seven, or even ten years ago. You've got the complexities of the different allegiances that change all the time, and the witnesses' fear of reprisals. You've got the complexity of the family background of the victim. Take — , for example. At one stage we had something like twenty family liaison officers on the investigation because there were so many issues coming out of the family set-up. You're talking set-ups where there can be a dozen fathers within that family group.'

Examples of the unpredictability of Trident's reactive investigations were given to me by an experienced detective:

'We had two similar jobs fairly close together. Shots had been fired in two separate streets and we went to them to pick up the empty bullet cases. In one street, on an estate, we got only one person prepared to make a statement. People didn't want to help because of fear of retribution. The other street, of private homes, was the opposite. They were nearly all happy to talk to us. These were people who were unaware of the extent of criminality.

'On another occasion, we followed a trail of blood to a house. It ended at the front door. The owner said he didn't know anything about it. He didn't want to know, and there was nothing we could do about it. At another place, a trail of blood ended on the doorstep. The victim had been taken to hospital. The owner said an unknown gunman had shot him at the front door. But then we were given information that this wasn't the case – that the shooting had been in the kitchen at the back of the house. We investigated and found bullet holes in the kitchen. The shooting had been there and the victim had been taken to the front, and then on to hospital. Even to this day, we don't know what happened. The most likely explanation is that the gun went off accidentally in the kitchen. That can happen quite easily. If you've got a gun in your pocket, or down a belt, and you pull it out, less experienced people can put their finger on the trigger and squeeze it accidentally as they pull it out. You can then shoot yourself in the leg or bottom.'

Analysis of Trident shootings and murders shows that about eighty per cent involve British-born young black men, with Jamaicans responsible for around eighteen per cent and the remainder from Somalia or other African countries. According to Coles:

Jamaicans tend to be more violent and vicious. They generally operate at a higher level – importing cocaine, whereas the British-born kids we're dealing with are street-level dealers. Jamaicans tend to carry the more dangerous weapons – the real thing, rather than conversions or replicas. Also they're from a slightly older age group, twenty-five to thirty-five years old, whereas the British-born tend to be younger, between seventeen and twenty-three. Then there are crossovers, because some of the youngsters hero-worship the Jamaicans, and they also have family connections. Even though they were born here, they still have connections going back to Jamaica.'

Coles said that prior to Trident being set up, police met a 'wall of silence' when investigating black community murders. That no longer exists. 'In most cases we know within twenty-four hours who did a murder,' he said. 'We are given names, and then we are expected to get the evidence. It may take us three years, but we get there.' Detective Superintendent Rick Turner, in charge of the department's reactive sections, agrees that Trident murder investigations are the most difficult and complex ones a detective will ever work on, largely because people are too frightened to give the police more than a name of who they believe responsible, refusing to take that extra big step of giving evidence in court. He said:

'They're in fear of having their brains blown out. If someone is arrested and charged with murder, and they think they can get off through taking out a witness, then they'll do it. In a normal murder in a pub, say, you'll get two people arguing and one pulls out a knife and stabs the other to death. Most of the people in the pub will give witness statements over what happened. But Trident murders are different with guns involved, and most of the people we're dealing with are still connected to Jamaica, even if they're two or three generations away. I went to Jamaica three months ago and was taken out in an armoured Land Rover by the Consul. On one street I saw two guys walking along with guns in their belts – nine people had been shot dead in that same road the week before and two of them were cops. It was very frightening. Life is cheap there. It made me realise why people will fill themselves with condoms full of coke and smuggle them in here. I can understand the motives of these mules. They want out. So while a victim's family may be law-abiding here, and while intimidation and reprisals may not happen in London, there's a possibility that in Jamaica there's an aunty or uncle etc., and there's a veiled threat, sometimes direct, that if they do help the police, then the family in Jamaica could suffer.'

Turner spoke of Trident criminals being very chaotic and very disorganised:

'Historically we can look at traditional crime families such as the Krays and the Richardsons, who, if they were involved in armed robbery or whatever, would often have quite meticulous planning. Black criminals involved in drugs bring an element of chaos, and often shootings happen on the spur of the moment, the reasons ranging from disrespect to just happening to see someone in the street. Lots of shootings happen that way. That makes investigation difficult.'

The callousness of some of the killers continues to surprise him.

'There's no conversation, no negotiation stage. It's simply going up to the person and at very close range, putting a gun to their head and pulling the trigger. Gratuitous violence from a very close range. To do that is a frame of mind difficult to understand.'

One investigation featuring 'disrespect' and problems with witnesses was also one of the most bizarre murder cases ever handled by Trident. It occurred at a New Year's Eve party when two men were shot dead by a single bullet. The party was continuing well into New Year's Day 2002 when local police and paramedics were called to reports of a shooting at a flat in Shore Place, Hackney, close to Victoria Park. They arrived at 9.30 a.m. to find many of the party-goers wanting to leave the murder scene. Aware that the gunman could still be among them and also that they could lose vital witnesses, the police tried to keep the crowd there until Trident officers arrived. One of those shot died at the scene. He was the party's DJ, Ashley Kenton, a 22-year-old from Deptford in south-east London. The second man, Wayne Mowatt, twenty-nine, from Clapham, died early that evening in hospital.

Although many of the eighty or so at the party were still there, few wanted to help the police. However, detectives managed to piece together what had happened. Two men had rented the flat for the night in an unofficial deal with a letting agent. The pair charged £5 a head for entry and hired Ashley Kenton, known as Creation DJ, to play garage music. During the night, things got a little rough on occasions, and there were scuffles. By nine in the morning, Kenton had had enough and declared he was leaving. But his way was blocked by someone who wanted him to play on. 'No one ain't going nowhere,' said the man. He punched Kenton, who hit him back. Shown disrespect, the man then fired a gun at the DJ, hitting him in the neck and severing an artery, so that he bled to death quickly. But the bullet passed right through his neck, hit a partition wall, came out the other side, and was then lodged in the head of the second man, Wayne Mowatt, aka Titch, who collapsed in a pool of blood. Mowatt was himself no stranger to 'diss' violence, having stood trial in 1995 for killing a taxi driver who had tooted his horn at his girlfriend. Mowatt was cleared of murdering father-of-two Raymond Ennis, but convicted of manslaughter and given a five-year prison sentence.

Trident detectives sent the glasses, bottles, cans and other party debris for DNA and fingerprint analysis to gather evidence and to try to establish exactly who had been there. The murder weapon was missing. The bullet which had killed the two young men was examined, but it was too badly damaged for experts to attempt matching it with any gun used in previous shootings. The bullet's case was also missing, which was unusual. Some gunmen are aware that casings are more likely to yield forensic evidence against them than bullets which, when fired, generally lose any DNA traces on impact. But because the cases are expelled from the gun, they can carry valuable clues, either DNA or even fingerprints. Some professional hitmen, if they have the time, try to recover the cases so they are not found by police. But that would have proved very difficult, if not impossible, in the middle of a panicking party crowd. Police think the gun must have been fired from inside a sock or a bag. The bullet would have passed through the fabric without any problem, but the casing, expelled from the weapon at low velocity, would be trapped inside the sock, if that is what was used, and could then be carried away along with the gun.

As for witnesses, it was the usual story for Trident. Through the dead men's families, appeals on Crimestoppers and informants, Trident were able to identify a man called Iain Davis as their main suspect. But he had disappeared from his home in Bellefields Road, Brixton, and people appeared unwilling to make witness statements while he was at large. Detectives believed he had fled to Jamaica. There the matter rested. Then suddenly, out of the blue, nineteen months after the murder, there came a lucky break.

In August, 2003, Scotland Yard received a phone call from the USA, from a Homeland Security officer at Long Beach airport, California. He was trying to establish the real identity of a man stopped for possible immigration offences. The man had flown to California from New York and on arrival had been asked some questions. Unhappy with the answers, and because the man was growing increasingly agitated, officials checked on the passport he was carrying. Although it carried a photograph of the man in front of them, the passport itself was registered as stolen. Under further questioning, the man admitted that he was Iain Davis and said he was wanted in the UK for assault. The US officer asked Scotland Yard for help, and was put through to Detective Inspector Andy Shrives, in charge of the Trident investigation into the two deaths at the party. The information Davis gave in California was only partly correct. He was indeed wanted for an assault at the Notting Hill carnival, but he was also the prime suspect for the double

murder. He was extradited to the UK a few weeks later and DI
Shrives met the aircraft at Heathrow. Davis had left the UK after
buying a stolen passport and putting his own photograph in it.

After charging Davis with the two murders, and with him
safely locked up in prison on remand, police found witnesses more
willing to come forward. They did so at the Old Bailey in May 2004,
giving evidence from behind screens with their voices distorted
through a special sound box, so that the defendant and those in
the public gallery could not recognise or possibly intimidate them.
During cross-examination, defence counsel are usually allowed
to position themselves so they can see the witnesses, in order to
better gauge from their reactions to questions whether they are
telling the truth. However, in Davis's trial, his lawyer could not
see some of the witnesses. After Davis was found guilty, security
staff had to clear the public gallery to prevent violence breaking
out between members of his family and relatives of his victims.
Judge David Paget sentenced him to two life terms, ordering that
he serve at least twenty years.

Another Trident investigation involved two warring gangs in
north-east London. The Beaumont Crew, based in Walthamstow,
were being challenged by the up and coming Beaufort Boys,
suspected of being connected to drug-dealing in clubs in Cyprus.
At least eight shooting incidents were attributed to the groups
in 2001 and 2002. In one, shots were exchanged around Church
Road in Walthamstow. An Uzi was used in another, in the same
area. A passer-by was almost killed in a shoot-out in Brick Lane.
As it seemed only a question of time before the gang rivalry led to
murder, Trident was asked to help out.

The team was led by Detective Inspector Nick Linfoot,
and the best chance of making successful arrests lay in the Brick
Lane shooting which had occurred mid-afternoon on a Friday
in January 2002. Five men were sitting in a Rover car, parked in
Brick Lane at the junction with Shacklewell Street, when shots
were fired at them. According to witnesses, one of the men
in the Rover beckoned to three men, as if inviting a fight. The
three men approached the car, pulled out guns, and fired between

ten and fifteen shots, hitting one of those inside, Dwayne Dyer, aged twenty. A stray bullet smashed through the windscreen of a passing car, and flew past the driver's right ear. The Rover sped off with the injured Dyer inside, a bullet lodged against his lower spinal cord and suffering from a slight head wound. Someone jumped from the car and flagged down a passing ambulance, and Dyer was taken to hospital. Meanwhile, one of those in the Rover when it came under attack in Brick Lane ran round the corner into the busy Bethnal Green Road, pursued by gunmen in a Saab, one of three other cars which had roared away from Brick Lane immediately after the shooting. Spotting him as he ran past a shoe shop, a passenger in the Saab fired at him. The bullet missed, but ricocheted round the shop, ending in a display area.

The man was later found by police hiding in a building site. One of the Beamont Crew, he said he had been in the Rover with four friends, including Dyer. They had stopped in Brick Lane to buy some trainers, but had been confronted by three men he described as robbers. Dyer asked police for protection, but as he claimed not to know who was responsible for the attack, this was denied him, the reasoning being that if he was unable to identify any of his attackers, then they would not be able to recognise him.

The Rover was abandoned a mile away near the Barbican. Witnesses gave police the registration numbers of the three other cars which sped off after the shooting. The Saab had false number plates and was never found. Another car, a BMW, was stopped with three men inside, two blacks and an Asian. They were interviewed, and bailed after it turned out that they had nothing to do with the shooting, but had simply taken off, worried about getting involved. The Asian was eventually charged with possessing a gun. Trident detectives had more success with the third car, a Peugeot.

Its description and number had been circulated to all police forces and, a few weeks later, police in Peterborough said that they had found it during an on-going drugs investigation. Trident told Peterborough police that the men with the car were suspected of attempted murder. Peterborough replied that they needed another ten days to complete their drugs investigation before moving in on those in the Peugeot in a joint operation with Trident. Only a few days later, however, Peterborough told Trident that it wanted to arrest the men quickly. With no Trident officers available to take part in the arrest operation at such short notice, Peterborough went ahead on its own. Three police cars moved in on the suspects' vehicle, but it manouevred through and past them. A chase ensued during which the Peugeot's occupants threw a package out of the car window. Eventually they were arrested and the package found. It turned out to be a gun wrapped in an old sock, and tests proved that it had been used in the Brick Lane shooting. Two of the men in the Peugeot were in their thirties and came from north London. Sean Stewart, of Walthamstow, and Joseph Pitkin, of Edmonton, were believed to be members of the Beaufort Boys. Searches of their Peterborough addresses revealed a set of body armour at Pitkin's, but there was nothing to interest police at Stewart's.

Trident officers arranged for an identity parade for the two at a police station in north London, with eyewitnesses to the Brick Lane shooting agreeing to attend. But there was a major traffic incident and subsequent jam on the appointed day, which meant cancellation of the ID parade because some of the witnesses were unable to get there at the agreed time. A second parade was arranged for a month later, but the man police believed to be their best witness, someone who had managed to get to the first parade, could not be persuaded to attend another one. Pitkin was not identified, but Stewart was and he was charged with the attempted murder of Dwayne Dyer. Both men appeared at the Old Bailey in February 2004. Pitkin was found guilty of possessing a firearm and ammunition, and was sentenced to three years' imprisonment. Stewart was found not guilty of murder. But he too went to prison, having earlier been found guilty of possessing a gun.

Two different worlds collided in another Trident murder. Pauline Peart and the young men who gunned her down came from vastly different backgrounds. Pauline, aged twenty-five, was from a respectable family and had a responsible job as a finance company's customer account manager. She lived in her own flat on the outskirts of London, in Waltham Abbey, Essex, and had taken out a second mortgage on it in order to buy her dream car – a silver and green Audi TT sports Cabriolet, worth £24,000. Her killers, however, had both grown up in a tough part of the Jamaican capital, before moving as youths to London, where they became immersed in the drugs and gun culture of Tottenham. Maurice Miller had been abandoned as a baby by his father Winston who became a drug dealer in New York, being shot dead in Brooklyn in 2002.

It was on 10th March, 2003 that Maurice Miller, then just nineteen years old, and his friend Nebra Bennett, twenty-one, encountered Pauline Peart. This attractive young woman was in the wrong place at the wrong time. At 11.00 that evening she was sitting in her sports car with a male friend, Yemi Johnson. He had chatted her up on a garage forecourt as they filled their cars with petrol. They exchanged phone numbers and over the next few weeks swapped text messages, occasionally meeting for chats. She already had boyfriends and he had girlfriends. Their relationship was not physical, but it was a close one which looked as if it could develop into more, given time. It was not to be. Maurice Miller and Nebra Bennett, along with a third young Jamaican, spotted them and the nice-looking car parked outside the home of one of Johnson's friends in Hampden Road, under a mile away from Tottenham Hotspur's ground in White Hart Lane. The car looked an attractive proposition to the three young men, or maybe it was the couple inside who seemed as though they had plenty of money, ripe for the taking. The three walked past and then, a few minutes later, at least two of them returned.

Yemi Johnson, in the front passenger seat, heard a rattling noise from the driver's side where Pauline was sitting, as though someone was trying to open the door. Then he saw a man in a hooded top thrusting a gun through the partly open driver's window. Johnson ducked down in his seat and did not see what happened, but he heard Pauline scream and the sound of a gun being fired. He shouted at her to start the car and drive off, but saw her arch her body in great pain. She had turned away from the gunman, and was shot in the back. Johnson carried her inside his friend's house. Police and paramedics arrived. But it was too late. She was dead. The single bullet had pierced her heart. Johnson was lucky. If the gun, a blank-firing handgun converted to fire live rounds, had not jammed, almost certainly he would have been shot too.

Trident officers were called in. Johnson was traumatised and it took time before he was able to explain what had happened. Meanwhile a man living in Hampden Road came forward and said he had witnessed most of what happened from his window. He saw three youths in the street. One, in a light coloured knee-length coat, was leaning against a van. The other two were opposite. He saw them walk along the middle of the road, obviously up to no good. Not wanting to be seen, he moved away from the window. He then heard the sound of a gunshot.

In a search of the area police found, next to the car, a piece of metal which turned out to be part of the slide mechanism of a handgun. The police also retrieved CCTV pictures showing three young men walking near the murder scene. The trio were on Hampden Lane which runs from Hampden Road to the High Road and the Red Lion public house which stands at the junction. When first seen they were heading towards the pub. Ten minutes later, just before the murder, the video showed them heading back the same way, towards Hampden Road and the Audi car. Detectives showed a still of the video to Johnson who said he thought at least one of the three had been at the car. A few days later, he saw one of the three in the Red Lion car park. But detectives were already aware that the three suspects used the pub. Undercover officers had visited it and had identified the three, Miller, Bennett and the third, another Jamaican, Morris Green, aged twenty-eight. By 4th June, Trident detectives had enough evidence to arrest the three, and it was known they would be in the pub that evening.

The officer leading the investigation, Detective Sergeant Richard Davies, held a briefing in the afternoon. He had wanted around sixty officers to take part in the arrest operation, which was to be at the suspects' homes rather than at the pub. Doing it that way not only minimised the chances of injuring innocent members of the public in any shoot-out but also meant there was more chance of gathering evidence from their belongings in their homes. Three eight-man surveillance teams were wanted to follow each of the suspects from the pub to their homes, and three firearms teams to make simultaneous arrests thus avoiding the risk, if done separately, of someone witnessing the first arrest and tipping off the other two suspects. Instead, Davies was allotted only two surveillance teams and one firearms team. It meant a change of plans. Miller and Bennett's addresses were not known, so it was decided the two available surveillance teams would follow them. It was known where the third suspect, Green, was living, and an observation point had been set up there to monitor his movements. The two officers manning it could report back when they saw him return home.

As expected, the three suspects met at the Red Lion on the evening of 4th June. Miller was with his girlfriend, Kenisha, and they were followed as they left the pub together, travelling by bus to their home in a flat in The Sunny Road, Enfield. The second surveillance team tracked Bennett to a flat in West Green Road, Hornsey. By midnight all the suspects were in their homes. The prime target was Miller and it was decided to arrest him first. When raiding drug dealers, police make a rapid entry to premises, smashing open the door and piling inside quickly, to prevent drugs evidence being flushed down the lavatory. But when suspect gunmen are to be arrested, firearms officers are called in and they use the 'call-out' tactic, smashing a door open and then calling for the occupants to come out. This minimises the chance of anyone inside firing their weapon and injuring officers. But call-outs do have disadvantages. They can lead to stand-offs, hostage-taking and sieges. Some evidence can also be destroyed, but a gun can't be flushed away, and police are obviously wise to the throwing of weapons out of windows.

At 3.35 in the morning, police smashed open the door to Miller's flat, calling for him and anyone else inside to come out.

Miller did as instructed, coming out along with his girlfriend, another couple and three small children. A police dog was sent into the flat to sniff out any guns and ammunition. A pistol was found hidden in a flip-top rubbish bin. It was loaded, ready to fire, with a bullet 'up the spout' – ready to discharge. Miller was arrested on suspicion of murder and the other adults were also arrested for possible possession of the gun. Almost certainly it belonged to Miller, but the arresting officers could take no chances. Miller could deny the gun was his, and forensic examination might show it had been handled not by him but by one of the others. The two remaining suspects, Bennett and Green, were arrested later that morning. A small amount of heroin, for personal use, was found at Bennett's home.

Trident officers spent a long time interviewing Miller, against whom there was strong evidence. The gun found at his home was an 8 mm pistol, converted from firing blanks to one that could discharge live bullets. Part of its slide mechanism was missing. That same piece had been found by police beside Pauline Peart's Audi sports car. Miller admitted the gun was his but denied having been at the murder scene, claiming to have been with his girlfriend at the time. However, he said he had heard that Green, Bennett and another man were responsible for the murder.

Eventually Miller admitted he had been at Hampden Road, but insisted he had not pulled the trigger: 'I didn't shoot her,' he exclaimed, alleging that another man, L— , was the shooter. He then went on to tell a tortuous story, which, although full of lies, reveals something of his lifestyle. He claimed there had been a dispute between L— and Yemi Johnson, who had shown him disrespect on an earlier occasion. L— had recognised Johnson as they passed the car, and had then run back and fired the gun, aiming for Johnson. Explaining his possession of the murder weapon, Miller said he had it for protection after two masked men had shot at him three months before, as part of a running feud involving those who had killed his father a few months before in New York. He said he had given the weapon to L— two weeks before the Hampden Road shooting, and a month afterwards,

L— had returned it. Miller said he hid the gun behind some trees in a park, and every day would check it was still there. He said that while in the Red Lion during the evening before his arrest, he had seen the two men who had fired at him three months before. So, sometime between seven and eight o'clock, he left the pub and collected the gun from the park. However, by the time he returned to the Red Lion, the two men had left.

Police knew he was lying. From observations on him before his arrest, he did not leave the pub in the early evening. Also, having checked through their records of previous shootings, although police did find that there had indeed been an incident where Miller claimed to have been shot at, it was not three months before, and there had only been one gunman, not two. That gunman had not been masked and there were believed to have been two victims, neither of them Miller.

On the day after his arrest, Miller was charged with murdering Pauline Peart, as were Bennett and Green. Bennett denied knowing Miller, and Green denied being at the murder scene. He said his girlfriend had just given birth and he would have been with her that evening. Before their trial was due to begin, lawyers decided that there was insufficient evidence to continue against Bennett and Green. Miller stood trial for murder on his own early in 2004. The jury could not agree on a verdict, but because Miller, giving evidence under oath, had blamed Bennett for the shooting, it was decided that Bennett should be re-charged. He and Miller stood trial at the Old Bailey the following September. It was a cut-throat defence, each blaming the other. The jury found them both guilty of murder.

No definite motive emerged at the trial. The officer in charge of the case, DS Davies, believes it was robbery. He told me that Miller and Bennett could have been after the car, aiming to hijack it, but it was more likely that they thought anyone with such an expensive vehicle would be carrying quite a bit of cash and credit cards. Whatever was planned, he said such robbers would first have threatened the couple and then tried to take control of the car, probably by trying to take the keys. If Pauline Peart, in the driving seat, had put up resistance, and Yemi Johnson's evidence was that she did scream, then the gunman could have squeezed the trigger in panic or frustration.

The judge, Mr Justice Astill, told the pair they had gunned down an 'utterly vulnerable and utterly defenceless' young woman. He said: 'You have the benefit of life, but you have deprived a young woman of her life, and deprived her family of seeing that life develop.' Flanked in the dock by big security guards, the two defendants looked even younger than their years. They stood like two schoolboys, unemotional, resigned to their punishment, not interested in what was being said. If anything, they looked bored with the proceedings, the judge's words wafting over them. Continuing, the judge said the two believed that carrying a loaded gun increased their esteem, but they had to understand that society took an opposite view. 'Carrying a gun does not demonstrate power,' he declared. 'It demonstrates that you are both despicable cowards... We don't want people like you here to roam free in our society, whether citizens from here, or whether you came here from another country.' He sentenced them to life imprisonment recommending that they serve eighteen years, with deportation to Jamaica at the end of it. They were led off, out of the dock, still showing not the slightest flicker of reaction, let alone remorse.

Shortly after the trial's end, the murdered woman's mother, Shirley Peart, agreed to record an appeal for a Met police radio advert, part of a new Trident anti-gun-crime campaign aimed at persuading more people to cooperate in ridding local communities of gunmen. The advert told how gun crime has a devastating effect on individuals and communities, and Mrs Peart said: 'We want to stop more people getting hurt. Perhaps more people will listen to us because they know what our family has been through. Our hope is that people will do something positive to help the community.'

'In Jamaica, you learn to see and be blind, and hear and be deaf. If you hear anything and you tell police, they will come and kill you and your family. I was scared for my life and family.'

A scene of carnage met uniformed police responding to the 999 call from an address in Peckham, south-east London on Saturday, 22nd June 2002. A man stained with blood sat crying outside the house which had been converted into an office building. Glass from a freshly broken first floor window littered the pathway near the front door. Inside, in the hallway, there was blood on the floor and radiator, and a big streak of blood trailed diagonally along and up the wall leading upstairs. On the first floor, there was a bullet hole in the door to the front room marked 'Managing Director'. Pushing their way inside, the officers saw more bloody horror: the bodies of two men. One had been stabbed in the chest and then shot three times in the head. Oozing blood saturated the carpet where he lay. The other man had a plastic bag tied tightly over his head. Thinking he could still be alive, one of the officers cut a hole in the bag so he could breathe. It was a vain attempt. He too was already dead, also shot through the head. Both men were tied up with thick electrical flex. It looked as though they had been tortured and then executed.

Outside the house, 29 Raul Road, the blood-stained man who had dialled 999 still looked extremely upset and shocked. Haltingly, he told the officers that he lived along the road at number 5. His name was Glen O'Brien and he owned number 29, running an estate agents from it. Shaking, he said that mystery gunmen had burst inside and shot the two men. Police treated him as a witness at first. But then they grew suspicious. There was no sign of the front door having been forced and, although there was blood on the man's clothes, he had not himself been injured in any way. Interviewed at Peckham police station, O'Brien altered his original version of events. He had said in his emergency call that two gunmen had burst their way inside the house. Now he said that two men – the victims – had come to his office to negotiate buying a house. As they came inside, they were closely followed by three masked men who attacked them. It sounded unlikely, and as Trident officers investigated, the story started to unravel.

A full search of O'Brien's premises revealed another side to him. Trident's Detective Constable Paul Lombard videoed the crime scene. 'I never like saying a particular murder was the most horrific I've ever dealt with,' he told me. 'It would devalue all the other murders I've investigated, and what would the families of these other victims think if they heard I was saying their murders were less shocking? It's equally shocking for anyone to lose a loved one. Let's leave it at this – the Raul Road murders were extremely brutal.' Lombard gathered various grisly exhibits and made an intriguing find in a cupboard. There, at the bottom, lay a set of police issue body armour. What was a man who said he was an estate agent doing with equipment to guard against attack? It was also discovered that he had come to the UK years before, claiming he would be studying for six months. His entry permit was never renewed.

Further clues that there was more to O'Brien than he was letting on came the following day. Rather unusually for those fairly early days of Trident, detectives found neighbours willing to talk about what they had heard and seen. They told detectives that the sounds of bangs and thumps had come from the house, and one person saw three men leave quickly from the back entrance, jump over a wall, and drive off in a car which looked like a Mercedes. The fact that a car had been waiting for them suggested that the attack had been planned, and possible confirmation of this came when another neighbour said she had seen O'Brien talking to the driver of a red sports car with darkened windows about two hours before the murders. According to the woman, it looked as though they were Yardies and were doing some kind of deal. The same car was seen at two other places nearby immediately before and after the shootings.

Events started slotting into place following the identification of the man shot once in the head. He was Kevin Barrington, sometimes called Ainsley Barrington. He was the nephew of the reggae star, Desmond Dekker, who had a hit with 'The Israelites'. Because of his lighter complexion, Barrington's street name was Brownman. One of his relatives, a half-brother, told police that he knew Barrington was going to number 29 Raul Road to see O'Brien. The two had been friends. Both were thirty-four years old. After coming from Jamaica to England, Barrington married a solicitor, Marcia Harris, who was expecting to do some conveyancing work for O'Brien. But police were to find that Barrington had a hidden side too. He was already married to a woman in Jamaica. And he was also a well-known gangster on the island – the 'don' of Kingston's Precinct 13 district. He was wanted there over a shooting.

The other dead man was identified as Leo McKain, aged twenty-one, who had stab wounds to the chest and three bullet wounds to the head. He was also known as Chris, and – because of his weight – as Fatman. Key evidence came from a friend of his, Patrick Wright, who had come to England from Jamaica in 2000. He told detectives that he, Barrington and McKain were all friends and they had met some hours before the murder, talking for three to four hours in a park in New Cross. Barrington said he was waiting for a call on his mobile phone from an estate agent about some money he was owed. The call came and Barrington drove his Suzuki jeep to Raul Road with McKain, followed in a separate car by Wright and another friend called Andrew. Barrington told them to park outside number 29 and wait for them. Wright saw the front door open and Barrington and McKain enter. He did not see anyone else go inside, let alone a group of masked men, as claimed by O'Brien. But after a few minutes he saw someone leave, talk on a mobile phone, and then, walking slowly back, re-enter the house. Wright recognised him as a man known as C—. Police entered the name into their criminal intelligence database and came up with at least twelve people with the same street name.

After another few minutes, growing worried, Wright phoned

McKain's mobile, but there was no response. He tried again a few times, but heard only the ringing tone. He realised there was something fishy going on, and drove to a nearby supermarket car park. While there he saw two black men in a red car staring at him in a threatening manner. Then came the sound of approaching police car sirens. The two in the red car drove off, very quickly. Wright then got out of his car and walked the short distance to Raul Road. He saw police activity at number 29, went back to his car and he too drove off. However, he had made a note of the red car's registration number and later passed it on to the police. It matched a car owned by a close friend of one of those eventually to stand trial for the murders.

After a full forensic examination of number 29, Trident police were able to piece together what had probably happened. The blood in the hallway belonged to McKain, so it looked as though he was stabbed on entering the house with Barrington and then manhandled upstairs, leaving blood smears on the wall. It appeared that one of the pair had broken away from the men who were lying in wait, and had tried to barricade himself inside the front managing director's office on the first floor. This was most likely to have been Barrington. He had been in the building several times before and would know the lay-out, and the stabbed McKain was in no state to make a dash for freedom. Whoever made it into the room rammed a metal chair against the door to try to prevent anyone entering. A bullet was fired at it. From the trajectory, the bullet had been fired from the stairs leading to the second floor. It passed through the door and hit the chair, shattering against the metal frame. Footmarks on a landing wall indicated that someone had put his feet up there and pushed his body against the closed door, trying to force it open. Once inside the room, the attackers at some stage flung McKain against a wall near the front window, blood from his chest wounds leaving a smear. The gang then set about completely disabling their two captives, a task for which they had come prepared.

They had brought thick electrical flex to tie hands and feet, a roll of plastic bin-liners and some plastic gloves. Maybe they had expected Barrington to arrive alone. There was enough flex to bind him to the metal chair and to fasten McKain's ankles, but not enough for the younger man's wrists. Instead, sticky parcel-type tape was used for that. The wrapper was torn from a new roll of white plastic bags and thrown on the floor, and bags were put over both men's heads. More sticky tape was wrapped round the pair's necks and jaws. One of the attackers used rubber cleaning gloves and the others wore transparent plastic gloves, the type freely available at some petrol stations. But as these flimsy hand protectors came in contact with the sticky tape, bits of plastic were detached, and even whole gloves came off, becoming entangled in the fastenings round the men's necks.

Pairs of small puncture marks were found on the men's bodies, which looked as though they could have been caused by a staple remover, used as a torture weapon. Police never worked out the purpose of hooding the two. Was it to disorientate or terrorise them, or was it to suffocate them? Whatever the reason, the tape used to secure Barrington was tied so tightly that it forced his upper dentures to the back of his mouth, and he started to suffocate. A pathologist found pinprick-size specks of blood on his face, one of the signs of asphyxiation.

Meanwhile, the wounded McKain fought back. He had somehow managed to free his hands, and then tear the plastic bag from his head and try to get to his feet. His efforts were in vain. He was shot in the head, three times, dying instantly. Neighbours had told police they heard three or four bangs close together, followed by another single bang a little later. The detectives concluded that Barrington had been shot after McKain, and the attackers had then made their escape out of the back door of the house, leaving the owner, Glen O'Brien, to concoct a story for the police.

It was a terrible way to die. But who was responsible? Fingerprint and DNA evidence from the murder room suggested that five men had taken part in the onslaught, one of them O'Brien. No guns or knives were found at the scene, but forensic examination of the bullets used showed they had been fired by two guns, a .45 revolver and a Mac-10 semi-automatic machine pistol capable of firing up to 1,200 rounds a minute. The Trident gun database showed the Mac-10 may have been a hire gun, rented out to killers. It had been used in 1999 when a gunman had walked into a travel agents and sprayed bullets around, killing a man behind a desk. It had also been used two years later in an attempted murder. The gun may have been at the root of the trouble between O'Brien and Barrington. At least one of the dead man's associates told detectives that Barrington had left it for safe-keeping with O'Brien, and he wanted it back. He may have thought he was safe in going to Raul Road unarmed because he believed that O'Brien did not have bullets for the pistol. However, Trident officers were also told that the dispute between the pair had been over a business deal, involving either diamonds or drugs.

Detective Inspector Nick Linfoot was put in charge of investigating the gruesome double murder. This was his first 'business' murder while with Trident. All the others had been 'disrespect' shootings. As with all Trident murders, someone on the investigating team always attends the victim's funeral. Family members are more likely to hear who is responsible for the death of their loved one, even when they are in Jamaica. The funerals of Barrington and McKain were in the countryside near Kingston, and DI Linfoot went to them. A tubby man with a dry sense of humour, he told me he met Chris McKain's partner and his mother and father, twenty-five miles east of Kingston.

'As we arrived, kids ran up to me. It seemed like they'd never seen a white man before. The mother lives in a ten foot by ten foot breeze-block shack with one room above, at the end of a track. She's a lovely woman and couldn't have been more courteous. It was a Catholic funeral. The "dons" came from K13 [a district of Kingston]. There were six of them in creamy white suits, and white fedoras on their heads, with guns in their belts. One came up and shook hands with us, saying thanks for coming to show respect. I must say I was a bit nervous. The next day we were up in the hills in beautiful countryside for Barrington's funeral. We found the chapel but there was no one there. We waited and were getting worried. The police protection officer with us said he didn't like it. Just then we saw coming round a bend a procession of twenty vehicles. It couldn't have been more different to Chris McKain's. The men wore proper suits and there were girls in hot-pants. The guns were much more apparent, stuck in belts. One man had a huge handgun. I've never seen one as big before… As we drove off we passed through a village, through a crowd of men, and two of them were having a go at one another with machetes – hacking at each other. The police escort officer with us told the driver not to stop. He said these kind of fights were very common, and wouldn't get reported to the police.'

Linfoot learned little more in Jamaica about who could have been responsible for the double murder. The main suspect was O'Brien. But suspicion had also fallen on two other Jamaicans, Courtney Palmer, a 23-year-old known as Tallman, and Linval Edwards, thirty. One of Barrington's half-brothers, Kifron Lodge, said Barrington had been friends with Palmer and Edwards, but they had fallen out. The three had a heated row two days before the murders, and Lodge said he saw Palmer lift his shirt, revealing a handgun, and that Edwards, also armed, warned Barrington: 'Pussy – pussy, you're dead.' Police learned that the red sports car seen outside 29 Raul Road belonged to Palmer, and they were told that he had been sitting in it with a gun in his belt and was overheard by a passer-by saying: 'We have to kill this man. This man have to be dead.' Both Palmer and Edwards disappeared after the shooting. Later police learned that both had gone to Manchester. There, Palmer and another man – believed to be Edwards – tried to rob a cannabis dealer, shooting him in the arm. But the dealer, a 76-year-old who said he had been smoking cannabis since 1945, fought back, slashing at his attackers with a kitchen knife. The two fled, leaving behind a trail of blood.

One month after the Peckham shooting, an attempt was made at apparently silencing some of Barrington's associates who were believed to be talking to the police, breaking the 'no grassing' rule. Two guns were fired at one of the Lodge brothers, Kimarly, in Edward Street, New Cross, near his home. Bullets recovered from the scene showed that some had come from a .38 gun, but more importantly, the other gun, a .45, was the same weapon that had been used at Raul Road.

Then a few weeks later, early in September, came the dramatic arrest of Palmer and Edwards. Trident received a tip-off that the pair were going to pick up some jewellery that had been left at a pawn shop in Peckham. A Met Police ARV was called in to assist the unarmed Trident detectives and the shop was staked out. ARV teams are in great demand. Their time is precious, and after a wait, the decision was made to pull these officers out. Just as they were about to leave, Palmer and Edwards and a third man arrived on the scene. The armed team moved in and caught Palmer as the trio left the shop. But Edwards escaped them, and started running down the street, towards two unarmed Trident officers, Detective Constables Phil Haake and Paul Davies who were about twenty yards away. 'There was no time to think whether he was armed or not,' Haake told me. 'You just act instinctively, and I grabbed him.'

Edwards was wrestled to the ground and in his belt was a fully loaded .38 handgun, a Brocock-style air-pistol converted to fire real bullets. One bullet was 'up the spout'. Test-firing showed that this was the weapon used in the Lodge shooting a few weeks before. The third man escaped, throwing away a loaded gun and T-shirt as he ran, pursued by police. DNA on the T-shirt matched DNA found at 29, Raul Road. Test-firing of the gun showed that bullet case markings matched those on a case found outside the murder house. It looked like the third man was one of the group seen at the killings, the man known as C— . A search of Palmer's home revealed another converted air pistol stuffed down the back of a sofa. Later, the .45 used in the murder and the Lodge shooting was found after an incident in west London. The other murder gun, the Mac-10 machine pistol, has still not been recovered.

Courtney Palmer, of Bellenden Road, Peckham; Linval Edwards, of Burwash House, Elephant and Castle; and Glen O'Brien, of Raul Road, were all charged with the murders of Kevin Barrington and Leo McKain. At their Old Bailey trial, O'Brien stuck to his story that men wearing balaclavas had burst into his offices, forcing him to help tie up Barrington and McKain. Palmer told the same story. He had been at number 29 doing cleaning work when the masked gang came in and had threatened him, telling him to keep quiet and not to talk to the police. 'In Jamaica, you learn to see and be blind, and hear and be deaf,' he said. 'If you hear anything and you tell police, they will come and kill you and your family. I was scared for my life and family.' He said Barrington had been like a father to him.

'More than a brother' was how Barrington was described by Edwards. He said: 'When my father died in 1998, Barrington was the only one there for me. He gave me money to help bury my father... I would do anything for him.' Edwards denied being at number 29 at the time of the murders. His alibi evidence gave an insight into his lifestyle. He claimed to have visited no fewer than four girlfriends in the course of twenty-four hours, and had then gone on to see others out of London. He said he'd spent the night before the shootings with his 'regular' girlfriend. He'd left her in the morning and went to see another girlfriend, staying with her until 3 p.m., when he had gone on to a third girlfriend in Peckham. He'd been with her until 8.30 in the evening and then went on to see a fourth girlfriend with whom he stayed the night. He left for Manchester and a fifth girlfriend the next day, and then went on to Birmingham for another. 'We checked it all out and it was basically true,' said DI Nick Linfoot, the officer in charge of the case. 'We reckon he went to Raul Road between the third and fourth girlfriends.'

The trial ended at the Old Bailey in February 2004 after the jury spent eighteen days deliberating their verdicts. Palmer was found guilty of the murders and O'Brien and Edwards guilty of manslaughter. Palmer showed no emotion during sentencing, when told by the judge, the Common Sergeant of London, Peter

Beaumont, that he had inflicted mental and physical suffering on both victims before killing them. He was ordered to serve a minimum of twenty years in prison before being considered for parole. O'Brien and Edwards were each sentenced to ten years for manslaughter with Edwards receiving an additional three years for possessing a gun.

But the story surrounding this horrific murder did not end there. A mystery man – someone with no real name – was also to end up in the dock charged with the killings. He was linked to the murder scene by forensic evidence, as well as a fifth man, C— , who is still wanted. During the trial, O'Brien said that one of the gang was called 'Red-Root' or 'Redwood' and that he was the man who shot Barrington in the head as the group left the office, having been instructed to make sure he was dead. Trident had a lucky break in identifying this suspect. A man calling himself Junior Bartley was involved in a dispute with a taxi driver in Luton. Police called to the scene found a small amount of cannabis on Bartley and cautioned him, taking his fingerprints and a DNA sample. Later these were fed as a matter of course into a police database, and a match was made to one of the two missing suspects for the double murder. Police decided to arrest him.

The usual risk assessment was carried out. Bartley was living with a woman called Joanne who had a stable job as a court-worker at Luton. She also had a young baby. Police decided to move in without armed back-up early in the morning, when it was thought unlikely that Bartley would put up much resistance, if any. The judgement was correct. DI Nick Linfoot rang the bell on the ground floor flat at 6.30 a.m. and it was opened by Joanne. Bartley was still asleep, with the baby in his arms. Linfoot shook him awake, then arrested him.

In interviews, police tried to establish his background, particularly his identity, because no one by his name showed up in any state records. He appeared not to have paid tax or claimed any kind of benefit. He told them that he came to the UK in 1995 at the age of sixteen. He could not remember his port of entry or the names of the people he was with who had left him in Camberwell, south London. He lived with a woman called Keesha but did not remember her second name or address. He left her for another woman, but could not recall her name either. Friends had given him money. He worked for O'Brien, doing odd jobs, running errands, decorating, and doing some cleaning. That must have been how his fingerprints and DNA had been found at number 29. He said he had been in Luton at the time of the murders, but before that had stayed in a Peckham flat with a friend called Orrill who lived with his wife, Beverley. He did not know their second names and gave an incorrect address for the flat, but police managed to trace it. They were also to discover how 'Junior Bartley' got his name.

The woman owning the flat was called Beverley Bartley-Richardson. The Bartley part of her name came from a previous marriage, and from an earlier marriage, she had a son called Clifford, who was nicknamed Junior. She remembered the arrested man had stayed in a room in the flat for several weeks. But she knew him as Jermaine and his nickname was Redwood, the same name given by O'Brien as the man who had killed Barrington. It was all too much of a coincidence, and from then on, police worked on the basis that the man they had in custody had taken the name Junior Bartley after staying at the flat. Unable to discover his real identity, police charged him with the two murders under the name Bartley.

When he appeared for trial at the Old Bailey in June 2004, it was still as Junior Bartley. Prosecuting, as he had at the first trial, was Richard Horwell. He told the jury that Barrington and McKain had been executed. The motive or motives of the killers may never be known, he said, but proof of motive was not a requirement in any criminal trial. Cases depended on evidence, he went on, and the criminals' greatest enemy was now science, with techniques available to investigators which were previously unimaginable. These methods had condemned the three men convicted in the first trial, and they condemned Bartley too. He was linked to the murders by two pieces of scientific evidence, said Horwell. His fingerprints were on the plastic bag which had been put over McKain's head, and his DNA was on a cigarette butt caught up in the sticky tape used to secure the bags.

After evidence from neighbours of what they had seen and heard at Raul Road, the public gallery was cleared so that evidence could be given by Patrick Wright, who had driven to number 29 with the murder victims. Defence lawyers at the first trial had given him a hard time and he was reluctant to appear again. Police persuaded him to go to the Old Bailey, but he wanted to give evidence from behind a screen, because he believed there would be people in the public gallery who might want to harm him. He said those people did not know what he looked like, and he did not want to give them a chance of seeing him. Because it was difficult to erect a screen in the court where the trial was being heard, the public gallery was cleared instead. Even so, Wright insisted on giving evidence wearing dark glasses.

He told the jury that Barrington had gone to Peckham to collect some money from O'Brien. Under cross-examination from Bartley's barrister, Patrick O'Connor, he denied knowing of any feud or that his friend McKain had accompanied Barrington as 'back-up', or that either of them had gone armed. 'If I had thought there was a feud, I would have advised Chris [McKain] not to go inside. We would have asked the real estate man [O'Brien] to come out. If my friend had been armed, he would have retaliated. He would have put up a big fight.' When it was suggested that he had been there outside in case of trouble, he retorted: 'If I had been back-up, they wouldn't be dead.'

Bartley did not go into the witness box. To have done so would have exposed him to searing cross-examination, not least about who he really was. Because what Bartley had said in interviews with police had been read in court, his counsel was able to use the information to spell out the defence case in his closing speech to the jury. O'Connor argued that Bartley had not been at number 29 at the time of the murders and that his fingerprint and DNA traces had been left by him earlier in the week. However, he went on to tell the jury that if they concluded that he had taken part in the attacks, then it did not necessarily mean he was guilty of murder. That theme was taken up by the judge, Peter Focke, who spelled out the differences between murder and manslaughter.

For a murder verdict, the jury would have to be convinced that the intention from the outset had been to kill Barrington and McKain.

After a day's deliberation, the jury returned its verdicts – not guilty of the murders, or of killing Barrington, but guilty of the manslaughter of McKain. He was set to join the three others sentenced earlier having been found guilty of either murder or manslaughter. Bartley showed no emotion as the judge sentenced him to nine years in prison, ordering that he serve at least two-thirds of that time. He was led out of the dock to start his sentence under the name Junior Bartley. His real identity is still unknown.

CHAPTER ELEVEN | The Gunman's Fatal Embrace

*'He hugged me and asked me how I was. We hadn't seen
each other for a long time… Then he pulled out a gun and
he shot me. He was really close. He just kept shooting me
and he didn't say a thing. I just kept getting hit.'*

Even at the best of times it is unusual for detectives to discover the
full motives behind shootings. Likewise, the origins of feuds can
be forgotten by even the battling gang members themselves. Such
was the level of violence in London in 2001 that even attempting
to learn the whole truth behind every shooting was pointless.
At that time Trident was inundated with gun crime, and officers
were finding it difficult to cope. But one of the many dramatic
incidents is worth recalling because its knock-on effect was still
reverberating more than three years later, with another killing.

May Bank Holiday Monday in 2001 was a hot one. But
what sparked off the afternoon gunfire in Burton Road, Brixton,
remains a mystery. Two men in dark clothing were seen arriving on
a motorbike, drawing up next to an Astra. They opened the car's
boot and put their helmets and other gear inside. Then, according
to witnesses, they emerged from the vehicle with guns blazing
– including what looked like an Uzi sub-machine gun. They used a
black Mercedes sports car as cover, crouching down behind it, but
it was unclear who or what they were firing at. No one appeared
to have been hit. Then the pair jumped into the Astra and sped off.
Part of its registration number was noted down by one witness.
That car was eventually to play a significant role in an investigation
started later that day into a major shooting incident in which a
man was left lying on the ground, badly injured.

That second incident was outside the Atlantis nightclub, off
Purley Way, in Croydon, south London. Cyrus Moses found that
his VW Golf was blocked in the club's car park. He remonstrated
with those in the other car, but they got out and started punching
and kicking him. Then another man emerged from a gold Audi
with a machine gun saying: 'I ain't having this.' He fired a spray of

bullets into the air, and then turned the gun on Moses, who was sheltering behind another vehicle. He was hit in the thigh and his attackers ran towards the Audi and another car, a BMW. As the club's security guards gave first aid, a man from the Audi ran back to the scene shouting that he'd lost the keys. The gunman told the guards: 'Turn away or you'll get it.' The men then sped off, but police, called to the scene by a 999 call, caught up with them and a chase ensued.

Police spotted the Audi parked at traffic lights in Purley Way and saw one or two men getting out of it and into their other car, the BMW. Shots were fired at the police car, which followed the BMW down a slip road and was joined by another police car, and an armed response vehicle. More shots were fired from the BMW's offside window and one of the police vehicles was hit. The BMW hit a wall, but managed to continue on past Thornton Heath railway station where it hit another wall, went out of control and crashed into some parked vehicles. All but one of the occupants escaped on foot, leaving Marcel Salami behind, trapped in the wreckage. He was wearing body armour and at his feet was a loaded pistol. Inside the car was a loaded Uzi, with a bullet in the breach which appeared to have jammed. On his way to hospital, Salami tried to wipe firearms residue from his hands, rubbing at them with a blanket in the ambulance. Detectives discovered that the attackers' other car, the abandoned Audi, had been stolen eight days earlier in Shepherd's Bush, west London. It had false number plates, and inside it was a loaded magazine from a handgun. In the glove compartment was a bullet hole and a bullet fired from the Uzi was lodged in the engine.

Salami refused to answer questions, but the Trident intelligence database identified him as one of the Peckham Boys, a black group involved in drug dealing and robbery. Four other men were suspected of involvement. Three of them were thought to belong to the Peckham Boys – Quincey Thwaites, Jason Tash and Junior Reid, aka Ramone Welsh. The fourth was a friend of Thwaites', called Jermaine Abbott, whose name was to come to prominence two years later.

Meanwhile, clever detective work led the Trident officers to link some of the suspects to the Astra car which had been driven off after the mystery shooting incident in Burton Road, Brixton, before the nightclub attack. A car wash receipt had been found in the BMW. The garage was traced and its CCTV showed that at the time the receipt was made out, an Astra car was going through the car wash. Its registration number matched the partial number plate taken down by the witness to the Burton Road shooting. The Astra was a hire vehicle and the manager of the rental company told detectives of its interesting recent rental history. A relative of Salami had hired it for a week on 16th May, twelve days before the two shooting incidents, but it was not returned on the due date. Two days after the nightclub shooting the hirer phoned and said the car had been stolen. Later he went to the hire company and said it turned out that a friend had taken it after a night out at a club. He took the manager to the car, saying he wanted to retrieve some motorcycle gear that had been left inside. As neither man had keys for the vehicle, the manager arranged for it to be transported later to a depot where it could be opened. The hirer was never seen again, probably because the police had been making arrests and he believed the net was closing in.

By then Quincey Thwaites, aged twenty-three, had been arrested with his 21-year-old friend Jermaine Abbott while in a car in Fulham. Abbott denied involvement in the shooting. Thwaites said nothing. Junior Reid, aged twenty-three, was tracked down through his use of his mobile phone. He had moved to Northampton with his girlfriend, and was arrested as he came out of a house with two packets of heroin. Inside the address was a further 1.7 kilos of the drug. Jason Tash was arrested at a later stage at his home. Evidence was found linking each of them to the two shooting scenes. Thwaites's DNA was on the trigger of the Uzi machine gun, and Marcel Salami's was on the trigger of one of the other two guns found. Reid's DNA was discovered on a halloween mask found in one of the cars. Those three men were all found guilty at the Old Bailey in March 2002 of firearms possession. Salami, aged thirty-one, was sentenced to ten years, Thwaites, to fourteen, Reid to six with another six, to run consecutively, for possessing the heroin. There was less evidence against Jermaine Abbott, whose fingerprints were found in the Audi, and it was decided that he should not be put on trial. That position changed, however, after Abbott was arrested for allegedly killing a man in a fast-food restaurant.

The Audi in the Croydon incident had been stolen in Shepherd's Bush, Abbott's stamping ground, and it was there, six weeks before the end of the trial of his friends, that gunfire erupted in Nando's chicken restaurant in Uxbridge Road. DJ Keiron Bernard, aged twenty-five, walked into trouble moments after entering the crowded restaurant. His killer passed a remark about Bernard's Afro hairstyle, and then both men pulled out handguns, scattering a group of black men at the counter. The killer cocked his pistol and pointed it at Bernard, who dashed behind the counter for safety. He was hit in the chest and thigh and another bullet hit the waitress, 28-year-old Gabriella Slegrova, in the arm. Although badly hurt, Bernard managed to run to his black Honda Prelude, parked outside. But he did not get very far before losing consciousness while in the driving seat. Just two hundred yards from the restaurant, the car smashed into the window of an estate agents. Bernard was dead. A witness reported seeing a gun in the car, but it had disappeared by the time police arrived.

The Trident officers had no great difficulties investigating the murder. The restaurant's CCTV had caught the whole scene, and Bernard's brother Janik had also been there. He not only named Jermaine Abbott as the killer, he also picked him out at an identification parade. Seven months after the murder, Abbott was on trial at the Old Bailey. He denied being the killer, claiming that it was another man shown on the CCTV footage. The jury could not agree and a retrial was ordered. Meanwhile, four months later, Abbott was on trial for the Croydon nightclub shooting, along with another of those arrested, Jason Tash. Tash was found guilty and given a ten-year prison sentence, but once again there was disagreement on the jury over Abbott and a retrial was ordered. In January 2003, Abbott was back at the Old Bailey facing his second trial for the Shepherd's Bush murder. This time he was acquitted. And the same thing happened in July 2003 at his retrial for the Croydon incident. After eighteen months in custody, Abbott was a free man. However, just days after his release from prison he himself was the victim of a deliberate, carefully planned attack.

Abbott was lured to Notting Hill to meet someone he regarded as a friend, whom he had not seen for some time. The pair hugged on the pavement in what was to be a fatal embrace. Less than a minute later, six bullets were pumped into Abbott's chest and abdomen at close range. Hearing the gunfire, people came to see what had happened. They found Abbott lying on the ground in a growing pool of blood, losing consciousness, his life apparently ebbing away. One man, trying to stem the flow of blood from a chest wound, asked who had shot him, and Abbott replied in a whisper that it was Hassan, the Moroccan from 'The Grove', the name given by locals to Ladbroke Grove. Paramedics took Abbott to hospital where his wounds were thought so severe that he would not survive. Police put the name 'Hassan' and information that he was Moroccan into their criminal intelligence database. The name of Hassan Abouzohour came up quickly. He lived near Ladbroke Grove and had also been questioned about another attempted murder. It looked fairly clear cut to detectives. An alert was put out for Abouzohour's arrest.

Luck was with the authorities. By sheer chance, the next day at 11 a.m., a police constable at a control booth at the entrance to the Channel Tunnel stopped an expensive-looking new jeep-type vehicle with dark tinted windows. There was something suspicious about the two young men inside. He asked: 'Where are you going, chaps?' The driver was another Moroccan, Samir Tahir, who said he was off to a wedding in Belgium. PC Peter Hathaway asked for their passports. These were handed over and he ran them through a scanning machine. Tahir was clean, but the same was not true of the other man in the car. Up came the message that the passenger, Abouzohour, was wanted for the attempted murder the evening before. The PC arrested the pair and they were driven off to Folkestone police station. In their vehicle was £1,000 in £20 notes and two mobile phones, one of them belonging to Tahir. It proved crucial to the Trident investigation.

Checks on mobile phones' memories and the sites used to make calls can provide police with key evidence, and so it was in this case. Jermaine Abbott was critically ill in hospital. Although he had indicated he knew who had shot him, he refused to break the criminal code and name the person to police. However, Abbott's mobile phone had been with him when he was shot and an examination of calls showed a series of messages with another mobile, ending in the three digits 116. The sites used to make the calls from the two mobiles showed a convergence at the time and scene of the shooting. It looked as though the 116 number had been used by the shooter to arrange a meeting with Abbott. The suspicion was that it was Abouzohour's, but he did not have it when arrested at Folkestone. However, Tahir's mobile, ending in 148, had been used to contact the 116 number, and it had also been used close to where Abbott had been shot. Tahir said that he had been dropping off his girlfriend in the area, but detectives did not believe him, especially when they found that he was visiting a prisoner awaiting trial for a very serious murder.

Further checks on the background of their main suspect, Abouzohour, also came up with more damning evidence. He had been held in custody on suspicion of attempted murder earlier in the year. Abouzohour was to have gone on an identification parade but a witness had cried off and that meant there was insufficient evidence to hold him. Abouzohour was released in March 2003. However, his clothes had been taken for forensic examination and he left a phone number for police to contact him when they were ready for return. A record of the number had been kept in police files. It ended in 116. Although Abbott was still refusing to cooperate, Trident officers felt that they now had enough against Abouzohour and Tahir. The former was charged with attempted murder and kept in custody. Tahir was charged with assisting an offender, the belief being that he had picked up Abouzohour after Abbott's shooting. Tahir obtained bail, with two sureties, each of £100,000.

When their trial got underway the following year at the Old Bailey, there were surprises, one of them dramatic. First came problems over witnesses. Abbott was still seriously ill, unable to give evidence even if he wanted to. Others were refusing to cooperate and warrants were issued in an effort to compel them to attend. Two men who had tended Abbott as he lay apparently dying on the ground were refusing to give evidence without assurances that their identities would be protected. Both wanted anonymity and to have the witness box curtained off so they would be shielded from the defendants and the public gallery. The court agreed to the requests but refused a further demand from one of the two that his voice be distorted through a special machine. When the two finally gave evidence, there was confusion over whether Abbott had named the man who shot him as Hassan or Hussain, and what exactly they had told police who arrived at the scene.

The drama came during evidence from a mobile phone expert who had examined the two mobiles recovered by the police – those belonging to Abbott and Tahir. He said he had tracked their movements on the night of the shooting through their use of different cell sites in London. He had also mapped the movement of the missing 116 handset, which the prosecution said was used by Abouzohour to lure Abbott to Notting Hill where he would be shot. What happened during the expert's cross-examination was an event very rarely seen during court proceedings. Certainly, no one I talked to in court had ever seen anything like it before, apart from in TV or film dramas.

The police had been looking for the 116 handset for months. Suddenly, without warning, Tahir's barrister, Brian O'Neill, produced it in court, and handed it to the expert, who confirmed that it was indeed the 116 phone. The prosecution was stunned at the move and the police were furious. Why hadn't the lawyer given the handset to them as he knew they had been seeking it, rather than introducing it so dramatically in court? They felt they had been ambushed. O'Neill followed up his advantage with the next witness, a friend of Tahir, who said he recognised the phone as belonging not to Hassan Abouzohour but to a Somali called Hassan, with whom Tahir did business selling trainers. The implications of what was being suggested by the defence were immense for the prosecution case, and the jury was asked to leave while the lawyers and the judge discussed the situation. The court then adjourned for each side to take stock.

The problem for the prosecution and police was that the case against Abouzohour was falling apart. First there was confusion by witnesses over whether Abbott had actually named someone called Hassan as the gunman and now there was doubt over the crucial 116 mobile. Abouzohour had certainly been using it a few months before the shooting, but did he have it on the night in question? Who was this other Hassan? Was the defence going to suggest that the phone calls between Tahir and the 116 number at the time of the shooting could be explained because Tahir was meeting the other Hassan? Then there was the 116 handset itself. Time was needed so that it could be properly examined and tested, and checks made on the incoming and outgoing calls in its memory. After further legal discussion, spread over a few days, the judge discharged the jury and adjourned the case until later in the year. Tahir, who had been on bail, was taken into custody.

After the aborted trial, the police went back to Abbott who was still in hospital and still desperately ill. Previously, he had always been reluctant to talk to police. Sometimes when detectives approached his bedside, he would pull the sheet over his head and tell them to go away. But Trident officers are persistent. Occasionally, he would chat, but he said almost nothing about events on the night he was shot, and making a full statement was out of the question. In his criminal world that was something you just did not do.

However when police told him that during the trial the defence had been suggesting that Hassan Abouzohour was the wrong man – that Abbott had been referring to another Hassan or even to someone called Hussein, he changed his position. He grew angry at what he called the lies being put forward. He knew he could still die, and although it was against all his principles to cooperate with the police, he said he wanted to put the record straight. He agreed to make a signed statement on 13th March, quoted here in full.

'It is with reluctance that I make this further statement. I've thought much about the night I was shot on the 14th of July 2003. I have previously made statements to you, the police, which do not tell everything. The reason for this is due to my past, I feel that I am being a hypocrite, but this needs to be said now. Police have told me of the development of the trial with Hassan. I'm still in a lot of pain. I could still die and I didn't deserve this. I want to make a statement for the record.

'On that night I was shot, I was with two good friends who you know, but I won't name. We were all in a car and I was in the front passenger seat. We were going to meet my friend Hassan, Hassan Abouzohour. I've known him for years. We had spoken a few times on the phone and had arranged to meet where I was shot. He told me he had a gun and he wanted bullets for it, proper ones. He thought I could help, so I said I'd look at it.

'When we got there, Hassan was waiting there, so I got out. He hugged me and asked me how I was. We hadn't seen each other for a long time. Hassan said he didn't want to show me the gun here as there were people about, so we agreed to go somewhere in the car. He said to me "you sit in the back because I've got the thing" – meaning the gun. He was worried about being stopped by the police. I got in the back of the car. He got in the front passenger seat. Immediately, as he sat down, he turned around and said, "this is what's happening".

'He pulled out a gun. All I can say is it was black. It all happened so quickly – I just wasn't expecting this – and he shot me. He was really close. He just kept shooting me and he didn't say a thing. I just kept getting hit. I couldn't move. I was in a lot of pain. I managed to get out of the car. I don't know where Hassan had gone. I was bleeding from all over. I thought I was going to die, there and then. To this day I'm sure the only reason why I am still here is because we had dud ammo. People then came up to help me. I remember telling them who had shot me. In my mind I was dying. I still don't know why he shot me, but I know he was paid by someone. I know he was on crack and [would] do anything for money.'

Signed J Abbott

The statement was explosive. As it had been signed by Abbott, he could be compelled to give evidence. But the new trial was not scheduled until the autumn, several months away and there was continued doubt about whether Abbott would ever recover from his serious injuries. In fact, he died from his wounds. His death raised further legal issues. If another trial were to go ahead, the charge against Abouzohour would have to be increased to one of murder. But the main question was whether Abbott's death-bed statement naming his killer could be used in court. The prosecution said yes, and the defence said no. The judge ruled in the prosecution's favour when the new trial started at Kingston Crown Court.

Even with the strong new evidence, the jury was out for two days considering the verdicts, eventually finding both men guilty by majorities of eleven to one. The verdicts came at 12.55, just before the break for lunch, and the judge said he would sentence the pair at two o'clock. The jury entered the court before the judge and, fearing trouble from the defendants, asked to sit out of their view. As the court waited, Tahir shouted angrily at the police. Abouzohour stayed silent, emotionless. The court was quiet and orderly when the judge entered. He described the murder as a pre-planned execution, and sentenced Abouzohour to life imprisonment with a recommendation that he serve a minimum of fifteen years before being considered for parole. Tahir was given four years for assisting an offender.

No firm motive for the killing emerged at the trial, but afterwards the officer in charge of the investigation, Detective Inspector Tim Neligan, speculated that it had been over drugs. 'Abbott had been in prison for a year on remand, and when he came out his drugs business had been taken over. He wanted to get back and others wanted rid of him. They took him out. I think it's as simple as that.'

'It looked like a classic hit. The few witnesses said they had seen two men on a motorbike. They wore dark clothing and had full helmets masking their faces. The pillion rider had fired the shots, stretching out his left arm to aim the gun. Several shots were fired and the bike then roared off.'

Unsurprisingly, most of London's shootings occur in the evening and night hours between 5 p.m. and 2 a.m. the following day, and Trident has a well-defined system for dealing with them. Until ten o'clock at night, cover is provided by Operation Trafalgar, which normally deals with non-black shootings. If it is a black-on-black incident, it is passed to Trident's night team on duty from 10 p.m., dealing with non-fatal shootings. That team would not normally deal with an overnight murder involving firearms. A non-Trident homicide assessment team, referred to as a 'HAT', is called out to murder scenes. The HAT detectives secure the murder scene, gather any CCTV footage, find out about the victim, possible suspects etc. and alert a senior Trident officer if it is thought to be a case for the specialist squad. Information gathered overnight is then handed on to a full Trident murder investigation team the following morning.

I joined Trident's two overnight shootings duty detectives on the third of their seven night shifts. Detective Constables Dave Milton and Diane Maiden had spent the previous two nights working at Trident's headquarters in Putney, undisturbed by any call-outs. They had caught up on their paperwork between their start time until their finish at six the following morning. They both told me they much preferred working on a shootings team, rather than as a mere part of one of the larger murder teams which usually comprise sixteen officers.

The reasons were spelled out by Milton, a big 53-year-old officer, balding and grey-haired, who has 'been around' the Met:

'The murder teams have massive resources, with officers having dedicated roles. One will be in charge of exhibits, for example. Then there'll be an interview expert and someone who deals with phones, and so on. I wouldn't want to go back to a murder investigation team because you're just a number there. With shootings, you deal with everything. I prefer that. I like getting the whole view, having full knowledge of an investigation. On a murder team you know your bit, but you never know the full story, unless you're working on the intelligence side.

'Murders are more likely to get cleared up, but it's not the same with shootings. We're involved in volume crime, and dealing with that you have to put a lot of effort in. When you go out on a shooting, the local police can't wait to get rid of it to Trident. It's certainly more challenging work. It's often the case that there are no witnesses to a shooting. No one wants to talk, and the victim doesn't want to know. I wish it was the case that we know who did a shooting within twenty-four hours. That may apply to murder cases, which are the ultimate crime, but not with ordinary shootings. "Someone will tell you" – I've heard that a few times from people. They want you to sort it out, but they want someone else to tell you who did it. It's hard work, and you get little thanks for your effort – not from the victim, not that you're out for that. If you get a result – a conviction – it's very satisfying.'

DC Diane Maiden, a black officer in her early thirties who joined the Met after several years with the Bedfordshire force says:

'It's easier on a murder team, but you're doing the same things all day – bagging out exhibits, taking statements… Beds had 1,300 officers and I knew ninety per cent of them. I could walk into any police station and know everyone there. It was a bit of a nightmare coming to the

Met. It was a case of "sit down and get on with it". In Trident, you just pick things up as you go along. I'm not shy now to ask. My parents are Jamaican. Out on jobs, younger Jamaican males – the twenty to thirty-year-olds won't speak to me, but they do to Dave. They see women as second class citizens. There are cases where some of them have ten babymothers pregnant at the same time. The situation can quickly reverse, when they talk patois, because I know what they're speaking about. British-born and the older generation Jamaicans are fine. They simply see me as a black police officer. Being a woman is not a problem for them.'

On my second night with the pair, an emergency call took us north of the Thames. Driving to the scene in an unmarked car, Milton explained that information on the shooting was sparse. There had been a fight involving IC3s [blacks] in the Kilburn area, which was linked to a later second incident, a mile away. One man had been shot and taken to hospital by a friend, who had then been arrested for alleged obstruction. 'Nine times out of ten we don't find out exactly what happened,' observed Milton. 'We don't know who are the goodies and who are the baddies, or whether they're all baddies. We'll find out more at the scene, but sometimes we never know, even after lots of investigation.'

Our first stop was in Kensal Rise in north-west London. Patches of blood on the pavement and shattered glass marked the scene on Chamberlayne Road at the junction with Leigh Gardens. Police from the local station, Kilburn, had cordoned off the area, diverting buses and other traffic. Ducking under the red and white tape, the two Trident officers examined the scene and heard that the victim, a black man in his twenties, had been alone in his Peugeot car when he was attacked by a group of blacks. Reported to have been shot, and trailing blood, he ran down the busy Chamberlayne Road, past the underground station, and then turned left into Kilburn Lane, where a second related incident had been reported.

That second scene was also still cordoned off, but to complicate matters the uniformed officers there were from another police station, Paddington, because it was in their area. Witnesses described how a car had cut in front of a second car, forcing it to stop. According to a woman bus driver, a man with big Afro hair got out of the first car, carrying what looked like a knife. He went over to the other car and kicked at one of its doors. A man with a bleeding arm emerged, and after a shouted altercation both cars drove off. The bus driver wrote down the registration numbers and called the police but, as she explained to DC Milton, she had been in difficulty because the bus passengers had been shouting at her to drive on. The bus carried a CCTV camera which, if it was working, could have caught the whole scene in Kilburn Lane. Milton arranged for the tape and camera to be examined.

Next stop was St Mary's Hospital, Paddington, to which the injured man had been taken, driven there by his friend, known as D— . As we arrived, there were shouts and screams from a disturbance near the entrance to the accident and emergency unit. A blue-uniformed nurse ran past calling out for a security guard. Ignoring what was probably a regular Saturday night commotion, the Trident pair went inside and established that the victim was in a small eighth-floor ward. Two uniformed officers there handed over various bits of evidence, including the victim's clothing, which would be going for forensic examination. D— had attempted to take some potential evidence – the victim's mobile phone – away with him, until prevented by hospital staff who told him he should wait for police. He had already tried to wash the victim's injured arm which could have resulted in the removal of firearm discharge residue (FDR). Even small traces of such gun residue can tell investigators the type of weapon used and from how far away it had been fired. D— had been arrested for alleged obstruction. But did he do what was being suggested deliberately, or was it the act of a friend helping to clean him up, relieving the pressures on nurses in a busy A&E department? Had he attempted to take away the victim's mobile phone through worry that it would go missing in hospital, or was he concerned that, if it fell into police hands, some incriminating phone calls would be revealed?

The victim was unable to answer such questions. He did not even know of his friend's arrest when, lying prone in his hospital bed, he was questioned by DC Milton, who spoke softly so as not to disturb the darkened ward's three other occupants, one of whom was gently snoring. The victim said he was in his X-registered Peugeot and on his way home to Wembley Park when a black car pulled in front of him with at least two men getting out and coming over to him. Both wore black T-shirts and baseball caps. He tried to drive off, but his keys were grabbed. He jumped out of his car, but then heard a bang, and saw that one of the men was holding a gun in a black-gloved hand. Although blood was dripping from his arm, he picked up a brick and hurled it at the car. Somehow, he managed to retrieve his keys, but they were bent and his car's steering lock was on. He could not start the engine, so he made a run for it. His friend D— picked him up in Kilburn Lane, the scene of the second incident. He was aware of another car there but took no notice of it. D— had helped him, taking off his T-shirt and wrapping it round his bleeding arm.

The victim described the initial attack on him as an attempted car-jacking, and said he did not recognise his attackers. 'I was not scared,' he told the detective. 'It's really crazy, but I couldn't believe it was happening. It was like a movie.' However, no bullets or cartridge cases were found at either scene. It was possible that a bullet could have been lodged in the victim's car, so it was important to examine the vehicle, but it was missing from where it had been abandoned. The victim said he had given the keys to his brother, who must have driven the car away. Milton did not probe further. That would be for other officers to pursue later when the victim had recovered sufficiently to make a statement. The detective phoned the victim's home, spoke to the brother, and made arrangements for the car to be hoisted on to a police vehicle and taken for forensic examination at a police pound at Charlton in south-east London.

Next stop was the nearby Paddington police station and a discussion with the duty inspector there about giving the victim an armed guard during his stay in hospital. The wounded man had said he did not know his attackers, but the police had no way of knowing at that stage whether this was the truth, or whether the shooting was part of a feud. If the man was shot while in hospital and there was no armed guard, the police would come under criticism. Against that was the manpower issue. With few officers to call on, mounting an armed guard could be a waste of resources. 'If we had an armed guard for everyone in hospital who was possibly under threat, we'd have no police left on the streets,' observed the duty inspector, who had the job of deciding the issue.

While he was wrestling with the problem, the Trident pair drove on with me to Kilburn police station for the customary debriefing of officers involved in the incidents, and the handing over to Trident of any evidence gathered at the incident scenes. 'These debriefings are crucial,' said Milton. 'It's surprising how much information you can lose if there's no debrief. Each officer relates their role – that's fairly straightforward, but things can come out in the discussion that could prove important to the wider investigation – small things, or bits of background that the individual didn't necessarily think were important enough to put in a written report.' There were fourteen officers waiting for Milton and Maiden in the canteen at Kilburn police station, and doubts about it being a car-jacking soon emerged. One officer said an X-registered Peugeot was not the kind of car to be particularly envied in the area. Another officer said he had recently arrested someone for robbery, and the victim was the 'appropriate adult' who sat in on police interviews.

D— , the victim's friend who had been arrested, was 'in the bin' at another police station, Wembley, and that was the next stop. On the way there, a call came through to Milton's mobile that there had been another, possibly related incident. A man had been stabbed in the eye outside Knightsbridge underground station. The attackers had fled the scene in a black car, the same colour as one of those used in the Kilburn Lane incident. But it was not another job for Trident. No gun had been used and it later became clear that the attackers were not even black.

When arrested, D— had given a different name and no permanent address, so had been registered as of NFA – no fixed abode. It was too late in the night for him to be questioned, so that task was left for the Trident day team. A report of the night's events had to be prepared for them, so it was back to Trident headquarters in Putney for the long job of writing it all up in the Crime Reporting Information System (CRIS) – and a check on the intelligence database. The victim's name drew a blank, but D— had 'form'. Completing the report took the two officers beyond the 6 a.m. end of their shift, and they expected to play no further part in the investigation into the incident. The day team would question D— , add to the report, and then the following day, Monday, Trident's north shootings team would take over the whole investigation because the incidents had been in their area. I asked DC Milton if he would ever check on the progress of this or other investigations with which he had been involved in their early stages. 'Of course, I'm curious,' he replied, 'but we just don't have the time because we're dealing with so many jobs. This one's someone else's now.'

Later I learned that D— was in the country illegally, and was to be deported. As for the shooting, it turned out that it had been nothing of the kind. A hospital doctor told the investigating team that there was no sign of any bullet wound to the victim. His injuries were consistent with him having punched his fist through glass. Witnesses were later traced and although they said the incident did appear to be a car-jacking, none had seen or heard a gun being used. One man with military experience said he had seen the whole incident from beginning to end, and if a gun had been fired he would certainly have recognised the sound. So, it was back to the victim who then told detectives that although it was an attempted car robbery, he was now unsure of what happened afterwards, adding that he *thought* he had been shot because he heard a loud bang. As a result of the follow-up investigation, the incident was reclassified as an attempted car-jacking. But the victim did not want the matter pursued further.

Trident officers are used to victims of shootings not wanting to cooperate in investigations. In such cases it usually means that detectives never get to the bottom of what really happened and the motives for it. What makes this case unusual was that it was not a shooting at all, and should never have involved Operation Trident. But unfortunately it did, and it took up many hours of police time to investigate, involving at various times at least thirty different officers. If there had been a genuine shooting that night, the Trident officers would have had difficulty dealing with it, running the risk of valuable evidence being lost or not acted on until it was too late.

Just a few weeks before going with the Trident night team to the reported shooting incident in Kensal Rise, I had been in exactly the same area trying to find out more about the circumstances surrounding a Trident murder, which had occurred literally yards away. A murder trial at the Old Bailey had left many questions unanswered. I tried to find out more, but had ended up no further forward, unable to penetrate the murk.

Shawn Perch appears not to have noticed the two young men on the motorbike, their heads covered by full dark helmets with tinted visors. As he walked along the one-way street, he was a happy man. It was Good Friday and he was the proud father of a baby just two days old. He had spent much of the day preparing for the birthday party that evening of Natasha, his baby's young godmother. Perch was a good friend of her family, and had volunteered to help with the cooking, taking charge of barbecuing the fish in the back garden of her home, overlooking a railway line. He had done a good job, and the party was getting into full swing. Now he was taking a break, on his way to buy some more beer and crisps from the corner shop at the end of the street of terraced houses. Leaving his five-year-old daughter at the party, he set off along Clifford Gardens with Natasha's fourteen-year-old brother, Santino. The pair chatted to the shopkeeper as Perch bought cans of beer and then they set off back to the party. They had gone only a few feet when three shots were fired by the man on the back of the motorbike. Shawn did not have a chance. Bullets hit him in the head and he slumped to the pavement, blood seeping from his body. Unhurt, but in shock, Santino ran back to his home. All he managed to blurt out was that Shawn was on the floor.

Natasha and Santino's mother, Sandra Vassell, ran along the street. She was no stranger to the effects of gun violence. One of her sons died and another was badly injured in a shooting incident a few years before in Hackney. As she approached this latest shooting, someone tried to shield her from the sight. Standing at her front door pointing along the street towards the corner shop she told me:

> 'They said I shouldn't look, but I did. I knelt down and he was still alive. I could see what looked like two cuts in his head. He'd bought the drinks and crisps and he was lying on the bag. There was blood at his stomach. He was breathing. I just started shouting "he's alive – get an ambulance". There were people from the shops standing there. I just couldn't take it. I couldn't take it in. I had to come back...his five-year-old girl was here and she just didn't understand what was happening. He had her things and the baby's things here... It was terrible. I'll never forget it. There's still a bullet hole in the door next to the shop. It's a constant reminder.'

The police had little to go on. They only discovered the dead man's full name from cards left on bunches of flowers which marked the spot where he had fallen at the junction of Clifford Gardens and Chamberlayne Road, close to Kensal Rise underground station. It looked like a classic hit. The few witnesses said they had seen two men on a motorbike. They wore dark clothing and had full helmets masking their faces. The pillion rider had fired the shots, stretching out his left arm to aim the gun. Several shots were fired and the bike then roared off. No one got its registration number, but one man said it was a yellow and black colour. That limited information, coupled with some good detective work and a tip-off a few weeks later, was to prove crucial.

Trident detectives took over the following day. People at the party were initially wary of talking to the police, who were presented with something of a puzzle. If it was a targeted hit, how did the motorbike gunman know that Shawn Perch would be coming out of the house at that time? It had been a last minute offer by him to go for the drinks. Was it a case of mistaken identity? Police discounted that possibility because he was wearing distinctive clothing. It looked as though the waiting motorbike gunmen had known exactly who they were after, perhaps tipped off by someone using a mobile phone at the party. If that was so, what had Shawn Perch been mixed up with that could have warranted his death?

He was a good friend of Natasha's brother Leon, who, although hit in the liver, had survived the shooting which had killed his brother Meshack. That incident was outside the Trenz nightclub in Hackney, formerly known as The Regency, frequented in the 1960s by the Kray twins. It was followed a few months later by another shooting. Rudi King, the man suspected of the Trenz murder, was himself shot dead, hit several times in the head as he sat in his car at Willesden, less than a mile from Kensal Rise. But those shootings had both been in 1997. Police discounted a possible connection as feuds were unlikely to last for six years. But was the motive for the killing more personal? The mother of Perch's five-year-old daughter was in Jamaica. Was someone sufficiently upset to kill him because he had taken up with another girl, who had just given birth? In Jamaica, Perch was known as Bad Ting [Bad Thing]. When he came to England he became Good Ting. Police suspected him of involvement with drugs. As with so many Trident shootings, detectives were never to establish a definite motive for his death, but as their investigations continued they were able to make a fair guess.

A tip-off led to the killers. Someone told the police that one of those responsible was riding around in a red car, a Mitsubishi Colt. The description was circulated to police as a vehicle to look out for. Then a month after the murder, early one morning, at about 1 a.m., a policewoman saw just such a car in north-west London. Following it, she saw it turn into the driveway of a house in Aldborough Road, Wembley. She saw a young black man and woman get out and enter the house. The Trident team was alerted.

The IO (investigating officer) Detective Inspector Stephen Horsley, drove with another officer to check out the address. The car was still there. It had tinted windows so no one could see inside. But they also saw, parked against a wall at the end of the driveway, a yellow and black Suzuki which fitted the description of the murder motorbike. It was too much of a coincidence. Armed officers were requested. The house was going to be raided. But before back-up arrived, the car was driven off. Local CID officers followed in an unmarked car, but it seems those in the red Colt spotted them, because it accelerated away to be lost by the following police. However, touring the area looking for the vehicle, they found it parked in a nearby street, abandoned and locked.

To avoid possible contamination of the scene, police who had not recently handled guns or ammunition were used to break into the car for a search of the interior. Under the front passenger seat, in bags, were two guns. One was a Smith and Wesson with a shortened barrel. The other was a Webley 'service' gun dating back to the 1920s. Police disabled both weapons, sending them and the bullets inside off for forensic examination. Meanwhile, Trident officers went armed with a search warrant to the Aldborough Road house, where the car had been seen parked. The black and yellow motorbike belonged to a young man called Reco Joseph who lived at the address with his parents and sisters. Joseph's background made him an unlikely killer. Bespectacled and serious-looking, he could easily have been taken for someone heavily into studying. He came from a loving family, with respectable parents, and he had no previous convictions. But the evidence against him started to mount. In his bedroom were small amounts of cannabis and crack cocaine, plus nearly £1,000 in cash, and a set of electronic scales, all the trappings of a drug dealer. There was also some firearms residue. More evidence emerged later. But of Joseph himself, at that stage, there was no sign. He had disappeared.

Checks on the red Colt showed that it had figured in an incident at a car pound to which police had been called. The car had been seized and the registered owner was a man called Nigel —, who had got into an argument with one of the workers at the pound. Police had been called to prevent a possible breach of the peace. Luckily for the Trident officers, CCTV footage had been kept of the incident and it showed Nigel arriving at the pound in a VW Golf. Its registration number was checked and the car was found to have belonged to the Joseph family, but they had sold it. From documentation at their house, it was discovered that the vehicle's windscreen had been replaced immediately after the Easter weekend of the murder. The mechanic involved was questioned. He not only remembered the job, but he recalled remarking at the time that the hole in the windscreen looked as though it could have been caused by a bullet. The VW's new owner was traced. Trident officers searched the car, and found a neat hole in the inner lining of its roof. After careful prodding, out dropped a bullet. It too was sent off for forensic examination.

Police checks on Nigel — revealed that he was a Jamaican and, although only twenty-three years old, he had several aliases. He had been deported from the UK, but had returned under another name, sponsored by Reco Joseph's mother, who said he was a distant relative. Nigel spent some weeks at the Josephs' home, sharing Reco's bedroom, before being thrown out, accused of stealing some jewellery. His fingerprints were found in the red Mitsubishi and on a motorcycle helmet found in Reco's room. Joseph's fingerprints were on a bag containing one of the guns. The results of the various forensic tests on the guns and ammunition showed that the bullet which had killed Shawn Perch had been fired by the Smith and Wesson found in the car. The bullet found in the roof lining of the VW Golf had come from the other gun, the Webley. Further police investigations into incidents around the time of the murder showed that a Golf of the same colour had been involved in a gun battle between warring groups in nearby Harlesden. A machine pistol had been fired at two or three people who ran off through estate gardens. Crucially, this was just a few hours before the fatal shooting. Piecing together all the evidence and the information, Trident detectives reckoned that Perch had somehow been involved in the feuding, and had been shot dead by Nigel — and Reco Joseph on the motorbike.

Eventually, Joseph surrendered himself to police. In a series of interviews, and later, on trial at the Old Bailey, he said he had been staying in a hotel and also with friends. He confirmed that he knew Nigel. He said that Nigel had sold him crack, but he denied dealing in it himself. He agreed that he had travelled in the Mitsubishi Colt but claimed that Nigel had driven it to his house, telling him that there was a gun inside. Joseph denied driving the car when it was spotted by the police, and he denied driving the VW Golf when it was hit by a bullet. He also said he did not know Shawn Perch, and claimed he had been at home and with his girlfriend at the time of the murder.

The jury was unimpressed. They found Joseph guilty of murder, possession of the two guns and ammunition, and possession of crack. It did not matter whether he was the one on the front seat of the motorbike or the one behind, the trigger man. Under the law, both were equally responsible. Whether Perch was the intended target, or whether anyone coming out of the house was to be killed, will probably never be known. In mitigation, Joseph's lawyer said he should not be treated as a professional killer, but rather as someone who had fallen in with more sinister people. The judge, the Recorder of London, Michael Hyam, sentenced him to life imprisonment with a recommendation that he serve eighteen years. It was clearly a planned killing, he told Joseph. 'Only you and your confederate know the motives.'

A few weeks after the trial, I went to Clifford Gardens to see whether Sandra Vassell and her family had heard more. She told me that Reco Joseph had been D-Jaying at her daughter Natasha's previous birthday, her sixteenth. They had never heard of the other man on the motorbike, who was supposed to be back in Jamaica. She was grateful for the way Trident officers had kept in contact, telling her of developments in the case. But she and others in the family had been forced to appear as witnesses at the Old Bailey. They had not wanted to go because they had nothing to do with the murder, and had no idea about the killers' motives. 'But we had made statements and Trident said because of that we had to go,' she told me. 'I didn't like it at the Old Bailey at all – all the nasty questions from the defence lawyer. They brought up my son Meshack dying in the shooting at Hackney. It was hurtful to hear that. Eventually I turned to the judge and appealed to him – why am I having to answer all these questions? It stopped after that.'

Now, reflecting on the killing more than a year later, she said her family were still affected by it, particularly Santino, her fourteen-year-old son who had been with Shawn when he was gunned down. 'What these people [the killers] don't know is that it affects everyone. Santino won't go anywhere near that shop now. It could have been him shot. I can remember how nice Shawn's five-year-old was – how she was over here from Jamaica and delighted to see snow for the first time. Now so many children are growing up without dads. When I was young, the worst that you'd hear was someone getting knifed or bottled. But now it's guns. You're lucky now if you reach more than thirty years old.'

At the corner shop, it was business as usual. The two local newspapers were splashing Trident stories accross the front pages. The *Willesden and Brent Chronicle*'s headline said: 'No drugs link in Trident shooting – The mother of an aspiring footballer gunned down on his doorstep last week has begged people to come forward with the truth about her son's death. Police found 21-year-old Leon Labastide in Mordaunt Road, Harlesden, suffering from multiple gunshot wounds shortly after 10.30 p.m…' The headline in the *Willesden Observer* covering the aftermath of the same murder said: 'Time to put an end to shootings – murder prompts police crackdown.'

CHAPTER THIRTEEN | Slaughter of the Innocents and Witness Problems

'A coat was put under the fourteen-year-old girl's head, and she asked for her trainers to be taken off. Bleeding from her wound, she appeared to be slipping in and out of consciousness. "I think she's gone", said a girl at one stage. "Keep her awake. Don't let her die," a boy pleaded. "Don't let her die."'

In 2005, the main problem facing detectives remained the same as when Trident was officially launched five years before as a cross-London operation: how to deal with reluctant witnesses. People tell the police what they know about a murder or shooting but refuse to repeat it in evidence in court. Some fear that their own wrong-doing will emerge if they agree to be a witness. But fear of reprisals is the most common reason emerging during Trident investigations. The situation has been improving, however, with evidence coming from Trident's very impressive 'clear-up' rate of past cases, that witnesses were overcoming their fears and talking.

A combination of factors has led to more people now being prepared to come forward. Trident's dedicated family liaison officers keep in contact with the murder victim's family members, those most likely to know or to hear about who was responsible. Trident is the biggest user of the Met's witness protection scheme, which operates on different levels according to need. The lowest in the range of measures is the giving of a special emergency telephone number for a witness to call if he or she thinks they are in danger of being 'got at'. At the other end of the scale, not only witnesses but also their immediate families can be given new identities, moved to other parts of the country or even abroad, and helped with finding jobs. Then there are the special measures that can be taken in courts to protect the identities of witnesses, whether it is withholding their names and addresses, or allowing them to give evidence from behind a screen or, in the most serious of cases where they know the defendant, having audio machinery distort their voices.

The one major reason over and above all others for changing attitudes has probably been the formation of the Trident Independent Advisory Group with separate sub-groups in different London boroughs. Trident officers and representatives of the black community get together to talk through gun-crime issues and the ways people can be persuaded to act against the gunmen. Each year Trident launches an anti-gun-crime advertising campaign and this is replicated by local groups in the gun hotspots, with some funding and backing from individual boroughs, the Metropolitan Police Authority and the Home Office.

However, despite all these special measures – the adverts and the campaigns for people to cooperate with the police – some investigations still run into that familiar wall of silence, even when they are high profile cases receiving considerable publicity, with the offer of sizable rewards for information. One such murder was in October 2003.

The tangled past of the crack-dealing gangster known as Bertram Byfield finally caught up with him some time after twelve on a Saturday night when he was shot dead in his bedsit. So common then were such London murders that his killing would probably not have merited even a paragraph in a national newspaper. But this one hit the headlines because shot dead alongside him was a seven-year-old girl, Toni-Ann, who he looked on as his daughter. The first bullet fired was into Bertram Byfield's groin, followed by another to his chest. Then the gunman turned on Toni-Ann who had witnessed the murder. She was shot in the back, cowering in fear on the floor.

When police and paramedics arrived at the old terraced house in Kensal Rise, near notorious Harlesden, and pushed the bedsit door open, all they could see in the dimly lit room was Toni-Ann's body, and she looked as though she could still be alive. Going inside to try to revive her, they saw Byfield on the floor as well, and they gave him medical aid, too. But both were most likely already dead.

The 999 calls had come from neighbours in the other bedsits in the house on Harrow Road, owned by a housing association and mainly used for the homeless and offenders released from prison. One neighbour described hearing a dispute, and amid the gunshots the sound of a female screaming. It sounded like an adult's scream, not a child's. Had a woman been with the gunman? Could the bullet to Byfield's groin have been punishment for sexual activity? It looked a possibility, and as police checked on his background they became more and more convinced that was the case. Although 41-year-old Byfield had been in prison for dealing drugs, he had many girlfriends, and had tangled with them and their boyfriends on previous occasions.

By Sunday afternoon the murder team had the name of a suspect, a love rival, who I will call 'SH', who had allegedly tried to kill Byfield a few months before. This new murder was being classed as a 'domestic', with, unfortunately, innocent Toni-Ann in the way. No need, therefore, to call on the specialist services of the black-on-black murder team, Operation Trident. That was to change, though, after the murders received massive coverage on TV and radio because of Toni-Ann's age. After high level consultation between London politicians and Scotland Yard's top brass, it was decided that this was indeed a case for Trident.

It was handed over to a team led by Detective Chief Inspector Neil Basu at a 6 a.m. briefing meeting the following morning. There was little to go on forensically, partly because so many people had been in the small twelve foot by twelve foot bedsit after the shootings. Four paramedics and at least six police officers had been there. Murder scenes are supposed to be preserved to avoid contamination, but no one was blaming the emergency services for rushing in and trying to save lives, especially that of a young girl. At that early stage in Basu's investigation, everything pointed to a revenge killing and to SH being responsible. He had the motive. They had shared the same girlfriend. The story behind that, what followed during the investigation, and how Toni-Ann came to be living with Byfield is very telling about the disjointed, chaotic lifestyles of those involved in black gun crime.

Back in 1997, Byfield was sentenced to four years for possessing crack cocaine. While in prison, his girlfriend abandoned him and shacked up with SH and had his baby. However, she started visiting Byfield during his sentence and she rejoined him when he left prison, taking the baby with her. SH then confronted Byfield and there was a fight during which both were stabbed with a screwdriver. The girlfriend then returned to SH who later on is alleged to have fired several shots at Byfield, hitting him twice while he was standing with SH's three-year-old son. Byfield told police what happened and SH was arrested and charged with attempted murder. He stood trial but was acquitted. It had largely been his word against Byfield's.

Within two days of the bedsit murders Trident officers tracked down SH's girlfriend's flat where their target was believed to be staying. Two detectives kept watch outside but the girlfriend appeared to have spotted them as she pulled up in her car outside the property. Believing they had been 'eyeballed' and therefore compromised, the two detectives were told that they may as well 'front her up'. They knocked on her door, and told her that they were Met officers looking for SH. She let them search her flat, but he was not there, so they left, leaving her a card with a phone number for him to contact them. A little later she left the flat and went to a telephone kiosk, and called SH. Later that evening SH surrendered to Trident, but under arrest and in custody he denied knowing anything about the murders. Accounting for his movements, he claimed to have been with his girlfriend throughout the weekend. However, his girlfriend gave a slightly different story. After further questioning, the stories diverged even more. It looked increasingly as though Trident had got their man. SH, a Jamaican, refused to cooperate any more and was remanded in custody as an overstayer, having exceeded his permitted time in the UK. Meanwhile, Trident set about researching his alibi, convinced the couple were lying.

The girlfriend's car was seized, but it was discovered that she had another one and that SH had been using it on the Saturday night of the murder. It took six to eight weeks of probing, arrests and searches before detectives got somewhere near the truth of where he had been – out and about in west London, delivering crack, in, amongst other places, Harlesden, close to the murder scene. It was discovered that at one stage that night he had been with another girlfriend, a sixteen-year-old. The Trident intelligence file on SH showed that he did have a sixteen-year-old girlfriend, whom he had met when she was fourteen and a year later had his baby. That relationship led to him being shot, interestingly, in the groin, the same place where Bertram Byfield had been hit by the first bullet. Police had interviewed SH after he had been shot, and he told them that he had gone to a flat to meet the young girl, but found her being sexually assaulted by some men. When he intervened, he was shot, but he was unable to identify the gunman.

The Byfield murder investigation team tracked down the sixteen-year-old girl who confirmed that she had been with SH for some time on the night of the murder. Police also traced another man who said that in the early hours of the Sunday morning he had been given crack by SH and driven around by him. He pointed out to police a petrol station they had visited. Trident detectives found some CCTV footage covering the scene, and discovered that SH was there in his girlfriend's second car at exactly the same time as the murder was taking place. The inevitable conclusion was that he could not have committed the murder. That was confirmed a little later when the results of DNA and fingerprint testing showed no link between him and the bedsit.

The Trident detectives were angry at what had happened, not because they had got the wrong man, but rather that SH himself should have been more honest, saving them much time and effort which would have been better spent trying to catch the real, brutal killer. SH and his older girfriend were both charged with conspiracy to pervert the course of justice. They stood trial the following summer, but were acquitted before having to mount a defence, the judge ruling there was insufficient evidence for the prosecution to proceed. Months later that particular episode still rankled with the officer in charge of the Trident investigation, DCI Basu. 'By charging him with perverting the course of justice, it made a Trident point: that we do not charge enough people with lying to the police,' he said. 'I think it would have sent a message that you don't lie to Trident, particularly, in my view, when you have subverted an inquiry. The cost of that meant that other lines of inquiry were put on hold and up to £300,000 was spent on a number of officers investigating his lies. I was horrified by that, as was the CPS and counsel.'

It was not exactly back to square one as the investigating team had established Byfield's movements on the night of the murder and they also knew more about Toni-Ann's disturbed upbringing. Byfield himself was born in 1962 in Beckenham, south London, but was brought up in Jamaica where he was known as Anthony Pinnock. He met Roselyn Richards, a part-time hairdresser from a Kingston ghetto, Olympic Gardens, who became his partner. The couple had two sons and, although Byfield returned to the UK, he continued to visit Jamaica, apparently on drug runs. Police believe he organised female 'mules' to carry cocaine to the UK. Richards was financially dependent on him. She gave birth to Toni-Ann in 1996, and the following year, after Byfield's imprisonment for crack dealing, she struggled to bring up her three children in an area renowned for gang violence, shootings and murders.

In 1999, to ease her money problems, Richards sent Toni-Ann to a family friend in Birmingham, a woman who was one of Byfield's former lovers. Teachers at the local primary school Toni-Ann attended remember her as 'a bright, lively girl who made friends easily', but there were problems at her home and she was taken into care by Birmingham social services in 2002, and then placed with a foster family. Byfield wanted to look after her himself following his release from prison, but he led a chaotic lifestyle which made it unlikely that the authorities would accept him as a suitable guardian, and he would have had difficulty in proving he was her father. However, a year later, during the month before the murders, Birmingham social services placed Toni-Ann in the care of a woman understood by them to be the girl's aunt. The woman lived in Willesden Green, no more than a mile from Byfield and he regularly visited her there. An inquiry has been launched into the placement and what steps were taken to alert Brent social services to the fact that Toni-Ann was now in its area.

On the day before the murders, a Saturday, Byfield took Toni-Ann and two women to Brent Cross shopping centre in north-west London to buy her some school clothes. Byfield then returned with one of the women and Toni-Ann to his home, but the two adults had a row about another of his girlfriends, and the woman left the bedsit at 9.45 p.m. Just over an hour later Byfield went out crack-dealing. Rather than leave Toni-Ann in his home on her own, he took her with him. They visited old friends of his who say he and his girl left at about midnight. Their movements after that, and at what time they arrived home, are not known.

After the brutal murders, detectives traced Byfield's girlfriends, still believing that he was probably killed by a love rival. At least five were questioned, their homes searched, and their bodies examined for signs of injury consistent with having been involved in a fight at the murder scene. Detectives dismissed the idea of a woman pulling the trigger on the pair. A woman could have been angry enough to murder Byfield, but for her to turn the gun on an innocent young child would have been, according to senior detectives, 'unique in criminal history'. However, although they have not ruled out the possibility that a woman was present, and only one gun was used, police believe that it is more likely there were two gunmen. Byfield was a big, hard, fit man, and anyone wanting to kill him would reckon that he would put up a fight, possibly have others with him, and that he may be armed himself. For one man to go on his own would have been a risky venture.

During the 2003 Notting Hill carnival there was a street party outside Byfield's home and he did a roaring trade dealing drugs. In 2004, the party, a regular feature, was moved a little further along the Harrow Road out of respect for his and Toni-Ann's deaths. The one and only gun murder during the 2004 carnival was at that party. It is thought to be unconnected to the Byfields' murders and is dealt with later in this book. A year after the murders in the Harrow Road bedsit, there was a peace march through Brent starting off at Kensal Rise, and pausing at various shooting sites. First stop was outside Byfield's flat, where DCI Neil Basu and anti-gun-crime campaigner Cheryl Sealey laid a wreath. At the same time, Scotland Yard announced a reward of £25,000 for information leading to the prosecution of the person or people responsible for the murders. A year later a man was charged with both murders. He is awaiting trial at the time of writing.

Two other high-profile murder cases occurred in the provinces, both of them 'drive-bys'. Such shootings from cars were not particularly rare in Nottingham. Not for nothing was this East Midlands city branded a gun-crime capital and nicknamed Shottingham. As in other places, gun use rose with the spread of crack cocaine, affecting first the run-down inner city areas of Nottingham before reaching largely white working-class estates on its outskirts, so much so that armed police patrols and road blocks became a common sight. By 2002 Nottingham police were investigating one shooting a week with more gun incidents that year than in the previous seven years combined. Headlines were made again the following year when the force became the first in more than a decade to fail a Home Office inspection on efficiency and effectiveness. Even so, few people, if any, could have predicted the shock and impact that followed a burst of gunfire from a car in the early hours of a Saturday in October, 2004.

The gunmen belonged to a gang from another area of the city. In the rival territory of St Ann's that night, they spotted a group of fifteen or so youngsters, most of them girls in their early teens, heading to their homes. It was just after midnight, and they were walking along together, happily recounting the evening they had just spent at the city's huge annual funfair, the Goose Fair. Some were carrying fluffy cuddly toys won on sideshows. The car passed the group and some of the girls noticed its distinctive gold colour and black tinted windows. It pulled up ahead of them. Then, suddenly, its headlights went on and its engine revved up. Its windows went down as it drove towards the group of youngsters. A black-gloved hand appeared holding a gun. Some of the girls shouted out to 'get down'. Up to six shots were fired sending the group scattering, looking for cover. One girl was hit. Fourteen-year-old Danielle Beccan fell to the pavement, clutching her stomach.

'Everyone screamed and ran,' said a sixteen-year-old girl, recalling the horror. 'I didn't think it was real at first. I didn't know where to go so I hid behind a tree. Then I saw Danielle lying there. She was just shouting my name and I ran back to her. Then I seen the car turning round again. I was so scared. I said, "Oh my God, Danielle, it's coming back". I ran to where everyone else ran but everyone was already gone. I shouted that Danielle's been shot and I think everyone heard me. I ran back to her and said, "Danielle, I don't know what to do". She said "help me – ring an ambulance". Then the others ran down and dragged her to the other side of the road.' A coat was put under her head, and she asked for her trainers to be taken off. Bleeding from her wound, she appeared to be slipping in and out of consciousness. "I think she's gone", said a girl at one stage. "Keep her awake. Don't let her die," a boy pleaded. "Don't let her die."'

One of Danielle's friends rushed to her home in nearby Rushcliffe Close. Her mother, Paula Platt, had been trying to move her family from the area because of its violence. In fact, Danielle had spent a year with her father in Derby but, missing her friends, had returned to Nottingham not long before. Now her mother's worst fears were being realised. She said she went numb on hearing what had happened, then, pulling herself together, dashed out of the house. 'I eventually came across Danielle lying on her back in an alleyway,' she recalled. 'I knelt down and spoke to her. She was conscious. I stroked her hair. She recognised me straight away and said: "I'm going to die". I told her over and over, "You're not going to die". I could see she had a wound to her stomach. I told her it was a flesh wound and that she would be OK. But I could see her eyes rolling into the back of her head. I was so horrified to see my daughter in such distress. I was in total shock and panic and I felt helpless. I did not know what to do. I was just trying to keep her conscious because I was convinced that if she became unconscious she might never wake up.' While Danielle was being taken into surgery at the Queen's Medical Centre, Mrs Platt told her: 'Come back to me, I'll be waiting'. Danielle replied: 'I will, but I'm in too much pain to talk.' Shortly afterwards, she died on the operating table.

It soon became apparent that the shooting was gang-related. Danielle's friends told police that one of the death car's occupants had given a victory sign after the shooting, holding his fingers up in a W sign, which stands for the Waterfront Gang, based on The Meadows estate, a mile away from St Ann's. Police were given a detailed description of the vehicle, Danielle's friends saying that as well as the gold colour and tinted windows, it had a silver twin exhaust, alloy wheels and coloured trims. The description was circulated and early in the afternoon, less than twelve hours after Danielle's death, such a car was seen being driven by Deborah Campbell in Nottingham's Meadows area. She shared the vehicle with her son Mark Kelly, a twenty-year-old with a police record who could not be found. It looked as though the police now had the murder vehicle, an X registered Citroën Xsara Coupé, and a prime suspect who was known to friends as Yardie Mark.

A warrant for the arrest of Mark Ontonio Kelly was issued, and two days after the murder he was caught, by chance, a passenger in a car stopped by police for jumping a traffic light in London. He gave a false name, and although he had changed his appearance by shaving off his braided corn-row hairstyle, his true identity was soon established. Kelly had fled from his home with his brother's passport and a large amount of money. He stayed with his aunt in the capital, telling her he had lent his car to someone who had then used it in a shooting.

Detectives believe there were up to five people in the Citroën, and they found telling evidence against one of them in the car's glove compartment. There were two mobile phones belonging to a 24-year-old mixed-race man, Junior Andrews, a heroin dealer, who, like Kelly, was on probation. Stored on one of the phones was film of him swaggering around the St Ann's area a week before the shooting, boasting that he belonged to the Waterfront Gang, and showing great bravery by entering enemy territory at 2 a.m:

'I'm on the creep. I haven't even got no gun. I go anywhere on my own. I'm a real killer. You can't see any Waterfront man come this way [St Ann's]. I robbed 'nuff man down here. Which Waterfront man can say they've been down here at two o'clock in the morning? I don't really know anybody like me who's a real killer. I come up here. I haven't even got my bullet-proof vest. I've got one at home. I'm walking about St Ann's ville this time of year with no gun, no vest. All I've got is one broomstick…Waterfront, I've been, I've sawn and I've conquered.'

Andrews had also disappeared from his Meadows home and, as detectives explored his background looking for clues as to his whereabouts, they discovered he was obsessed with gang life, and felt a burning hatred for St Ann's people. How and why that had developed is unclear, but after being born in Northampton he moved to Nottingham and actually lived in St Ann's until he was thirteen when his family moved to The Meadows. Probing his background, police learned that he had worn a bullet-proof vest after being shot at by people he thought were from St Ann's. One of his girlfriends said he spoke of wanting to go to St Ann's to 'shoot up' people, while another said that he had harboured his hatred for the area for all of the four years she had known him.

Andrews had several tattoos on his arms including a revolver and bullet, the words 'thug life' and the initials 'WFG', standing for the Waterfront Gang. Tattooed on his neck was The Meadows postcode 'NG2', which he referred to on a rap tape he recorded. 'NG2 killers – ya – NG2 killers,' he sang. 'Murder at the scene. Trying to gather evidence. You ain't gonna find any evidence on me. I never bow down to ya…going to St Ann's, looking for my enemies. I'm gonna get there.' Andrews was traced to Aberdeen where he had gone by taxi, paying the £350 fare with cash. His mother lived there, and he told her he had problems and was fleeing from the mob. He was arrested nine days after the murder.

More evidence was needed against the two men, and over

the weeks the police were to obtain it. To establish a stronger link between the Citroën and the shooting, police scoured five hundred hours of Nottingham's CCTV footage, eventually finding an image of what looked like the murder car leaving St Ann's just a few minutes after the shots were fired. But the pictures were so blurred that not only was it impossible to read the car's registration number but even the make and model could not be established beyond doubt. The images were sent to a specialist centre in Cambridgeshire which concluded that it was indeed a gold Citroën Xsara. There are only around 150 such vehicles in the country and police traced every one of them. All but one of the owners were able to give descriptions of their whereabouts at the time of Danielle's killing. The odd man out was Mark Kelly.

In the car was further evidence linking Kelly and Andrews who were at the murder scene together. Their DNA was found on a DVD player, DVDs and a watch found in the car. The property had been stolen from a house two hours before the shooting. Analysis of the pair's mobile phones showed they were associates and that they had both been in the St Ann's area on the night of the killing, although the phones had been switched off at the time of the actual shooting. Afterwards, a panicking Andrews had tried to contact Kelly and his mother because he knew he had left his phones in the car. After the pair were arrested, police secretly recorded their incriminating conversations during prison visits and phone calls. But perhaps the most important single piece of evidence came from an examination of gun residue found in the car. It matched traces found on the bullets fired in St Ann's.

Despite all the evidence against them, both men decided to take their chances in front of a jury. They pleaded not guilty and their trial started at Birmingham Crown Court in September 2005. Lawyers for both sides, prosecution and defence, painted a bleak picture of life on the two estates, St Ann's and The Meadows. A 'pathetic and absurd' gang feud was behind the shooting, and Danielle was the innocent victim, the jury were told by prosecuting counsel, Peter Joyce. He said that Danielle's group were in good spirits and not behaving badly as they returned from the funfair:

'Danielle Beccan was in the wrong place at the wrong time, going back from the Goose Fair after that good night out.' He said Kelly and Andrews were driver and passenger in the Citroën and that the fatal shot had been fired by Andrews who had then given the Waterfront Gang victory salute.

Kelly did not go into the witness box to give evidence, but his co-defendant did. Andrews said he had not been anywhere near St Ann's at the time of the murder, claiming instead to have been in the city's Bomb nightclub until 3 a.m. The jury found both young men guilty, but only by majorities of 10–2. The judge, Mr Justice Butterfield, tore into the pair. 'This was a terrible killing,' he said. 'You armed yourself with a handgun and set out cruising around St Ann's looking for likely victims. Your pathological and illogical hatred of everyone from St Ann's was so intense that you did indeed want to kill. You found a group of young people, most of them children. You stopped your car and fired at them at a range of no more than ten yards.' After jailing them for life with a recommendation that they serve at least thirty-two years before even being considered for parole, he turned to Danielle's friends and family, offering his heartfelt sympathy and praising them for the quiet dignity they had shown.

In a moving interview, Danielle's mother, Paula Platt, spoke of her family's feelings. She could have been articulating the thoughts of everyone who has lost a very close family member to gun crime. She said:

'Some days are good, and some are not so good. On the good days we can all have a laugh and it seems like we're a normal family, but we don't feel normal. There's always in the back of our minds the knowledge that someone is missing. Danielle was bright, she was bubbly, very intelligent, very capable of moving on and achieving great things. And sometimes she was moody, a typical teenager. I don't want to paint a picture of a perfect child, but she was beautiful. She was the girl next door that everybody knows – a friendly, happy girl.

'When we're having a good time, quite often there's this slap-in-the-face moment when you realise that Danielle is not here – and then you feel guilty for being happy. It's just a rollercoaster. There's not a day goes past – even an hour goes past – when I don't think of Danielle. The simplest things remind me of her. I can be in the local supermarket and see a carton of yoghurt she used to like or walking down the road behind a young girl that looks a bit like her. Or even something totally unrelated can trigger that feeling. Everything comes back to her. Only on two occasions have I ended up crying on the street. Once was in the fruit and veg aisle of a local supermarket. Another was in the Victoria Centre, at the fountain outside Boots. I just sat there and cried – and again, I really don't know what triggered it. There's just this tremendous sense of loss – a cloud that comes over you. Sometimes I can talk about Danielle in a matter-of-fact way. I don't get emotional about it.

'I think about the day it happened all the time. It's like a videotape. You think: when am I going to get some peace in my head? I can be doing something completely unrelated, going about my everyday life, and the videotape starts playing, and it rewinds and plays again, and on and on. You just think: please stop. But it won't. I have to focus on other things to get some sort of respite. Sometimes I think being so mad busy is a negative because I haven't allowed myself to think about things too much. I don't know if I've fully grieved. I haven't released a lot of the things pent up inside me.'

Danielle's murder on 9th October 2004 was big news, with headlines and background stories that gun crime was out of control in Nottingham. In fact, at that time the police, working alongside community leaders, were just beginning to make an impact on the city's gun gangs. The fourteen-year-old's death spurred on the efforts. Two weeks after the shooting the city centre was brought to a standstill as 5,000 people gathered in her memory in the Old Market Square under the 'Nottingham Stands Together' banner. That event inspired a poster campaign – 'Not in My City' – and a two-week gun amnesty during which fifty firearms were handed in.

It was in 2002, after a marked increase in gun crime, that Nottinghamshire police started to tackle the problem in a serious way, by launching their own version of the Met's Operation Trident, calling it Operation Stealth. The initiative resulted in a steady drop in shooting incidents. In 2003 the number of people fired at, injured, or killed stood at sixty-three. In 2004 there were forty-eight, and in the first half of 2005, only twelve. In a joint statement after the trial of Danielle's killers, the city council and the police observed that far from being the country's gun crime capital, Nottingham compared very favourably with other areas. There were sixteen times more firearms offences in London, and five times more in both the West Midlands and Manchester. 'The majority of people who live, work or spend time in Nottingham will never see a gun,' declared council leader Jon Collins. 'It is simply not the reality of normal, everyday life in our city.' That may be true for most of the city, and, indeed, for the country's other gun hotspots, but the reality of life for young black people in some parts of Nottingham is still grim, according to Danielle's mother, Paula Platt.

After the murder, she and her family managed to move from St Ann's to a quieter area of the city, Wollaton.

'We all know about the problems that inner city areas and estates have. We wanted to get out of St Ann's because of what we had seen going back a couple of years. We wanted to raise our children in an environment that was less problematic, if you like. We didn't want them to think it was normal to see people being chased by the police every day or drug dealers on the corner of the street. I didn't want them thinking that was normal life. That was why we had to get away. I just wanted the kids to have something better.

'My major hope was for the children, the teenagers, to take stock of their lives and have a long, hard look at where they're going. Living in St Ann's we used to see a lot of teenagers with no hope. They had absolutely no expectation for the future. The thought of going to college or university was totally alien to them. I wanted this to shock them into a realisation that life can be too short. I think more recently they've become complacent again; they're back on the streets. That really saddens me. It makes me think: what does it take? You've seen one of your peers lose her life. I hoped Danielle would be the last, but I knew she wouldn't be – and I was proved right. As a family we want to put something back into that community. The kids have youth groups and clubs and whatever, but obviously there's something still amiss because this attitude and mentality persists – and it needs breaking.'

The trial of Danielle Beccan's killers ended in mid-October 2005, just a few days after the first anniversary of her murder. During the court case, several witnesses were allowed to give their evidence anonymously, fearing retribution if their identities became known. There had been major problems with witnesses at an equally important Midlands trial which had attracted even more publicity earlier in the year. More extreme measures to protect witnesses had been introduced in the case of the men who gunned down four teenage girls from Birmingham, killing two of them, Letisha Shakespeare and Charlene Ellis. As well as the use of pseudonyms, screens, and voice distortion for some of those giving evidence, there were other parallels between the two cases. Gang rivalry was behind both of them. The fatal shots in each were fired from cars with tinted windows, and, again, innocent girls were left dying.

The four teenage girls from Birmingham laughed and joked as they posed together for a photograph that was soon to become iconic. They were heading off for New Year parties. Their first stop was to pose for that photograph in front of the Christmas tree in the centre of Solihull, then on to a nightclub in the town. After that they went to a party at a hairdressing salon in Aston. Although it was a private party, details had been broadcast on a pirate radio station and the salon became so crowded, noisy, hot and stuffy that a few people there decided to go outside for some calm and fresh air. Among them were the four friends, Letisha Shakespeare, Cheryl Shaw and twins Charlene and Sophie Ellis. As the group chatted, a car with tinted windows drove up, sinisterly, with its lights off, despite it being the middle of the night and not yet dawn. Suddenly, exploding from its windows, there came a hail of bullets. Nearly forty shots were fired from three different guns, most of them from a 'spray and pray' Mac-10 machine pistol. Seventeen-year-old Letisha Shakespeare was struck four times. She died from a bullet that went right through her, hitting her in the chest and passing through her heart and lungs, before leaving from her back. Charlene Ellis, aged eighteen, was hit three times, first in the arm, then her shoulder, with the fatal shot being to her head. Her twin, Sophie, was seriously injured by two bullets while the fourth friend, seventeen-year-old Cheryl Shaw 'escaped' with a hand injury.

Cheryl told police that the death car looked like a red Ford Mondeo. 'I noticed it because I saw a gun outside on the passenger side, and someone with a balaclava on,' she said. 'I saw the gun and I heard gunshots, like a machine gun. I just stared at the gun in shock. I raised my hands to my face. I fell to the floor, and got up and started running.'

Immediate speculation on what lay behind the attack centred on the rivalry between two notorious Birmingham gangs – the Burger Bar Boys and the Johnson Crew – who had been at each others' throats for years. The hairdressing salon on Birchfield Road in Aston is just off the A34 which marks the border area between the two gangs' territories. The Johnson Crew was the biggest gang in Birmingham in the 1980s, controlling much of the city's drug trade from a café in Handsworth. But then a dispute occurred whose origins are themselves in dispute. One version is that it arose during an argument about a PlayStation game. The more likely reason is that it was about how to spend the huge drugs profits rolling in. Whatever the cause, a group split away and set themselves up elsewhere in Handsworth, naming themselves the Burger Bar Boys after the café where they based themselves. Rivalry between the two gangs is thought to have resulted in around twenty murders and innumerable shootings over the years. Gradually the police were to gather evidence that feuding was indeed behind this latest killing, and that the Burger Bar Boys were the culprits.

Not content with mowing down the group standing outside the salon, the gunmen in the red Ford Mondeo had driven for only a short distance before firing another volley of shots at a man sitting nearby in a car. Police believe the man, who was not injured, was connected to the Johnson Crew. Detectives also learned that the four teenage girls were not the only ones at the salon who had been at the earlier party in the Solihull nightclub. Some associated with the Johnson Crew were there too and one man in particular had been taunting the Burger Bar Boys from on stage. This man had also been standing outside the salon, close to the four girls, at the time of the attack. Could he have been the real target, with the girls simply getting in the way of the bullets from the Mac-10, a notoriously difficult gun to control? Detectives were also receiving tip-offs that the Burger Bar Boys were seeking revenge for the earlier murder of one of their members. The Johnson Crew were believed responsible for the murder a month before of a man called Yohanne Martin. That killing was itself reckoned to be a tit-for-tat affair. Martin had been charged with the murder of another man three years earlier, but the case against him had been dropped and he had walked free.

Rumour and speculation that the Burger Bar Boys were behind the attack was just that – rumour and speculation. Despite the horrific nature of the shooting those who had been at the salon party were reluctant to give evidence out of fear that they too could become victims of gang feuding. Solid evidence was needed and, as happens so often in such cases, detectives were to obtain it by technical means – in particular through mobile phone tracking and CCTV. A Mondeo car was discovered in Smethwick, burnt out in an apparent attempt to destroy fingerprint or DNA evidence. But two bullet cases found inside matched those picked up outside the hairdressers, proving that it was the same car used in the attack. Police had seized CCTV footage from the surrounding area and appealed for information after learning the same car had been spotted a mile away from the salon just a few minutes after the shooting. The three men inside were talking animatedly to the occupants of another car which had pulled alongside. Were they reporting on what they had just done?

Working on the theory that the murders were a Burger Bar revenge attack for the Johnson Crew's killing of Yohanne Martin, detectives started looking at those who were close to the dead man, especially his brother Nathan, whose street name was 23, a man with six previous convictions including attempted robbery and escaping from custody. An examination of his and others' mobile phone records showed his involvement in the purchase on New Year's Eve of the high-performance Mondeo from an unsuspecting dealer in Northamptonshire. The men buying the car, one Asian and the other of West Indian origin, were unidentified, but the dealer, Anthony Hill, recalled the sale as unusual. The two men told him they had travelled from Birmingham, but they had no car with them. Their mobile phones kept ringing, and they did not bother to have a test drive. They were in a hurry, handing over the agreed price of £1,850, and then they realised they had left themselves with no money for petrol. The dealer handed back £10 to allow them to buy fuel to get them back to Birmingham.

Police found CCTV footage of the Mondeo being driven along the M1 from Northampton to Birmingham. It was being shadowed by a Vauxhall Vectra with two men inside. A further search of CCTV cameras found that the same Vectra had been on its own when travelling out from Birmingham earlier in the day. A check on its number-plate established that it was owned by Nathan Martin. Detectives worked out that the man with Martin was his close friend, Michael Gregory, whose sister was Yohanne Martin's partner, and that the two men had driven the pair buying the car for them to a Northamptonshire trading estate, parking round the corner out of sight of the dealer, to avoid being seen by him. Gregory, aka Chunk, appeared to have organised the purchase of the gun car, using a new mobile phone for that purpose. Police tracked fourteen calls either to it or from it during the Northamptonshire trip. Crucially, it had been used as the Vectra and Mondeo arrived in Birmingham to call a 'high-up' in the Burger Bar Boys, Marcus Ellis, apparently to let him know the hit-car was ready. Ellis, known as E-man, had four previous convictions. Ominously, he had also been accused of murder in 2000, but the charge against him was dropped because of a lack of witnesses. Ironically, he turned out to be Charlene Ellis's half-brother and Letisha's cousin, although he had little or no contact with either girl.

That same mobile used to contact Ellis was again very active on the night of the killings with several calls to and from another of the Burger Bar Boys, Rodrigo Simms, aka Sonny and SS, who was at the salon party because he was related to the owner. Starting at 3.52 a.m., the mobile calls finished fifteen minutes later at 4.07 – thirty seconds before the shooting. Simms had six previous convictions including one for false imprisonment. Police suspected that his role had been as 'spotter' for the gunmen in the Mondeo, letting them know if Johnson Crew gang members were outside, and then guiding the car in for the devastating hit.

It was not until more than four months after the shooting that police issued a press release confirming that the gun car had been recovered and that it contained two bullet cases which had been positively linked to one of the guns used to kill the girls. It was a deliberate ploy to smoke out the suspects and gather more evidence against them. Unknown to Martin, he was under surveillance by undercover officers. Fearing that it was only a matter of time before the Mondeo was linked to his Vectra, Martin took his car to be valeted the day after the police announcement. He then abandoned it.

Although his move could be used as evidence against him, along with the stronger CCTV and mobile phone evidence, it was all only circumstantial. What the police still wanted after weeks of investigation were eyewitnesses prepared to say they had seen the suspected gunmen tooling up, or actually at the scene. Problems with getting witnesses to come forward were evident from the outset. No one wanted to talk to police. Within two days of the murders West Midlands police were appealing for help, and, unusually so soon after a crime, they set out the precautions that could be taken to guarantee anonymity. 'People should not be frightened to make a call to the police or Crimestoppers,' said a spokesman. 'We have a wide range of support in place to protect people's identity so they will not be revealed. These range from screens in courts where someone giving evidence will not be seen to far more extreme measures. We know that some people may be frightened to call us because of fear of retaliation but if they have information they must come forward. We are experienced in dealing with people who are frightened to give evidence and can offer a wide range of protection.'

A month later, after interviewing fifty-five people who were at the salon party, police were almost no further forward. They again appealed for eyewitnesses, repeating the call a few weeks later, with the officer leading the investigation, Detective Superintendent Dave Mirfield, expressing frustration that people were withholding information: 'There is still a fear among some of those who witnessed this horrific act to speak to my team. All I can say is that you can speak to me personally if you wish. There will be no pressure, and I will explain fully what we can offer through support and, if necessary, protection.'

Eventually, courtesy of the prison service, the police got that crucial witness. Prison officers told them that a prisoner was claiming to have been at the murder scene and was saying he could identify two of those inside the Mondeo just before the murders – Nathan Martin and Marcus Ellis. He claimed Ellis had been cleaning a gun, and that he had seen a third man, Rodrigo Simms, making mobile phone calls. However, there was a problem. The prisoner was not only tainted because he had serious 'form' but he also wanted total anonymity and protection if he was to give evidence. His demands were met. Given the name 'Mark Brown', he was the only one to come forward to say he had seen some of the killers at the scene. It worried police and prosecutors, but they believed they could tie the other suspects to the murders through phone and CCTV evidence.

When the trial opened in November 2004, the prosecuting counsel said the dead and injured girls had been 'collateral damage' in a bloody gang war. The main defendants, Nathan Martin, twenty-five, Marcus Ellis, twenty-four, Michael Gregory, twenty-two, and Rodrigo Simms, twenty, were said by Timothy Raggatt QC to have had no regard at all for the lives of anyone getting in the way of their aim to kill members of the rival Johnson Crew. 'This attack was no random event,' he said. 'It was coordinated, organised, and planned in the widest sense.'

No fewer than eighteen witnesses were allowed to give evidence anonymously, under pseudonyms, hidden from the defendants by screens, with their voices distorted electronically. The measures were described as unfair by defence lawyers, particularly those for the key witness, 'Mark Brown', who, in addition to the other safeguards, had a fifteen-second time delay installed during his evidence, so he could be broken off if he said anything which might identify him. It emerged during cross-examination that he had convictions for robbery, affray and assaulting a police officer. One defence lawyer told him: 'The truth is you are a hoodlum, a crook, a gangster criminal who has found a way to get the prison authorities and police to bend over backwards for you. And despite all that, you get the privilege of giving your evidence anonymously.'

After a trial lasting five months at Leicester Crown Court, Martin, Ellis, Gregory and Simms were all found guilty of the murders of Letisha Shakespeare and Charlene Ellis, and the attempted murder of Sophie Ellis and Cheryl Shaw. They had shown complete indifference to the lives of others, said the judge, Mr Justice Goldring: 'Those who were killed were wholly innocent people,' he said. 'Not a shred of remorse has been exhibited, and public interest demands the highest possible deterrent.' He gave the four gang members life sentences, recommending that Martin, Ellis and Gregory each serve at least thirty-five years before being considered for parole. Because of Simms' lesser role, it was recommended that he spend twenty-seven years behind bars. Defence lawyers said there would be appeals against the convictions, all of which were by majority verdicts, apart from Ellis's which was unanimous.

Police used the heavy sentences to hammer home a message. 'Four men will today be starting a total of 132 years in prison,' said Detective Superintendent Mirfield. 'The message this sentence sends out is that guns and gangs will not win. Justice will always win and any youngster who sees this today, take it as a wake-up call while you still have a chance.' These were bold words, and backing them up, West Midlands police listed extra measures being taken to reduce gun crime. Within days of the murder, a joint police and community coordinating group to tackle armed criminality in the West Midlands was being set up by Assistant Chief Constable Nick Tofiluk, aiming for long-term solutions. This was coupled with an increase of fifteen in the number of the force's firearms officers, and an expansion of the existing anti-gun-crime section, Operation Ventara. The latter's emphasis was changed so that its officers would take part in more operations themselves rather than simply passing on information for action by other units. Figures put out a few months later showed that offences involving firearms in the area had fallen by almost five per cent over the previous year.

However, the main problems facing detectives at the beginning of their investigation into the double murder still remained in the trial's aftermath – witnesses' fear of reprisals in coming forward to give evidence, coupled with continued distrust of the police. Recognising the reality during his sentencing, the trial judge said that the killers were to some extent right in believing that people would be too frightened to testify. But he added that what they had not reckoned with was the painstaking mobile phone evidence built up by the police, tying them to the murder scene. The silent witnesses were also criticised by the dead girls' mothers. 'You have to live with it,' they were told by Letisha's mother, Marcia

Shakespeare, while Bev Thomas, Charlene's mother, said: 'There are people there that saw and became blind, and heard, but became deaf. Today for me can be tomorrow for you. Don't wait for it to reach your doorstep.'

There are often problems getting witnesses to come forward over shootings which do not result in death. People are more likely to come forward and offer help and evidence when there has been loss of life. Even the injured victim who knows the identity of the gunman is reluctant to help out of fear of reprisals, believing that the defendant, if found guilty, will soon be out of prison because a sentence for attempted murder is lighter than one for murder.

However, this was not the case over a dramatic shooting in a busy high street in London, involving shots riddling a car and its occupants. This shooting was different. Detectives had no serious problems with witnesses. That was because a baby and a two-year-old were amongst the victims, and this was no accidental shooting. The gunmen knew a baby was inside the car. But they still sprayed it with bullets, firing up to fifteen rounds. The baby was hit and two men seriously injured but, astonishingly they escaped death.

The motive for the shooting in mid-October 2004 may lie in a dispute a week earlier when shots were fired outside a well-known Hackney nightclub, Geneva's. Two men, Dwight Charlton, aka Bagga, and Horace Gordon, aka Easy, had been handing out flyers at the club. They were advertising an event the following month entitled: Bagga – 'da girls dem lemon cream' – presents his 'Birthnite Bashment'. The flyer pictures the pair surrounded by girls, with Bagga in the middle holding what look like several $1,000 bills. 'Home Office style' security was advertised for the event. This generally means strict checks for weapons and drugs at the entrance, but these can also leave the field open for unscrupulous organisers to distribute drugs inside the venue. There were objections to Charlton and Gordon promoting an event at a rival venue, and the dispute continued outside the club, with at least one weapon being fired. Joining the argument were two other men who were to become victims.

A week later, Charlton and Gordon struck back. With them

was another man pictured in the flyer, their close friend, Michael Nelson, known mainly as Klinsman because he wore a football shirt carrying the name of the former Tottenham Hotspur player. But he also had at least four other street names – Kingsman, Sky, Sky High and Sky Topper. Nelson took the lead role in the shooting which happened in the early evening outside a West Indian takeaway, Too Sweet, on Chatsworth Road.

The three, all armed, spotted some of the men from the Geneva's dispute. Their targets were sitting in the back of a car, with two children, a baby and a toddler. (To protect the identities of the children, a court order prevents the naming of those inside the vehicle.) Approaching the car, Nelson was slightly ahead of Charlton and Gordon. None of the three wore masks or any disguise, apparently confident or arrogant enough to believe that no one would appear as witnesses against them. The car's occupants saw Nelson pull out a gun. A woman in the front passenger seat jumped out and shouted to him that there were babies inside. The two men sitting with the children in the rear seats tried to get out but, unknown to them, there were child-proof locks on the doors. They were trapped.

Undeterred by the warning of the babies' presence, Nelson calmly walked to the offside of the vehicle and fired shot after shot. The man sitting with his baby in his lap in the rear behind the driver was hit several times including in his chest and back. He played dead, leaning forward, attempting to protect his baby, who was also hit in the leg. Nelson then walked round the car and fired at the man in the other back seat. He was hit three times. Bullets struck his arm and leg and the third smashed into his mouth, entering his right cheek, passing through his tongue and out through his left cheek. Another of the three gunmen fired at the front of the car, his bullet shattering the windscreen. Amazingly, although badly injured, neither of the two men in the back died.

Ten cartridge cases were recovered at the scene. They had been fired from three guns. Michael Nelson was the first to be arrested, five days after the attack. He denied being there, as did Dwight Charlton who was arrested a few hours later. Gloves in his car were sent for forensic examination and were found to have residue consistent with three different types of ammunition, some of it similar to residue found in the car attacked at Hackney. Horace Gordon fled to Birmingham where he was arrested five days after the other two. 'I was just in the wrong company at the wrong time,' he told police after being cautioned for the attempted murder of four people. Gun residue on some of his clothing also linked him to the attack. All three men were picked out at identification parades, and their mobile phone use showed them in the area at the time of the shooting.

The three were found guilty at the Old Bailey in June 2005 of attempted murder, and the judge, the Recorder of London, Peter Beaumont, told them: 'For reasons beyond the comprehension of the court, you chose to open fire in a way which was intended to be a cold-blooded execution of the people who were in the car. That you didn't succeed is not due to you... The court has only one weapon in the fight against gun crime, and that is to pass sentences which anyone reading about this case might pause to reflect on what you did.' Nelson was given twenty-five years, and Charlton and Gordon each received sixteen-year sentences.

CHAPTER FOURTEEN | British-born Shooters and more Witness Problems

'The Met's record of protection for witnesses who cooperate is outstanding. But it's very difficult for a person who's lived twenty years in the same area, having the same job, speaking to the same people, having an extensive family network, to say goodbye to all that. It's very, very difficult. Our clients are the hardest to deal with. There's no doubt about it.'

Another murder and the bringing to justice of the killers became important for reasons other than the usual problems with witnesses. Not only did the investigation and court costs reach an estimated £5 million but, more interestingly, those involved in the murder – the victim, his friends, and the killers – were not Jamaican. They were British-born; young black men, mostly no-hopers, who had given up on leading more normal lives. Disaffected, they had joined gangs, dealt drugs and lived violent lives. What was to emerge about their callous lifestyles shook even hardened detectives and lawyers.

It may have started as nothing more sinister than unwelcome attention being paid to a girlfriend. Two boys, teenagers in a car, cruising the streets of east London, had tried to 'pull' the girl. Her boyfriend was outraged when told of what had happened. Although just out of his teens, he had a long record of violence, glorying in his reputation as his area's 'god' and its 'baddest gunman'. Anyone messing around with his girlfriend was showing disrespect, and should be taught a lesson. However, the revenge taken far exceeded the original 'offence'. An eighteen-year-old was gunned down and killed, and that in turn led to gang warfare – a spiral of violence over the following weeks with more shootings, torched cars, people fleeing London, and at least one more murder.

It was a hot summer evening on 9th June 2003 when the killers' guns blasted at the group of youngsters, playing 'money-up' in the shadow of a towerblock just north of London's east end. These teenage friends were throwing £1 coins at a low wall, trying to win all the money by getting their coin closest to the brickwork. They were the younger members of a gang known as the London Fields Boys, LFB for short, named after the nearby patch of worn green in the centre of Hackney. There were fights and feuds between them and other gangs in the area. Some of the fifteen or so youngsters either gambling, or watching, had elder brothers, uncles or fathers who made up the LFB proper. But many of them were not around that day. They had been at a funeral late that afternoon of a murdered Jamaican, and by the evening were at his wake.

The young vengeance-seeking gunmen were taking advantage of the absence of protection. They were certainly organised. A 'spotter' had seen the two disrespectful youths in the 'money-up' group, and a convoy of three cars set off for London Fields with at least nine youths and young men inside, nearly all of them wearing hooded tops or balaclavas to mask their faces. They were not to know it, but by the time their cars screeched to a halt next to the 'money-up' group, the two erring youths had left the scene.

The sound of sudden braking did not cause much of a stir. There were often joy-riders and others messing about in cars in the area. But the alarm was raised with warning shouts after someone saw what one of three men emerging from the cars was carrying. It was a long-barrelled handgun, according to an eyewitness, just like the one wielded by the star of the film *Dirty Harry*. 'It's what Clint Eastwood rolls with,' he recalled. Another gunman was seen taking aim from the back of one of the cars. After shouts of 'guns', 'drive-by' and 'machines' – a street reference to guns – the 'money-up' group started to scatter. Some ran for shelter to a nearby shop, where the owner quickly brought the shutters down.

It all happened quickly with the hyped-up attackers determined to get someone. Four loud gunshots were heard. One bullet smashed into the windscreen of a car. Another whizzed by the head of a ten-year-old on a bike. Young Jadie Brissett, eighteen years old, was hit twice. Rather than being singled out, it could have been because he fell over when trying to get away, making an easy target. A handgun bullet smashed into his upper left thigh, and a shotgun blasted a two inch hole in his chest, penetrating his heart and lungs. Somehow, despite his wounds, he managed not only to get to his feet but also to clamber over a wall, run across a small patch of grass, over a low fence, then, with life ebbing away, stagger on, eventually ending up at the side of the tower block. He finally collapsed there, bleeding heavily, his whole body shaking. He died shortly afterwards, next to some dustbins.

Jadie was popular, coming from one of the area's big well-known families. When police arrived at the murder scene, there was almost a riot. Officers were even being blamed for contributing to his death because an ambulance had been a long time in coming, the suggestion being that this was because the victim was black. Word soon got around about who was responsible. The prime suspects belonged to two rival gangs – the nearby Holly Street Boys, and those from a little further north in Hackney, the stamping ground of the Clapton Square Boys who, like the LFB, were heavily into drug-dealing, particularly crack cocaine. Three names headed the list. All were drug-dealing criminals. By the next day, they were being hunted down by the LFB, intent on vengeance.

Heading their list was Pepe Brown, a hulking, lumbering youth, who although just out of his teens, already had a fearsome reputation for violence. Like so many others, Brown had a disturbed family background. As a child, he presented serious behavioural problems at four different schools, eventually being shunted off to a special needs boarding school, returning home to Holly Street at holiday times.

From 2000 onwards, he was committing serious violent crime. At the age of sixteen, he stabbed a man three times during a fight at a New Year's party and was sent to a young offenders prison for twelve months. Then came a conviction for threatening, abusive behaviour, assault and possession of a knife. Later, he was one of a group of twenty youths arrested in connection with the murder of an Asian, stabbed to death at the Notting Hill carnival. Brown had been 'steaming' – one of a pack charging through the crowds, stealing as they went, fighting or intimidating anyone brave enough to put up resistance. Found guilty of violent disorder, he was sentenced to twenty-one months, reduced on appeal to a year, after he had given evidence for the prosecution at the trial of the boys charged with the murder of ten-year-old Damilola Taylor. He said he had heard some of the defendants discussing the boy's stabbing while on remand in prison.

Several weeks before Jadie Brissett's murder, Brown was caught up in a dispute which may have contributed to the London Fields shooting. It was between his Holly Street gang and the LFB and involved the earlier shooting of a Fields man. During an argument outside a court, Brown was stabbed in the back. Seeking shelter, he ran across the road to a police station. Fearing a further attack from the LFB, Brown asked for police and local authority help in moving out of the area. He got it and moved to south London where he started dealing in cars. He bought 'write-offs' in scrap yards, patching them up with the help of a friend in a garage who passed them off as roadworthy by giving them MOT certificates. Brown paid no tax, and although owning a VW Golf, had no insurance and had never passed a driving test. He carried and used false identification papers, and also dealt drugs.

He disappeared after Jadie Brissett's murder, frustrating the Field's Boys who wanted revenge. Two days after the killing, his half-sister was confronted in the street while wheeling her baby along. A man held a gun to her head demanding to know where her brother was. Protesting that she had no idea, she was told: 'Your brother is an idiot and has to pay for what he did.' Fearing worse was to come, she and her mother moved home.

The LFB were also after one of Brown's close friends, another one of the Holly Street Boys believed to have been in the murder group. Bullets were fired at his house. Another of Brown's gang suspected of involvement was himself shot dead a few months later. A bullet hit Lamont Silcott in the head as he sat in his Mini Cooper. Joseph Ashman, the 21-year-old found guilty of his murder, and sentenced to twenty-five years, had killed before. He had been been released from prison the previous year after serving under half of a six-year sentence for killing a shopkeeper in a bungled robbery.

Another youth being sought was only seventeen years old, and he had a different motive for hitting the LFB. Aaron Salmon had been dealing crack cocaine for over a year along with three others. They bought the drug from a Jamaican known as Yardie T, and each made about £1,000 a week in tax-free profit. Salmon dealt under the name 'King', using three mobile phones, on which he referred to crack as 'food'. His relative wealth and girlfriends led to trouble from rivals. He was arrested on two occasions for carrying a knife as protection, and later, in 2002, at a family barbecue, some armed Jamaicans came looking for him. Shots were fired, but he escaped, running down an alley.

Then, a few weeks before Jadie Brissett's murder, he came under attack again. By that stage, Salmon was flaunting his wealth, wearing a big expensive platinum chain and cross round his neck. While he was out driving one evening in Hackney with a girl by his side, an armed gang of about ten black youths ambushed him, surrounding his car. The driver's window was smashed, and a youth reached in, tearing the chain from Salmon's neck. He saw another youth with a gun at the passenger side. When he got out, Salmon was stabbed in the chest, and his car and mobile phones were stolen.

He was taken to hospital, the police were called, and he told them that he recognised Jadie Brissett and two other Fields Boys as his attackers, and that he thought the incident was over a girl, but he did not want police to pursue the matter because he was making his own attempts to have the car and chain returned. He had phoned one of his stolen mobiles, and spoken to one of his attackers, who told him that he had been hit because he was 'boastie' – too flash. After threats of violence from Salmon, the chain was given back to him at a café and his car was left outside a police station with the keys in the ignition. Meanwhile he had a growing reputation for violence among the Clapton Square Boys. During an argument with one, he pulled out a gun, and in the ensuing struggle, a youth was shot in the leg. He was also said to have stabbed someone in a crack house.

Just a couple of hours after Jadie Brissett's murder, Aaron

Salmon learned from a friend that the London Fields Boys were out to get him. One of the gunmen, although masked, resembled him in stature, being slim and smallish. That youth had carried his gun in his left hand, and Salmon was left handed. Fearing retribution, and to protect himself, Salmon bought a bulletproof vest. One week after the killing, revenge seekers struck. In what appeared to be a case of mistaken identity. They got the wrong man. A friend of Salmon's, driving the same type of car, was shot and injured.

The police were also receiving information on who was thought to be responsible. Although the crowd at the murder scene had initially been hostile, officers were given the names of at least three suspects, including Brown and Salmon. But it was the usual story. No one was prepared to name them in a statement, let alone appear against them in court. The detectives needed evidence and they were to receive it after eyewitnesses told them of three cars arriving in convoy at the Fields. In the lead was a black Renault Megane, followed by a green Ford Escort, while a white Orion brought up the rear. Someone had noted a registration number. A trawl through footage from Hackney's many CCTV cameras turned up video of just such a three-car convoy nearing London Fields just before the killing time of 8 p.m. on 9th June, 2003. It also caught a cyclist almost falling off his bike as he appeared to glance inside the Orion as it passed by. Had he seen those inside tooling up? The registration number of the Escort matched that of a car reported missing four days after the murder.

The registered owner, Dean Da Costa, gave police an important break. He told them that their main suspect, his friend, Pepe Brown, had taken it during the afternoon of the murder. A few days later, shortly before midnight, the Escort was torched and burned out on waste ground behind a block of flats. A black Golf car, the type being driven by Brown, was seen leaving the area. The police now had enough evidence to arrest him. When stopped in south London in his Golf, and told he was being arrested on suspicion of murder, he said: 'What murder, you fucking pussies?' Asked his occupation, he replied 'professional rugby player'. In his car were a drug dealer's calling cards. Taken to a police station, and aware of his rights and procedures, Brown asked if he could phone his brother to arrange for a change of clothing. But instead he phoned Da Costa, trying to stop him revealing that he had the Escort at the time of the murder. Overhearing the conversation, an officer stopped the call. When interviewed, Brown refused to answer questions. He was charged with murder. Police also arrested the second main suspect, Aaron Salmon. But he gave an alibi and because of insufficient evidence had to be released.

The third man fingered for the murder was Mark Lawrence, a drug-dealing associate of both Salmon and Pepe Brown. He got a phone call from one of his mates called Deadgoat who told him: 'People are saying you're involved [in the murder] and that Pepe and the Square Boys done it.' His friend gave him a number for one of Jadie Brissett's relatives. Lawrence phoned the man and was told: 'You're dead. You're fucking dead. All you lot are dead.'

Aged twenty-one, Lawrence used to live in the Clapton Square area but had moved north, out of London, to Borehamwood in Hertfordshire where he lived with his girlfriend and child, and from where he dealt drugs – 'serving up' crack, cocaine and cannabis. Lawrence, tough and arrogant, was another with a violent record, including convictions for robbery and assault. His first serious offence was at the age of eighteen, after his car collided with another one. He chased after the other driver, a seventy-year-old pensioner, and catching him, beat him up, savagely kicking him while he was on the ground. The man was so frightened that he refused to give evidence. Nevertheless, Lawrence was found guilty and given six months in prison.

He had a black Megane, just like the one on the CCTV seen leading the three-car convoy to London Fields. Two weeks after Jadie Brissett's murder, police spotted Lawrence in his car. They called up reinforcements and followed him to a housing estate, where a police car blocked the only exit. After a struggle, he was arrested and was found to be wearing body armour. 'That's the sort of life I lead,' he explained. In the boot of his car was a bottle of ammonia, and some cling-film used to wrap 'rocks' of crack.

Under the arm-rest in the car's back seat was a ski-mask, which Lawrence used to hide his face when out drug dealing. Opening up about his lifestyle to Detective Constable Alan Stimson and Detective Sergeant Ian Wade, Lawrence said he was aware that he had been picked out as a drug dealer on CCTV, but his face could not be seen, and that police wrongly thought his name was Danny. He had wanted to keep it that way by continuing to wear the mask. 'When I go into crack houses, and when I lick the shots [CCTV] – you know when there's cameras there and that, I put it on. When I sell drugs, if I go into a crack house, I'll put it on because of the smell, and sometimes I don't want to show my face – like some of them know my face and there's CCTV everywhere.'

Lawrence appeared to be equally open about events leading up to Jadie's murder, claiming it had happened because of Pepe Brown's girlfriend. Recounting events, Lawrence said Pepe Brown had invited him to the fight, telling him: '"It's beef – we're rolling, are you coming?" I said: "what's going on" and then he said the Fields Boys have been following my girl – tailing her. So I goes "alright then" – cool like.'

In a later version of what happened, Lawrence said Aaron Salmon showed him a rucksack containing guns and said: 'No need to worry if it comes on top, I'm strapped [carrying a gun].' Brown said he was also strapped. 'He was wearing a glove on his right hand,' said Lawrence. 'It means he's carrying a firearm – that's the hand you're carrying a gun in, so you don't get fingerprints on it.'

Beside Lawrence in the Megane was a twenty-year-old called Robbie Thomas, who had just been released from a young offenders' prison after doing a two-year stretch for drugs. 'We've been sort of looking after him,' Lawrence told police. 'Robbie's got a lot of size and plus we grew up together. We used to go to the fair when we was young and fight with the boys and that. In 1999 he got stabbed in the back, two years after I got stabbed. He's just come off his tag, but he's still on recall license.' Lawrence denied that Thomas had a gun and had fired it after getting out of the Megane, as one of the witnesses had claimed. 'Robbie didn't get out. Nobody didn't get out and fire no gun from my car. If Robbie had got out and fired my gun in my car, do you think I would still be driving that same car?'

Lawrence gave police the names of a number of people involved to varying degress in the hunting party. In particular, the third car in the convoy, the white Orion, had been driven by another eighteen-year-old Clapton Square boy, Danny Williams, who was known by his initials, DW. The following day, knowing the vehicle would be traced, and worried that it would provide clues to the police, Williams asked a friend to dispose of it. With revenge shootings taking place, he wanted to escape the area, and to raise money to get away, he joined others in a robbery at a car auction, where £5,000 was snatched from a dealer. Williams ran off, but became separated from his mates. He jumped into a passing van and, pretending to have a gun, forced the driver to take him to a mini-cab office. Without money for a cab fare, he left his mobile phone at the counter as security to cover the cost of the ride home. But the hi-jacked van driver had stayed in the area and seeing Williams in the cab, noted the registration number and called the police.

When arrested, Williams maintained that Pepe Brown, Aaron Salmon and Mark Lawrence forced him to join the convoy, along with three friends. They were told two boys who had interfered with Brown's girlfriend were going to be beaten up. Of Brown himself, Williams said: 'He's not someone to mess around with. He's like a God in Hackney. Everyone is scared of him... I didn't want to go 'cos London Fields has got a reputation of shooting people and I didn't want to go there at all.'

Describing the shooting scene, he said someone got out of the Escort wearing a mask and carrying a gun. 'He was crouching down with a silver gun,' said Williams. 'As I drove past, everyone was running.' He saw three youths run from the cars towards the flats – amongst them was Pepe Brown. Williams continued: 'I swear to God, I just drove off straightaway, sir.' Williams had a mild epileptic fit during his questioning, and his story evoked some sympathy with Trident detectives. But much of that disappeared when his mobile phone was examined. Its screen saver showed a picture of him pointing what looked very much like a gun, and there was a slogan – 'DW Gangsta'. Detectives labelled him 'the wannabe gangster'.

Another in the pack who had been in Williams' car did manage to get away from London. Nineteen-year-old Jermaine Allen, aka Faghead, was attending a college, where he heard that a Fields Boy was looking for him and a close relative. He recalled:

> 'For my own safety, I wasn't saying nothing to no one on the streets. This boy would park his car, and run out with his bulletproof vest and a gun, shouting "where's Jermaine? Tell them they're dead, yeah. Tell them they're dead."
>
> 'At college the next day someone says that someone's driving around outside looking for me in a tinted car. When I got home, an hour later, I heard there's three cars in the Square looking for me. They're all tinted – just parked out with boys – looking to kill me. Then the next day, I thought this was all getting on top. My mum's gonna get hurt in some way. I was thinking, oh man, what am I gonna do?'

Then he received a threatening call on his mobile phone.

> 'He phoned and said "come to the square now – I want to lick off your head" – meaning he wants to shoot me. "You was there when Jadie was murdered. We can't catch Aaron [Salmon] and Pepe [Brown], so we're gonna lick off your head."'

Allen changed his mobile phone and fled to Nottingham, staying with the babymother of a relative.

Arrested there four months after the murder, Allen told police he was frightened of the three main suspects. Of Brown, he said: 'Everyone knows about Pepe – he's just the baddest gunman.' Lawrence was handy with a knife, and Allen said he was terrified of Salmon, still having a bullet in his leg after being shot by him the year before. Allen explained he had been sitting on the boot of his mum's car, a BMW, with his cousin.

'We were just talking, jamming like, and Aaron comes out of nowhere with Mark Lawrence. First he was talking to me saying "you're alright – you're safe". I'm just trying to walk off 'cos I don't like being around him, and he said "give me your phone". Then he took my phone. I snatched it back and then he pulled out a gun. I grabbed his hand and then the gun went off and through my leg. Then he ran off and I was screaming in pain. It burns, and I went to hospital. The police came and asked if I wanted to continue, but I said no 'cos if they [the police] continue it, then he's gonna come back and shoot me or my family.'

Allen knew of the LFB's reputation. 'They don't fight you,' he said. 'I've had so much trouble with them Fields Boys. They kill you.' But he had joined the expedition to the Fields because his fear of Salmon was greater. 'If I had got out of the car, Aaron would most probably have said "where you going? – get back in the car! Do you want me to shoot you again?"'

At London Fields he saw four people get out of the two other cars, some wearing balaclavas and carrying guns. He recalled:

'I see Pepe with a gun – a long one – eight or nine mm. Another one came out of Pepe's car – he was kneeling. I goes "blood". I said to Daniel [Williams], "Them boys got guns. We're going. Hurry up! Breeze, 'cos I'm not getting shot again." Breeze means go. I goes to Daniel – "please just get us out of here – 'cos a shot could just ricochet." Get the hell out of here like – kind of move man… That day was so dangerous. Any of us could have ended up dead like. We just got out of there.'

With Mark Lawrence, Danny Williams and now Jermaine Allen confessing to having driven to the murder scene, Trident detectives made more arrests, including Robbie Thomas who admitted being there in the black Megane. Another of those arrested was found with a loaded gun which he said was to protect himself from LFB retaliation. Although that young man was convicted for possessing the weapon, there was insufficient evidence to charge him with involvement in the murder.

However, the additional evidence meant detectives could again move against the second main suspect, seventeen-year-old Aaron Salmon. He was re-arrested while in a car with a friend; they had body armour and wraps of crack. On this second occasion, he too refused to answer questions.

Salmon, Brown, Lawrence, Thomas, Williams and Allen were all charged with the murder of Jadie Brissett, the view being that they all knew guns were being carried. Although the firearms used had not been recovered and there was no forensic evidence to tie any of them to the killing, four had confessed to being there, and the remaining two, the main suspects, Brown and Salmon, as well as being named by the others, were also linked by other evidence.

Once again, powerful corroborating evidence came from the suspects' mobile phones. Analysis of Brown and Salmon's mobiles showed calls to and from the others in the run-up to the murder and its aftermath, and the cell sites used showed them to have been in the London Fields area. By offering anonymity, Trident detectives also managed to overcome the reluctance or refusal of some witnesses to give evidence in court. So it was that a series of people who had seen the three cars arrive at London Fields entered the witness box at the Old Bailey under pseudonyms, with their voices distorted, and a heavy curtain shielding them from the defendants and from the public gallery upstairs, where two groups of friends and relatives sat separately – those supporting the accused, and those connected to the murdered youth.

The trial of the six young men, all pleading not guilty, was beset with problems and surprises. The first arose straightaway. The judge, the Recorder of London, Peter Beaumont, ruled that some of the police questioning of Robbie Thomas was improper, and it was decided that he would stand trial separately after the others. To avoid possible conflict in the dock, the remaining five defendants were separated by security guards who sat between each of them. Three of the accused, Lawrence, Williams and Allen, had broken the 'no grassing' rule by naming others and it was clear the trial would develop into a cut-throat affair.

Outlining the prosecution case, Orlando Pownall said that it was impossible to determine who fired the fatal shots because those getting out of the three cars were masked with balaclavas, hoods and baseball caps. But it did not matter. For a murder charge to stick, the jury had to decide whether those in the cars knew that a gun was being carried and that it was intended for use at London Fields. If it was thought a defendant did not know anyone was armed but expected that severe violence could result, then they could still be found guilty on a second charge against them of conspiracy to cause grievous bodily harm.

Keeping the identities of witnesses secret led to another surprise. Statements from all witnesses are given to the defence teams before the start of trials so that defendants can suggest particular lines of cross-examination for their lawyers to pursue. When the real names of witnesses are not known, defendants often study the statements for clues as to the true identities. One of the most important eyewitnesses in this case was known simply as G, and had been one of the 'money-up' group. Believing he had worked out G's identity, one of the defendants briefed his lawyer accordingly, suggesting G would be vulnerable to a particular series of questions. The barrister prepared his cross-examination carefully, but when he moved forward to tear into the witness, and seeing him for the first time, he visibly jolted. The man in the witness box was clearly not who he was expecting. The lawyer had been led to believe G was black. But the man facing him, waiting to be cross-examined, was white.

Throughout much of the prosecution evidence, the main suspect, Pepe Brown, behaved strangely in the dock. He was the closest of the defendants to the public gallery above, where members of the Brissett family were sitting, including Jadie's mother Lana, who never missed a day of the proceedings. A big, powerfully built young man, Pepe Brown, with a background of violence, sat there for hours on end, sucking his thumb. Most people in court, including myself, saw this as a sign of emotional immaturity, rather than as an attempt to gain sympathy with the jury. But some of those in the public gallery saw it as neither. They complained that Brown with his thumb in his mouth and his stretched index finger resting on his nose, was, in fact, making the sign of a gun. He, in turn, said he felt threatened by those above, and that some of them had been making gun signs at him. The judge warned everyone to behave.

Then, eight weeks after the start of the trial, it had to be abandoned after one of the defendants, Salmon, became so ill that he required an operation. The retrial started in March 2005 with once again five defence QCs, each accompanied by a junior barrister. Again, many of the prosecution witnesses gave evidence anonymously. One of them, the girlfriend of one of the defendants, was reluctant to do so again as she felt she had been intimidated since her last appearance. Photographs of her had been stolen and suspicion had fallen on her boyfriend's associates. One important witness was missing altogether. Witness G, Jadie Brissett's friend and one of the money-up group, refused to attend. The judge ordered his arrest but, before he was found, prosecution and defence lawyers agreed that his evidence in the earlier trial could be read to the jury.

Pepe Brown was the first of the defendants into the witness box, declaring that at the time of the murder, he was riding around with his friend Lips, smoking weed and looking for girls. But neither Lips nor anyone else who could have backed his story appeared in court. Brown was just about to leave the witness box when one of the defence lawyers accused him of having threatened his client, Mark Lawrence, the evening before when the defendants had arrived back at Belmarsh Prison. Brown had apparently threatened Lawrence, saying: 'If you give evidence, just remember I know where your brother works – in a clothing shop in Dalston – and XXX will deal with it.' In the witness box, Brown responded furiously to the accusation, shouting that it was all lies, from a proven liar.

Lawrence was the next to give evidence. Cross-examined by Brown's QC, he denied ganging up with the other Clapton Square Boys and forming a plan that if questioned by police everything would be blamed on Brown and the Holly Street Boys. Lawrence and the next two defendants giving evidence, Danny Williams and Jermaine Allen, stuck largely to their original accounts that they had little idea of what was going to happen, and had left as soon as they saw guns produced.

Last into the witness box was Aaron Salmon, speaking in a confident manner, unlike the other defendants who had tended to mumble and give short answers. Questioned by his QC Michael Borrelli, he described how gangs in the north-east of London were mainly named after the estates where they were based. There were the Pembury Boys, Jack Dunning Boys, Stamford Hill Boys, and those from Tottenham. The Holly Street Boys were also known as the Rowdy Bunch. He told matter-of-factly about selling cocaine and crack from the age of sixteen, but denied any involvement in the murder.

The jury was out for four days considering its verdicts. Brown, Lawrence and Salmon were all found guilty of murder, and Williams and Allen were acquitted. As the guilty verdicts were given, clapping broke out in the public gallery. Lawrence and Salmon stayed silent, but Brown bellowed that he was innocent. 'I weren't there,' he shouted at the jury. 'I am an innocent man going down for murder – for life!' The judge ordered his removal and police to clear the public gallery. But the drama was not yet over.

Following the guilty verdicts, Mark Lawrence's lawyers said he was prepared to give evidence against Robbie Thomas, his friend and fellow drug dealer, who had travelled with him to London Fields, and was still to stand trial. It was a very big decision for Lawrence to make. When arrested he had been the first to drop others into the plot, but turning into a full grass by giving Queen's evidence was the ultimate step. Although by cooperating he could expect up to a third off his prison sentence, that had to be weighed against possibly having to serve all his time in a segregated prison unit to avoid reprisal attacks, not only from friends of the murdered youth but also from the Clapton Square and Holly Street Boys. And then there were potential problems for his mother, his girlfriend and her child.

Lawrence was the main witness for the prosecution at Thomas's trial which lasted for only five days and ended with a guilty verdict. Brown, Salmon and Thomas were sentenced together, each receiving life sentences with a recommendation that they serve a minimum of fifteen years before being considered for parole. Apparently expecting longer sentences, Salmon and Thomas were led away smiling, with the former remarking 'that's nice'.

To avoid any of the three turning on Mark Lawrence, he was sentenced later, receiving a life sentence with a recommended minimum behind bars of ten years. Neither he nor any of those convicted have expressed any remorse for taking the life of young Jadie Brissett.

The motives for many shootings are often no clearer at the end of exhaustive police inquiries and lengthy trials than they were in the immediate aftermath of the gunfire. This is a murky world, one full of shades of grey. Families and friends of the victim are unlikely to volunteer information that the shooting was because of a drugs turf war, for that would mean admitting knowing the dead man was involved in dealing, probably of class-A drugs. Similarly, the gunman, unless faced with strong evidence, will not admit to having had any past problems with the victim.

Even when the evidence is overwhelming, guilty pleas to murder are very rare. The defendants weigh up the situation, and see little advantage in admitting their guilt. If convicted, they receive life sentences with judges usually recommending that they serve at least twenty years. Pleading guilty would result in a reduction of about a third off the normal life tariff. So the vast majority prefer to take their chances at trial, pleading not guilty, hoping that they will be acquitted through the skills of their lawyers, or by going into the witness box and brazening it out, or by a combination of both. Even if found guilty, it could be on a lesser manslaughter charge with a lighter sentence.

The vast majority of criminals are beneath contempt, according to one of Operation Trident's most senior detectives, DCI Neil Basu. He deals with about ten gun deaths at any one time, and with eighteen months of Trident work behind him when we met, he told me: 'Trident criminals are amoral, with no concept of life whatsoever. Even the Krays and Richardsons had problems being able to pull the trigger and kill someone. Some of those we're dealing with just don't think about it. They have a complete disregard for public safety, for example using a machine gun in a high street, or youngsters who think it's flash to have a gun and a car, who'll shoot someone for pushing into a queue.'

In charge of the Byfield murders, he is also well aware of the difficulties surrounding witnesses, particularly over their protection or the payment to them of rewards. Such measures can be viewed as inducements for them giving evidence and result in their branding as unreliable. Basu said:

> 'It's difficult because you have to hear what they say first and judge the value of it. Inducement is clearly something that can't be allowed to happen, because if the witness has got any kind of background which might make them difficult, then the addition of an inducement on top of that will make the case a non-starter. You can't offer people the world, and of course protection isn't within Trident's gift, anyway. It's within the gift of the Metropolitan Police.
>
> 'A significant witness for me is someone who has actually seen the crime itself or heard a confession, or given a vital piece of evidence. But they wouldn't get protection unless they sign a witness statement and are prepared to stand up and give evidence in court. It's a purely voluntary thing. You get witnesses who don't want protection and are prepared to give evidence in

court. The most important thing is that when you protect a witness there's a contract between you and that witness. The witness should obey the rules and do what they're advised to do. But if they continue with their lifestyle, living in the same area, associating with the same people, then they're at risk and protection can be withdrawn. The Met's record of protection for witnesses who cooperate is outstanding. But it's very difficult for a person who's lived twenty years in the same area, having the same job, speaking to the same people, having an extensive family network, to say goodbye to all that. I can understand that and have every sympathy. It's an incredible thing to have to do and some are unwilling to do it all. They want to go to family events, social events, funerals, parties, and see and have regular contact with their family, keep the same cars, live in the same areas. It's very very difficult. Our clients are the hardest to deal with. There's no doubt about it.'

Another fairly high-profile case highlighting serious problems with witnesses eventually reached the Old Bailey in 2004. No one could have appreciated the far-reaching effect Damian Cope's murder would have when he was shot dead outside a nightclub in 2002. Cope's death led to his mother, Lucy, forming an influential group called Mothers Against Guns, with branches set up in other parts of the country, including Manchester and Birmingham. The group worked with Operation Trident and campaigned for tougher gun crime laws which were introduced early in 2004. Later that same year, after a long and frustrating police investigation, the man alleged to be the killer was brought to justice at the Old Bailey. But the case against him was to end with howls of anguish from Mrs Cope.

Damian Cope, aged twenty-two, was of mixed race, with seven brothers and sisters. His mother is white and her husband, Winston, was a Jamaican who died in the 1980s. Police believe that Damian was a member of a street gang based near his home in

Peckham, south London, but this is disputed by Mrs Cope who denies that he was mixed up with either crack cocaine dealing or firearms. Where she and the police agree is on the sequence of events which led up to his death. Damian had been playing football near his home at Burgess Park on the morning of Sunday, 29th July, and scored what he told his mother was a 'wonder goal', winning the game for his team. Later, however, Damian was involved in a confrontation at the park with an African-Caribbean man from a rival group called the New Cross crew, who apparently objected to Damian's celebrations. Threats were exchanged.

Later that night, Damian and some of his friends went to an expensive nightclub in Holborn, central London. CCTV shows him arriving there with a big smile on his face at 12.35 a.m. A few minutes later he is pictured walking out to make a phone call. While outside, out of range of the cameras, a bullet from a converted handgun hit him in the stomach. He staggered the fifty yards back to the nightclub and was picked up again by the CCTV stumbling through the doors. The video shows one of his friends spotting him clutching his chest. The friend drops his glass, runs over to Damian and catches him as he collapses. He died later in hospital.

Later, that friend told a grieving Mrs Cope that he had asked Damian: 'Who blazed you, blood?' [Who shot you, brother?] He said that Damian then named the killer as the man who had confronted him after the soccer game – Andrew Wonoghu. Damian's friend confirmed to police that Damian had named his killer, but he refused to repeat the name to detectives, apparently either out of fear or because he did not like talking to police on principle, or a combination of both. Without a statement from the friend, the Trident detectives were stuck. Although they had learned separately that Wonoghu had planned to go to the nightclub, no one had seen him there, and there was no video or mobile phone evidence placing him there. Tests showed that the gun used was believed to have been a blank-firing pistol converted to fire real bullets. The bullet which had killed Cope, extracted from his back, provided no clues. It was home-made, probably from melted down airgun pellets, and had been bent out of shape.

Seven months after the murder, another of Damian's friends came forward and said that he too had spoken to Damian as he lay dying in the nightclub foyer, and that Damian had named Wonoghu to him as well. The new witness gave Trident detectives justification to arrest Wonoghu, aka Sparks, twenty-four. But the suspect had fled to America, breaching a bail order he was under for an alleged burglary. Inquiries there drew a blank. Then it was recalled that Wonoghu had been a keen boxer, fighting professionally under the name of Weston. One of Trident's civilian workers, interested in the sport, discovered him boxing in Florida, under the name Andrew 'The Assassin' Weston. Trident contacted the US authorities, hoping that he would be deported as an undesirable. But they said they could only act if an extradition order was served. That was done, and Wonoghu was arrested in July 2003 just as he was about to step into the ring for a boxing match at Fort Lauderdale. He was extradited to the UK two months later, charged with the murder, and held in custody.

However, before the judge came into court for the start of the trial, it was clear that all was not well. Lucy Cope was there with family members and supporters. She was extremely distressed, crying uncontrollably and howling 'God help us'. Later, more calmly, she remained standing as the defendant was led into the dock, staring at him throughout the short proceedings, hearing Richard Horwell, prosecuting, explain to the judge that there had been developments over the preceding month.

Horwell said police had been back to Damian's first friend, trying to persuade him to give evidence, but he was still refusing. Without his evidence, said the lawyer, the prosecution case had not been very strong, depending as it did on only one witness, Damian's second friend who, in a police statement, had named Wonoghu as the killer. Now that friend, referred to as Witness A, was refusing to come to court to give evidence, and there was also doubt about what he had told police. Horwell said the CCTV footage showed Witness A going to Damian more than seven minutes after he had collapsed. Four doctors who had examined

Damian's body had each said independently of one another that his wound was so severe that, after such a length of time, it was extremely unlikely he would have been capable of having any kind of conversation. Further doubt on Witness A's evidence came from one of the club's bouncers, who had returned to the UK from abroad to give evidence at the trial. He had been with Damian shortly after he collapsed, staying with him until paramedics arrived with an ambulance. He said Damian had not uttered a single word during that time. Consequently, said Horwell, there was no realistic prospect of a conviction, and he was offering no evidence against the defendant.

The judge formally declared Wonoghu not guilty and said he would be freed on bail awaiting trial on the outstanding burglary charge. As he turned to leave the dock, he had a slight grin on his face. Lucy Cope shouted at him: 'Don't smile!' Prior to his release, Wonoghu was seen in the cells by Trident detectives, who warned him, as they were obliged to under the law, that a threat had been made against his life. They offered him protection, but he declined. 'We had to do it,' one detective told me. 'Think what would have happened if we had not told him of the threat and made the offer of protection, and he was then killed. Luckily for us, he said he did not want our help.'

Later, outside the court, Detective Inspector Tim Neligan, in charge of the Trident investigation, said the outcome was very disappointing, unfortunate, and represented something of a setback for Trident in that witnesses had failed to cooperate. 'We did our best given the situation,' he said. 'We had enough to bring the suspect to court. I don't think we could have done more.' Condemning the 'cowardice' of the witnesses who would not give evidence, Lucy Cope said: 'I am devastated. Nothing can heal my broken heart.' Like several others, she became an anti-gun-crime campaigner after being touched by personal tragedy. Others started to speak out against guns after they themselves had paid the penalty for being gunmen. Having been up against the law, these outlaws started cooperating with it.

'What you now see on the streets is chaos, and nobody's safe. It's hell, really. The shootings were once a year. Now it seems like they're everyday.'

A huge collective gasp went up from the two hundred or so young teenagers at the anti-gun-crime conference. The vast majority were black and they were not too impressed by the previous speakers, three tall hefty police superintendents, all white. These senior officers had found it hard going, trying to get through to this different generation, outlining the reasons why they should not turn to violence to solve their problems. One of the teenagers' teachers blamed some singers for encouraging a gun culture. She told the three officers that the young people in the audience at the conference in the Greater London council chamber were more influenced by music than by what police told them: 'You're talking to these people and they're looking at you, and without being disrespectful, they're not relating to you. They're relating to the music.'

One of the officers, Superintendent Dave Grant, second in command at Waltham Forest, replied with passion:

'Stereotyping works from all sides. People have a view of the police and people believe that police have a view of their community – whether you're young and black or white and middle-class. It doesn't matter who you are. Part of the problem is that those views never meet... We have a thing called "defending the 'hood". We took some kids off the estates [interrupted by derisive laughter] – yes, you can laugh. We took them off the estates for a start because they're the people who are going to be the most vulnerable. We want to have events like this which are led by young people which influence us, and not the other way round. I make no bones about it. I cannot understand some of the music. I cannot understand this culture of carrying guns. I don't think it's flash. I don't think it's smart. What you see at the end of the day is a lot of young people, young adults, who end up in the criminal justice system, who end up going to jail. What have they got to show for it? A little bit of flash, a little bit of money and at the end of the day, they haven't got anything, no hope. We're trying to break down the barriers and give you a chance to have your say, and say it's not worth doing drugs. And, no, it's not worth carrying a gun.'

However, it was the next speaker who had a greater impact on the young people. They could relate to him. He was black and he could talk their talk. Barrington Foster, wearing a T-shirt with a hemp leaf emblem, said he had been born in the UK, but had gone to New York at the age of eight, living in harsh inner city areas of Brooklyn, Queens and the Bronx. As a teenager he joined a gang who were into guns and robbery. He said:

'I thought I was cool doing that, I thought this was the way. Why should I rush up out of my bed and go to work, when I can go out and rob and make silly money. When you've got silly money in your pocket, it's very hard for someone to come round and say forget that, let's do something positive. I didn't listen to that. I thought, yeah, I'm cool. I can go out make some money, and wear nice clothes, have fast cars, plenty of girls.'

He returned to London when he was eighteen.

'I linked up with a crew that was carrying guns, and it weren't cool. We were going out, and I'll tell you straight, keep it real, we were robbing post offices, people out in the street, and involved in things at parties, dances. We were riding with guns, and a lot of people feared us. We thought they were respecting us, but they feared us. Respect and fear are two different things. And I went on a mad little six-month spree with some of my friends. Now that six-month spree ended up with me being arrested in 1982. I was charged with a very serious offence with a few others. I was sentenced in October 1982. I got sent down and I got released in 2000.'

Foster paused, and a succession of gasps and 'Ooohs' rose from the audience as they realised that this man in front of them had spent eighteen years behind bars for murder. He went on:

'So maybe you can relate to these police officers and to what this is all about. Eighteen years, seven months of my life in prison. No play stations, no Nintendo – hardcore jail where you've got someone telling you what to do, where to go, when to take a shower, when to go to bed, when to wake up, no chicken and chips and kebabs for me. It was real. This is what it's all about. I met many people in that stretch. Some have died because they couldn't hack that long sentence, some have ended up on crack, some have ended up on coke, some have got released and are walking the streets doing nothing. It took a lot out of me as a person. It also developed me. If I hadn't been to prison with the life I was leading then, I would have been shot or could have been on crack, or coke, because everything I was doing at that time was negative. If you hang with a crew and when you do negative things, it's going to rub off on you. You've got to be responsible for your actions…

'I'm here today to tell y'all that if you think carrying a knife or a gun or even hanging with people who've got a gun or knife, is cool, then you're making a sad mistake because if you're living that kind of life on the street, there's no law, every man makes their own law. If you're in a gang, your mother's in that gang,

your father's in that gang, your brother's in that gang.
Everyone's in that gang. Because if someone can't catch
you, they think they're gonna catch his brethren, going
to lick his mum. That's the reality of the situation. I've
lived in it. I've been in it. I've seen it in prison. I've seen
it now.'

He explained that since serving his murder sentence, he had been
working with older teenagers as a social worker.

'I've had people coming up to me, saying what are you
doing all this youth work for. Come let's get into this
and let's get into that and make some silly money. I look
at those people and think how many of them have been
inside jail. Guns and knives are not the way. If you know
someone with a gun or knife, distance yourself from
that brethren [applause]. Because if you don't distance
yourself from that brethren, you're going down, one
way or the other. If you're carrying a gun, I'll tell you
straight – you're either going to get shot by somebody
you don't know, or you're going to end up in prison
– hardcore jail.'

Later, at his home in Brixton, he told me he had decided to become
involved in youth work while in prison, having met young people
hovering on the edge of criminality who were allowed into prison
for a few hours to see the conditions they would have to endure
if they became involved in serious crime and were caught. Now,
when working with a group of young teenagers, he tells them that
they have choices. He said:

'I don't tell them "don't do this or that" because then
they're going to want to do it. That's how I was when
I was younger. I say that if you do this, this is the
consequence. If you want to go out tonight and rob
someone of a mobile, you know that when the police

catch you, you can go to youth offending. It's like giving them the information. They empower themselves, and then they make their own decisions.'

Barrington Foster is one of several black ex-offenders now working with local authorities, the police or anti-gun-crime groups. Steve Korsa-Acquah is another. He is part of a remarkable double-act, going into schools with the police officer he shot. Brought up in Tottenham, north London, Korsa-Acquah was expelled from school and, unable to find a job, joined a gang which robbed banks and ambushed security vans. In 1983, while making a getaway after stealing £35,000 from a bank in Bristol, his car was approached by a uniformed officer, Billy Burns, who tried to arrest him. Korsa-Acquah shot him in the face. The bullet from the .38 revolver shattered the officer's mouth, smashing five teeth, and passed through his tongue before ending in his throat. Burns survived but was invalided out of the police. Korsa-Acquah served nineteen years in prison for attempted murder and armed robbery. Towards the end of his sentence he was visited by Burns, a committed Christian, who forgave him for the shooting. The two became friends, and Burns now sometimes joins Korsa-Acquah, a totally reformed character, touring schools with community groups, trying to ensure young people don't make his mistakes and opt for crime. When he speaks of the wrong choices he made and his experiences in prison, he, too, connects with the youngsters.

Those young people aged nineteen and upwards are viewed as something of a lost cause by Operation Trident's head, Detective Chief Superintendent John Coles. 'The challenge is to get through to kids of the next generation. We have lost the current nineteen to twenty-four-year olds. We struggle to get the message across to them. We want to get the young generation, the five- to ten-year-olds. We have to stop the next generation going down the path of the current generation.' In addition to supporting work with teenagers, Trident, the Metropolitan Police Authority and the Home Office are now helping initiatives in primary schools aimed at encouraging self-respect, respect for others and responsibility.

This is done through programmes or short videos dealing with gang culture and questioning the use of guns and knives, topics leading on to classroom discussion.

The question of how influential music is in creating a gun culture has raged for years. Gangster rap, the kind glorifying guns, has faced criticism since the late 1990s, but a series of controversial attacks on it, and on one group in particular, caused headlines in 2003. First came the Metropolitan Police Assistant Commissioner, Tarique Ghaffur, the officer in ultimate charge of Operation Trident. He singled out the south London group, So Solid Crew, one of those providing a 'backdrop of music' for alienating young men and encouraging them to use weapons as fashion statements. At that stage three of the group's thirty members had been convicted of gun offences or were awaiting trial. Next was the Culture Minister, Kim Howells, speaking on radio in the aftermath of the killing of two teenage girls, Charlene Ellis and Letisha Shakespeare, at a New Year's party in Birmingham. 'For years I have been very worried about these hateful lyrics that these boasting macho idiot rappers come out with. It is a big cultural problem. Lyrics don't kill people but they don't half enhance the fare we get from videos and films. It has created a culture where killing is almost a fashion accessory.' He said rappers who carry guns in their videos were particularly sick, and described So Solid Crew as idiots who glorify guns and violence.

The attacks resumed a few weeks later after a man was shot dead following gunfire at a nightclub event associated with So Solid Crew. The police had been warned in advance that there would be trouble at the Turnmills club in Clerkenwell, central London, where Lisa Maffia, one of the group's singers, was to be promoting her debut single. The anonymous tip-off to Crimestoppers was passed to local police who discussed cancelling the party. When the organisers refused, police parked a marked van outside the venue, hoping that would be enough to deter any gunmen. However, in the early hours, with the party in full swing, several men burst into the nightclub firing shots, injuring one person and sending people scattering for cover. Outside, the gunfire continued. Gunmen in a BMW chased after two men in an Audi TT sports car, leaning out of the windows, firing at least twenty shots at them. Jason Fearon, twenty-six, the passenger in the Audi was hit in the head and died at the scene.

The then Home Secretary, David Blunkett, condemned violent gangster rap as appalling. However, various commentators and those involved in the record industry said it was too simplistic to blame music alone for the rise in gun crime. Even the Home Office played down such an approach. 'We accept that there is a lot more to the problem, not least poverty and lack of opportunity,' it said in a statement for a black music conference in the summer of 2003. 'But music is influential,' it continued. 'The glamorisation of violence and gun culture in a medium listened to mostly by young people could affect perception of how acceptable it is to carry guns among some of those who may be tempted to do so.' The Home Office praised singers who were prepared to take a stand against gun crime, showing that music can reach out to young people in a positive way. Award-winning singer Ms Dynamite was amongst those trying to raise awareness of gun crime in the black community, as was soul singer Mica Paris, whose brother Jason Philips was shot dead outside a house in south London in an argument over his girlfriend.

The calls for positive role models in the music industry were joined by Cindy Butts, the deputy chair of the Trident Independent Advisory Group. She agreed that black music was often used as a scapegoat, an easy excuse for social problems, but she went on:

'I also think that black musicians need to take more responsibility for the influence they have over young people… I think that some prominent members of the black community are terrible role models. Some musicians go out of their way to flaunt the status symbols they have gained through their music – money, cars, clothes, women, guns. Some bands do promote gun violence as part of this lifestyle, both in their lyrics and by their actions. Young people need to be offered alternative role models, musicians who have achieved success without guns.'

Following the Birmingham New Year's party killings, three local musicians recorded a song written by a young man going under the name Witness, who is in no doubt about music's influence: 'Music is a very powerful medium and so easily influences the minds of people. What you listen to and what you see is what you become.' His anti-gun-crime song 'Ghetto Cry' has this chorus: 'Momma's crying in de ghetto... Daddy's crying in de ghetto... Brother and sisters crying, 'cos of the violent killings.'

Another hip-hop artist singing an anti-gun-crime message is Adrian McFarlane who uses the name Slim Dutty. Slim because of his build and Dutty because it stands for Don't Underestimate True Talented Youth. Living in tough Harlesden in north-west London, he was attracted after leaving school to what he saw as the glamour of the gang lifestyle, and wanted to fit in with his contemporaries. But he drew back, partly because of his mother's influence and also, he told me, because he realised he would either end up in jail or in a coffin.

'Most people I know are selling drugs. They didn't do too well at school and thought "we gonna hit the street and make money fast that way". People feel little or no opportunity. They're from single-parent families. It's difficult to see mum struggle on her own. People started selling drugs to make ends meet. It seems a simple transaction if you're drug dealing, but then you have to think about the other dealers. They may want you out of the way. The next thing is you have to own a gun to protect yourself. You may think you're not necessarily going to use it. But if you have a gun, probably, sooner or later, you are going to use it. Being part of that crowd, means you're probably going to die.

'My cousin got in with a drugs gang. One day he

went with them on a deal in a hotel. It went wrong. A guy tried to "short" them. Shots were fired. When the police arrived they found a man bleeding in the hotel reception. My cousin was the only other one there. He got eight years. People I'd known since I was seven or so were being killed, people I'd been to school with. One was shot dead at the end of the road. I felt personally that I should speak out against it. I didn't want to be part of that lifestyle. I wanted to be positive and I can express myself through music.'

McFarlane wrote the song 'Blood Puddles' to explain how some turn to guns as a way out of their social conditions.

> *...Representing London Harlesden*
> *where gunshots falling like leaves in autumn*
> *everyone's a target nowadays regardless*
> *we wanna eat right*
> *sick and tired of hardship*
> *you can stop me if I'm talking garbage*
> *there's little peace*
> *lot of carnage...*
> *guns charged and blasting*
> *start wars without asking*
> *loose lips grassing*
> *end up in a wooden casket...*

His reference to 'grassing' sums up the continuing problem for the police. McFarlane supports the Not Another Drop anti-gun-crime campaign which receives Home Office funding and help and resources from Brent Council and the Metropolitan Police. I met him on a 'No More Guns' peace march through the borough, where he sang and laid a wreath to the memory of all those shot in Harlesden. Senior Operation Trident officers were there, including its overall head, Commander Cressida Dick, and the detective leading the hunt for the killers of seven-year-old Toni-Ann Byfield and her father, Detective Chief Inspector Neil Basu. With Cheryl Sealey, a long-time anti-gun-crime campaigner from south London, he laid a wreath outside the house where they died.

But even someone like McFarlane, who presents himself as a positive role model, has little confidence in the police to protect those giving information. He cited the case of Sophie Lewis, the Harlesden woman who was shot after giving police information about a killer, an episode detailed earlier in this book. Although it had occurred in 1999, before Trident's formation and its great use of the Met's witness protection scheme, he said people's attitudes to giving evidence were unchanged: 'The police don't care what happens. Protection is secondary to them, and it doesn't take long for the criminals to find out who's been grassing.'

Wayne Rowe, a reformed character after serving a seven-year sentence for possessing a Mac-10, and now working with young people, is another with doubts about some anti-gun-crime initiatives. Speaking to me after the launch of an advertising campaign aimed at persuading people to call Crimestoppers to report gun crime, he said:

> 'I don't want to knock poster campaigns. They might touch some people but the hardcore guys out there walking about are not going to take a blind bit of notice. You've got to have evidence. I can phone up Crimestoppers saying it was such and such, then the police start looking at that person, but they can't secure a conviction. The only way you can secure a conviction is to get somebody to stand up in the court and say I know it was him because I saw it, and they can't be offered proper protection to do that. That's why some of these guys get arrested and they get let out again.'

Rowe is now working with various youth projects aimed at keeping young people out of trouble, including one introducing them to the music business. He said:

'What I know is about the street and survival on the street, and the youth know that as well. They know that I'm not like a guy who's just come with a degree in social work – someone who's never lived that life, but is analysing them. You've got to be able to relate to them and I think that's half the problem. When you start analysing them, trying to get inside their brain to find a solution – that's where the problem is. First of all I relate to them. They know where I'm coming from and I know where they're coming from, and I know where they're going. They can't turn round and say you don't know what the fuck you're talking about, 'cos they know that I do know what I'm talking about. I'm a grassroots man – someone on the pavement. I know how to talk to the youth. You need a grassroots person on the road, to make that contact with the youth. The message doesn't get through otherwise.'

Asked what advice he would give someone who told him that he had witnessed a shooting, he replied:

'I'm more than aware that there are guys who've gone to the police and said things, and they've ended up dead, or their families get terrorised. I'd ask that person to weigh it up. I wouldn't say to anyone – go to the police, because that might be the wrong thing to do. If they're in fear of their life, and they feel comfortable about going to the police, I wouldn't say don't do that, but I wouldn't persuade them. The street is a very delicate thing, on a knife edge, so you have to be very careful how you do things. I'm not being negative. I know of so many incidents where things like that have happened. These people have been left vulnerable. It's not just them. Some of them can deal with it because they've been a bit naughty, but they've got to think about their mum, their little sister. There are guys out there who are going to go out and kill your family.'

Aware of police witness protection schemes, and of court measures to protect those giving evidence against alleged killers, he said he knows another reality:

> 'What I do know is that people are arrested for things and the next thing is that they're out and on the road. If you've got a whole community that knows that A has killed B and the court case has happened and he's got found not guilty, and he comes out, that doesn't look good for the rest of the community. That's why everyone keeps their mouth shut.'

Rowe said of the young people he meets on projects:

> 'They've all lost friends to guns. Somewhere along the line, they know someone who's been shot or has gone to prison. The sad thing is that it's become normal. Solutions? All I can say is to tell the youth, "don't go down that road in the first place". Then you don't have to worry about witness protection and all the other things. The rest is a difficult subject. There are no easy answers. But I think if I can stop just one person from being killed then I've achieved something.'

Tony Miller is another reformed character trying to save people. A former drug dealer involved in gun crime, and jailed for robbery, he had a life-changing experience after taking too many drugs and finding himself alone on Clapham Common in south London. He told me:

> 'This strange feeling came over me as though I was having a heart attack. I couldn't breathe. Then this thick black smoke appeared from nowhere, and I thought I was walking to hell with my eyes wide open. I'd never experienced anything like it before or afterwards. This smoke was so thick, I couldn't see the lights on the

street. It was engulfing me, taking me over. I couldn't see my hand in front of my face. I knew I was dying. I was gasping for breath. I said if there is a God, I'll do anything but please don't let me die like a dog in the street. The pain started to ease up – disappear. I got in my car, drove to hospital. I was keeling over and told the doctors what drugs I'd been taking. Other doctors came and while they were doing this, a small voice said to me get out of this place and go home. I had loads of cocaine at home and illegal things. I would have got eight years for it all, so I went home, slept with my clothes on, and woke up in the morning thinking what the hell is going on. I thought I was having a nervous breakdown. That experience changed my life. I got out of the whole madness in a flick of time. It was the right time to get out. When I came off the street, that's when the guns really started up.'

Tony Miller, formerly known as Little T, became a born-again Christian, worked with the probation service, and eventually founded a church called *Brixton Shall be Saved*. Now Pastor Tony Miller, he is a member of the local police advisory group, and works with the community to reduce crime:

'To be a good law-abiding citizen is very hard. I knew I had to do it otherwise I'd be dead or in prison. I tell people that you can't survive on the streets. Your biggest problem is not the police. You know where they stand. It's your best friend. A lot's changed since the 1980s. There was a code then, a structure. Some things you couldn't do. You couldn't go rob a lady. You'd be looked down on. You couldn't inform on anyone. Now that's all been taken away. The underworld structure has crashed. Now there's no morals, no loyalty to anything. It's a dog-eat-dog world out there. Now these young kids have got Mac-10s and they'll kill you for next to nothing. The younger generation have lost all sense of respect, and they've got no respect for themselves. Everything has crashed. What you now see on the streets is chaos, and nobody's safe. It's hell, really. The shootings were once a year. Now it seems like they're everyday.'

Another minister heavily involved in anti-gun-crime work is the Reverend Nims Obunge, who is based in Haringay, one of the hot-spot boroughs in north London, next door to Hackney. Aware of a rise in gun and knife violence in the late 1990s, he organised an ecumenical peace service at Broadwater Farm, the estate which had been the scene of rioting and the death of a policeman. That was followed by another big service, a peace week and an anti-violence seminar, which launched his organisation, the Peace Alliance. He had also started talking with the local police, trying to understand their problems. Then, in October 2001, he was approached by a grieving mother. Her eighteen-year-old son, Tyrone Rowe, had been blasted in the head as he sat in his car in Tottenham at four o'clock in the morning. He died in hospital a few hours later. Operation Trident officers, following their usual practice, tried to keep in touch with Mrs Rowe, but somewhere along the way there was a breakdown in communication, and she turned to Nims Obunge. He brokered a successful meeting between the two sides which strengthened his standing with the police. He recalled:

'The police were desperately wanting to engage the community. Policing is based on intelligence and the community were giving them nothing, so they had little to run with. There'd always been conflict between the black community and the police – a big wedge. There was a need to repair burned broken bridges. There was a distrust – deaths in custody, stop and search. The police had tried but they had identified the black community as a hard to reach group. The notion in the black community was that all the police wanted from us was information...

In Haringay a lot of work has gone into engaging. There are two tiers of police. There's no racial tensions with the black community in the first tier – senior officers. But I've heard of tensions with the street officers. There has to be a filtering down of attitudes from the senior officers to those on the street.'

Nims Obunge has helped bring about dialogue between the local black community and the police at a series of meetings. These include 'get-togethers' with young probationary police officers who are posted from the nearby Hendon training centre to Haringay for six weeks of street duty. 'Some of them are coming to London for the first time,' he said. 'Seeing so much diversity here comes as a shock for them, especially for those from the countryside. Getting together is good for everyone.'

Obunge is in contact with another black man involved in anti-gun-crime initiatives in that other hotspot, Harlesden, in Brent. Kola Williams runs a club, Dreams, above shops on the High Street, an area which has witnessed several murders and shootings over the years. The building houses a snooker hall, health club and a dance area, and Williams wants funding to expand to provide workshop and IT facilities for youngsters in trouble with the authorities, whether with the police or through being thrown out of school, just as he was. A tall, big 32-year-old, he sat talking to me at the club's entrance, with police 'wanted' posters behind him. Pulling his left trouser leg up, he showed me two bullet wound scars just below the knee, and explained how he had avoided turning into a gunman himself.

After trouble at school in north London, he was sent to a military-style college in Nigeria, his father's home country. Returning to London at the age of seventeen, looking older than his years, he felt hardened, ready for anything. He became a doorman at clubs and pubs and says he was strict in searching everyone, including guest singers and DJs, and making sure everyone paid entry fees. He said:

'Because of that I would get respect from everyone. I would give respect and I would get it. If someone pulled a gun, because of my upbringing, I wouldn't bat an eyelid. I would explain to them what had happened to me in Nigeria. I'd been shot at there by soldiers. My best friend got hit and I was spattered by his brains. The people coming into the clubs would say they needed a gun for protection, but I'd say that everyone inside had been searched and that it was cool – that no one else inside was strapped [carrying a gun] so there was no need for anyone to have one there.'

There were stabbings and glassings at the clubs, and a bullet grazed his shoulder when he was himself at a rave, but he was only targeted and shot on one occasion when he says his guard was down.

'I was too confident. I fell into the trap of standing round talking to two women. I had my back to the door and a bottle of champagne in my hand. I saw a guy coming towards me out of the corner of my eye and he shot me twice. I'd had an argument the week before and I should have been on my guard. Everyone ran away – people who'd told me how much they loved me. I remember running after the guy, but I'd lost blood and collapsed. Then I saw two holes in my trousers. I walked back to the club, sat down in the office and ran a metal detector over my leg to see if the bullets were still in there. One was. I was taken off to hospital.'

He told police he did not know his attacker's identity. Then in his late twenties, a cousin asked if he would manage Dreams. He jumped at the chance.

'From working in clubs, I could now have my own place and do things my way, making sure there is a secure environment. When I worked at other places, the owners would say to me "let him in. I know him". I didn't like doing that. That could be the guy to put a hole in my head. In the late 1990s people were getting shot who I knew, and I thought something needed to be done. We knew the police would join. It just needed someone to make the first move to keep a bit of equilibrium.'

Through applying for licences for dances, Williams met local police.

'We tried to give them some understanding of dealing with black youth. In previous years, the police would say "fuck you, Kola" and I'd say "fuck you". They had no respect and there was no dialogue. Then I found myself sitting down with them, telling them that they could have dealt with people better in the 'hood. They're supposed to be providing a service. They don't have to swear at us, beat us up, disrespect us. You don't do that to white people. Now I have good relations with the police.'

When Trident was set up and the Not Another Drop Campaign was launched in Brent, Kola Williams helped promote it, joining the local police advisory group. But he, like just about everyone else with an interest in anti-gun-crime campaigns, including police, acknowledge that it is part of a much bigger problem summed up in the phrase 'lack of opportunity'. It begins at home where there is often no male role model, continues at school, and then into employment. Williams is now a member of the London-wide Trident Independent Advisory Group, along with the Reverend Obunge, who agrees that there are no easy answers. 'I used to think of gun crime as an issue by itself, but it's much broader, not in isolation,' he said. 'It involves dysfunctional communities, and you have to get rid of the symptoms. You've got a headache – why have you got a headache? You've got guns – why? We have to look at the root causes.'

'I'm delighted to say that the days of us banging on the doors of the police saying "you're not interested because it's black drug dealers killing other black drug dealers" have faded into the past.'

'The coming together of the police and the black community over the last two years has seen the death knell of that type of political persuasion.'

Surprisingly little research has been produced on young people and gun crime in the UK. Even a report commissioned by the Metropolitan Police Authority in 2003 on the links between guns and drugs said that there was simply not enough information to reach any conclusions, and those figures that were available were contradictory. Some London boroughs with high levels of drug abuse have little gun crime, but the reverse applies in some others. The report's author, Phil Hutchinson, called for more research on the appeal to the young of crime, violent crime and gun crime culture.

More of an insight into the relationship between drugs and guns came from new research in 2004 based on probing interviews with fifteen men, all of them convicted of firearms offences, ranging from murder to possession of an imitation firearm. With about seventy per cent of gun crime in London involving black people, the ethnicity of these fifteen roughly matched the incidence of gun crime in their communities. Eleven were either black or of mixed race, one was Asian, three were white, and their ages ranged from sixteen to the mid-sixties. Although the study by Gavin Hales was in Brent, its significance was recognised by the Home Office and the author was asked to carry out research on the problem in other urban areas.

Hales, a strategic crime analyst with Portsmouth University, has found the link between the drug market and guns to be the most consistent theme in both sets of research. Thirteen out of the fifteen gun offenders interviewed in Brent had either directly dealt drugs themselves or were closely associated with those that did. Some of them described robbing drug dealers, and the need to be armed. One interviewee said: 'We were going to go into a drug dealer's house… Even though he's a white drug dealer, he might have a strap [gun] there. So, we went to a bit of trouble because we thought it was worth it – likely to be goods. We were going to get probably a nice bit of money out of it. So, I had the strap.'

'On the basis that drug dealers are targeted by other offenders,' says Hales, 'it is not surprising that they take measures to protect themselves.' One offender said guns were needed because his associates were dealing with fairly large quantities of drugs: 'If something does go wrong, they can't go asking for legal advice or for the police to come and help them, or for insurance companies. If someone comes to take your things, you have got to defend you. It's you by yourself. You're by yourself out there.' Another said: 'Every big drug dealer is most likely to have a strap [gun], or have a strap man to do it for you, get me? Or someone to hold it for you. That's how they do things… They can't phone the police and say, "yea, someone just put a gun to my face and took all my drugs". You're going to jail for drugs. So they have to do it themselves, in the street – you go and get your gun and do your stuff.'

The offenders also described shootings occurring over what had started as fairly trivial arguments, involving respect issues or a girlfriend. These then escalate. 'You beat someone up, they go and get a gun, and come back on the street,' said one man. 'Then you hear they're looking for you, and you wanna do them before they kill you.' Such disputes do not necessarily involve drugs, Hales observes, but he points out that it is the drug business that has led to guns becoming more readily available. He believed young people start drug dealing because they see a world that 'champions wealth, conspicuous consumption and instant gratification', with few legal prospects for achieving any of these goals. They see in their neighbourhood that the most conspicuously successful individuals – those with the most money, the best cars, and the most girls – are involved with drugs or robbery. The choice made by some is understandable.

Underachievement at school narrows opportunities for young people, especially blacks. Few of those involved in gun crime have remained in education beyond the age of sixteen. Without qualifications, jobs are very limited, with the best prospect for many being poorly paid employment in the retail trade. 'There is a massive amount of hopelessness amongst our young people,' said Lee Jasper, chair of the Trident Independent Advisory Group. 'Unemployment is sky high. Education failure is high, and has been so for the last twenty- to twenty-five years. It has created pockets of despair and cynicism. I'm afraid these people are then all too easily seduced by a crack cocaine gangster with a high octane lifestyle, who is able to offer that young person £1,000 a week on immediate entry to this kind of criminal world. Where these pools of unemployment reside, they are ringed by criminal opportunists who are seeking to recruit and seduce these young people.'

Detailed education research was published in the autumn of 2004 in a report for the London Development Agency called *The educational experiences and achievements of black boys in London schools 2000-2003*. In a foreword, London's mayor, Ken Livingstone, spells out the problem.

'It has been clear for some years that Britain's education system is failing to give black boys the start in life which they and their parents are entitled to expect.

'African-Caribbean boys, in particular, start their schooling at broadly the same level as other pupils, but in the course of their education they fall further and further behind so that in 2003, for example, roughly seventy per cent of African-Caribbean pupils left school with less than five higher grade GCSEs or their equivalents. This represents the lowest level of achievement for any ethnic group of schoolchildren. In national examinations African-Caribbean boys have been the lowest achieving group at practically every key stage for the last four years. Unsurprisingly, the 2001 Census indicated that African-Caribbean men were the least likely of all men to have a degree or equivalent qualification. Gaining good GCSEs is the first stage to securing employability and establishing a skills base for further training and higher education. Deprived of these qualifications, generations of black youth are effectively consigned to low paid, unskilled jobs and years of unemployment. The effect of years of failure to educate black children has been catastrophic for those young people and their communities.'

The report said that low teacher expectations played a major part in African-Caribbean schoolchildren's underachievement. Black pupils complained of racism. They were overlooked when it came to answering questions, suffered verbal aggression from teachers, and harsher reprimands than other students for the same misdemeanour. They were also wrongly accused, watched with suspicion at lunchtimes, and subjected to negative stereotyping. Several said that when a black boy had a reputation for behaving badly, it was very difficult to prove to teachers there was a genuine change for the better.

However, black teachers were seen as playing a critical role in supporting, encouraging and educating black pupils. They validated pupils' culture and identity and provided positive role models. 'In general, black pupils felt that black teachers took extra time to explain and were more prepared to trust black pupils with responsibilities,' said the report. 'Black teachers were seen as pushing black pupils to achieve and being positive role models.'

But the numbers of black teachers in London schools was hugely disproportionate to the numbers of black children – 2.9 per cent of teachers were black compared to nearly twenty per cent of children. Mayor Ken Livingstone called for action to ensure that the proportion of black and Asian teachers should rise to nearly one-third. 'The composition of the teaching staff, governors and other professionals dealing with the education of our children must change dramatically to fully reflect the diversity of London's children.' The report recommended that black teachers should be fast-tracked and offered 'golden hellos'. It also called for urgent action to reduce the number of black pupils excluded from schools, and suggested that headteachers should not suspend or expel pupils for a first serious offence, unless the incident involved a knife or gun.

The report was greeted with dismay by the general secretary of the National Union of Teachers, Steve Sinnott. 'It is grossly unfair to blame teachers alone for a phenomena which is more complex than the report appears to make out,' he said. 'Even academics in this field do not agree on any one reason for the continuing underachievement of Afro-Caribbean boys. Teachers and their unions want to work with the African-Caribbean community – pupils, teachers and parents – in tackling an issue which is long overdue. But this has to be done in a spirit of partnership, not blame.'

Sinnott is not alone in drawing attention to the role of black parents in the educational underachievement of their children. Although the report made headlines over the blaming of teachers, in fact it also touched on home backgrounds. It says that African-Caribbean boys were the least likely of all groups to believe they received good levels of support and encouragement from home. Black boys experiencing difficulty in school did not like to talk about school at home. The report hints at a much greater problem affecting black families – the absence of a male role model at home. It says: 'Some boys in single parent households led by their mothers, and where they did not have access to their father or other older male relatives, were unhappy about not feeling able to talk to someone at home about male issues.'

What the report is quietly acknowledging is that there may be particular problems for black boys in lone-parent families. This goes far wider than simply education. Nearly all the gun crime offenders I spoke to, or those featuring in court cases, come from one-parent families or were brought up by uncles, aunts or grandparents. When only one parent is around, invariably it is the mother, often working long hours in a lowly job. Anti-gun-crime campaigners and police have long recognised that the lack of positive male role models is one of three main reasons for black boys turning to the gun, the other two being education failings and poor job prospects.

Hard official figures about the number or proportion of one-parent families in the ethnic minorities are not easy to come by. But buried away in a social trends report put out by the Office of National Statistics is data gathered in spring 2002 on four different groups. The lowest proportion of families with only one parent are people of Indian origin. Only one in ten of such families have a lone parent. The next group is of white families. A quarter of them are described as having only one parent. But it is double that for those of black Caribbean origin. Just over half of such families are headed by only one parent. The figure is even worse for mixed race families, where three out of every five are headed by one parent.

Of course, not all boys in black single-adult families turn to crime, but there is certainly a connection, and it is not surprising that some in the black community do not want to engage with it, when even a veteran black-rights campaigner such as Darcus Howe has his failings as a father. In autumn 2005, he had a fierce argument with the US comedian Joan Rivers on BBC Radio's *Midweek* where he was promoting More4's TV documentary about his relationship with his twenty-year-old son. A father of seven children by four different women, Howe revealed he had only seen the boy a few times during his first eight years. Accusing him of calling her a racist, an angry Rivers told Howe that he had a major problem: 'You had a child, you left them. Your wife said you weren't there. You married a woman. You deserted her. Now your son comes back, and he's got problems. Where were you when he was growing up, until he was eight years old?'

Earlier in the year, an excellent feature film, *Bullet Boy*, brought home the realities of gun crime in the black community, depicting a family in which the father is missing. Ashley Walters, former lead singer with So Solid Crew, starred as a troubled young man who took to guns, badly influencing his younger brother. A three part BBC TV 'fly-on-the-wall' documentary series, *Murder Blues,* was equally graphic, showing how the Met's Operation Trident dealt with shootings and murders. In December 2005, the Met launched a London-wide campaign called 'Operation Blunt' against another lethal weapon – the knife. With offences involving knives running at more than 12,000 a year, it announced the formation of a knife crime advisory group, chaired by Nims Obunge, a leading member of the Trident Advisory Group. The Met was keen to stress that knife carrying was not confined to any one group, pointing out that the victim and the perpetrator belonged to different racial groups in the majority of non-domestic knife incidents. However, a more detailed look showed that in two-thirds of these cases the person wielding the knife was from the African-Caribbean community.

Whatever the reason for young people turning to serious crime and taking up the gun, whether through lack of job prospects, education failings, fractured family background or a combination of all three along with other factors, it is the police and the criminal justice system who have to deal with the immediate effects, while social workers and anti-gun-crime campaigners do longer term work. For reasons that can only be guessed at, some measure of success is shown in recent UK gun crime figures issued by the Home Office. A staggering thirty-four per cent increase in gun crime in 2002 was followed by a rise of only three per cent in the twelve months leading to June 2004, an increase that the Home Office declared was acceptable and predictable. The number of fatal shootings fell from seventy to sixty over the following twelve months, with the total number of firearms incidents up by five per cent to 11,160, most of that figure being accounted for by a twenty-eight per cent rise in the use of imitation firearms, according to ACPO. New laws had come into force earlier in the year clamping down on the carrying of replicas and imitations, and the latest figures led to renewed calls for their total ban.

At a news conference, the then Home Secretary, David Blunkett, said police and the government would target particular areas affected by violent crime linked to drugs. He said: 'We have a situation where crack and guns go together and because crack is a dangerous drug, that stimulates violence.' He said further measures would be taken in London, the West Midlands, Greater Manchester and Nottinghamshire, all areas where there are already special police units targeting gun crime and the drug trade. A few days before, Blunkett had spoken in the House of Commons about the death of Danielle Beccan, the fourteen-year-old Nottingham girl shot dead while returning home from a funfair. He had hinted then that he might increase the newly introduced five-year minimum sentence for possession of an illegal firearm.

But Blunkett was also criticised over what Nottingham City Council's chief executive, Gordon Mitchell, described as an obsession with short-term targets and initiatives, which left the police lacking direction and stability. In fact, Nottinghamshire police had come in for criticism in recent government reports, being rated amongst the worst in the country. Shootings were averaging about one a week, and although there had been a decrease in the months before Danielle's death, Chief Constable Steve Green agreed there were still problems. However, he recognised, as other senior officers had done before, that solving the gun crime problem required the police acting in partnership with other agencies.

For some time, such an arrangement had been working very successfully in Manchester, beset for years by gang rivalry in the southern part of the city, in the Longsight area together with neighbouring Moss Side and Hulme. Local people eventually started to do something about it, forming groups, including the influential Mothers Against Violence. Then the more official Manchester Multi-Agency Gang Strategy (MMAGS) was set up with Home Office funding. Police-led, it works with Greater Manchester council and other agencies and voluntary organisations, including an independent advisory group, aiming to enforce the law through joint agency work, and to deter young people from entering a gun-gang culture.

Police in the West Midlands started developing a similar strategy in early 2004. Assistant Chief Constable Nick Tofiluk said a multi-agency approach was needed over gun crime because total reliance on police to enforce the law could result in youths at risk feeling that they were being 'kept in their place'. The Home Office pumped money into the Birmingham-based 'Disarm Trust', Gun crime fell by fifty-five per cent in 2004 in Bristol, another city with an independent advisory group where police and the community work together successfully. The Government should continue to support such efforts, said the all-party parliamentary group on gun crime in a report at the end of 2003. Chaired by Diane Abbott, the MPs also recommended that police forces improve their coordination and exchange of information at an operational level, and that more money and resources be put into witness protection schemes.

Although London's Operation Trident and its collaborative work with the Trident Independent Advisory Group has been recommended by the Home Office as good practice for other areas, there is a sometimes tense relationship with the Metropolitan Police Authority, which is responsible for policing in London. A Gun Crime Scrutiny report by an MPA committee in 2004 questioned the very basis on which Trident was set up, claiming that focusing on only the black community was no longer helpful. 'There is a perception that black-on-black crime is marginalised by the media as it is seen as simply "bad-on-bad" – the implication being that no one cares if black gun dealers are shooting each other,' said the report. 'The extended focus on black gun crime may be demonising the black community and fostering a belief that everyone who is shot is automatically a criminal.' It recommended that widening Trident's remit to include gun crime in all minority ethnic communities be considered as well as an expansion in TIAG.

When the MPA's committee chair, Cindy Butts, expanded on this at the report's launch she received a frosty response from Cressida Dick, the commander in overall charge of Trident. Dick calmly pointed out that the facts spoke for themselves – in about seventy per cent of gun crime incidents, gunman and victim were both black, a hugely disproportionate figure when compared with the percentage of black people in London as a whole. She, like Trident officers and the TIAG, is against any dilution of the skills the team's detectives have built up over the years for dealing with the black community and this chaotic or unpredictable form of gun crime. In fact, the Met had anticipated the MPA's recommendation and attempted a compromise. Operation Trafalgar, which deals with all non-Trident shootings, was brought under the command of the Trident head, Detective Chief Superintendent John Coles, but it remains completely separate from the main team which continues to deal with shootings within the black community.

Looking back over the years since Trident's start, Coles said:

'Forming one unit showed the black community that we're serious in dealing with the problem. It increased the confidence of people in coming forward. The relationship between the black community and Trident officers has improved significantly. That's seen by the sheer numbers of people who have come forward and been prepared to give evidence. They've been through the criminal justice system and have come out the other side and survived, without there being a reprisal attack. What Trident said it would do in terms of witness protection and ensuring the safety of them and their family has been delivered. We've gone from where people didn't trust us at all to where a lot of people view Trident as almost their own personal police service.

'The final icing on the cake is that the Met's management have realised that we can't just spend our time reacting to black gun crime. We need to get ahead of the game. We now have another fifty officers, which has allowed us to create more proactive teams and have a crime reduction unit. It's a double-pronged attack. We're targeting the gun suppliers, the drug dealers and converters of the weapons – taking people out before they commit the crimes, and we're trying to get into the next generation, the six- to eight-year-olds, to divert them away from guns in the first place. Without doubt we're developing a culture where the criminals fear us, but the community feel safe and secure because we're there.

'It's in part throwing money and resources at the problem, but it's also changing entrenched views on the police side and on the black community's side. Police are unhappy with the MacPherson view that they're racist. They go out and do their best. A lot of the time we didn't understand a lot of things in the black community. Now most the of the Trident officers have an empathy and understanding of the black community issues and about how the kids end up in the situation they're in – social deprivation, the lack of job opportunities – all these things have an impact on where the kids are going. And the black community has understood that we're not all bad, that we are actually trying to help them.'

However, a common criticism voiced to me by some Trident officers and others involved in anti-gun-crime initiatives was summed up by one frustrated detective with these words: 'We're not trained to be social workers. We're cops and we should be catching criminals.' That issue was picked up by the Met's Commissioner, Sir Ian Blair, in November 2005, when he gave the Dimbleby Lecture and called for a national debate on the role of the police and how society intends to cope with pressing problems. He said police are now expected to be doing everything from social services to special forces, a situation that had come about because of a decline in other forms of social authority by such organisations as the church and trade unions, coupled with the disappearance of what he called 'agents of social enforcement' such as park-keepers, caretakers and bus conductors.

They are being replaced in London by Safer Neighbourhood Scheme police officers, who work with local communities to reduce the level of antisocial and criminal behaviour. By the end of 2005, there were 265 such initiatives in the capital with nearly 5,000 meetings taking place over the year. 'We are denying the habitat of criminality,' declared the Commissioner. 'Even simple things like cutting back of hedges and improving street lighting help reduce antisocial behaviour, and that in turn cuts street crime, out of which comes gun crime.' The Met claims the value of such schemes is proved by the fact that safer neighbourhood officers have handled 110,000 intelligence reports which have resulted in 7,000 arrests.

However, Trident officers continue to be perplexed by what from the outset has been their main problem in tackling black gun crime – the difficulties presented by witnesses to shootings. These range from a refusal to make a statement and appear in court, to going into the witness box and then, through fear of reprisals, not giving the evidence expected, therefore letting down and jeopardising the whole prosecution case. Having suffered because of relying too heavily on witnesses in the past, there is a growing tendency among police across the country to use different evidential methods in court. Technical evidence such as DNA, CCTV or mobile phone details are increasingly being used, backed up by testimony from expert professional witnesses. Some of the biggest cases are being won almost entirely on technical evidence, painstakingly put together by detectives. Perhaps the best example of this was provided by the trial of the young men who murdered Letisha Shakespeare and Charlene Ellis. They were convicted through detailed mobile phone evidence which tied them to the murder scene.

Another development, according to Trident's John Coles, is that fewer people are now trying to exploit black deaths or shootings by turning them into political issues. 'Two or three years ago, people would try and use a Trident murder for their political ends,' he said. They'd try and get into the family, and influence their relationship with the police. They had their own political agendas, trying to stir up anti-police feelings – that it was the black community against the police – to further some political ends. Fortunately that's a rarity these days. The coming together of the police and the black community has seen the death knell of that type of political persuasion.'

Much of the credit for that changing of attitudes must go to the Trident Advisory Group, which includes seventeen black members from the black communities in the London boroughs labelled as gun crime hotspots. When police have found doors closed following a shooting or murder, TIAG members have helped open them. TIAG advises the police on their policies and operations, develops effective media campaigns, and lobbies the Home Office and Government to provide funding for community projects.

'We in the black community have to take full responsibility for the violence in our areas and it is hugely disproportionate,' said TIAG's head, Lee Jasper. 'But I'm delighted to say that the days of us banging on the doors of the police saying "you're not interested because it's black drug dealers killing other black drug dealers" have faded into the past.' He told me that he was not going to be deflected by those concerned that Trident's role continued to be in dealing only with black gun crime. 'I understand the sensitivities,' he said. 'But they are nothing compared to the mothers of the young people who are dying or are maimed and injured in hospital because of this problem.'

The ruthlessness and the waste of young lives was summed up by 2005's final black-on-black court case. Marcus Paul, a 22-year-old, was driving his red Fiat Punto near his home in Ilford in July 2004 when he got stuck in the evening rush-hour traffic. Hilary Iwegbu, from nearby Manor Park, spotted him and went up to his car. After a short conversation, Paul got out of his Fiat, only to be shot by Iwegbu, who then ran off. A passer-by drove the badly injured Paul to hospital but he died there three hours later. Unusually for a Trident trial, a motive was put forward for the killing when the case reached the Old Bailey in December 2005. Iwegbu, a dealer in both heroin and crack, had been shot and injured in the autumn of 2003, and he believed Marcus Paul to have been one of his attackers. That shooting had apparently been carried out because Iwegbu had stolen someone's car.

Found guilty, Iwegbu, aged twenty-five, was sentenced to

life imprisonment with a recommendation that he serve at least thirty years before even being considered for parole. The officer in charge of the case, DCI Andy Shrives commented:

> 'Two families have been ripped apart. Marcus Paul died and his killer will not be out of prison until he's at least fifty-five years old. Making it more awful is that they used to be the best of friends. They lived next door to one another when they were youngsters, growing up together, and going everywhere together. It's such a waste.'

As for the future, although the police and the various groups involved in tackling gun crime are now working together to a much greater extent, everyone accepts that the problem plaguing sections of the black community is one that is probably never going to disappear, certainly not in the short term. Optimism in recent years that the worst appears to be over turns to disappointment with sudden surges in the rate of gun murders and shootings, illustrating the chaotic and unpredictable nature of this black-on-black crime. In London, Trident murders fell by half in the first six months of 2004, but then started rising rapidly, so that by the end of the year they were back at 2003 levels, dropping only slightly in 2005. Non-fatal shootings show similarly wide fluctuations, with detectives unable to explain why this should be the case.

Trident's head, John Coles reported:

> 'The first three months of 2005 were a nightmare, with shootings going through the roof, and, quite honestly, we don't know why it happened. Many of these were lower level shootings, where no one is injured, with the gun discharged in the street, to demonstrate authority, power and machismo. We were being overwhelmed at the beginning of the year, with so many reactive investigations coming in to the shootings team that they didn't have time to investigate and target those

responsible. They got in a vicious circle where the detection rate started to plummet and our availablitiy to become proactive became less. This meant that those engaged in the shooting had more freedom and liberty to do what they wanted to do, which meant shootings increasing and increasing. The only way of stopping that was by a concerted effort with all our proactive units really focussing on the main suspects and trying to stop the supply of guns. It worked. We took out some of the gangs, and broke the vicious circle. Our detection rate started to go up, shootings came down, and we were back on track.'

In 2005, confirmation came for Coles in the form of two worrying trends – the killers getting younger and gun crime spreading to other groups.

'In the last few months we've had people as young as fourteen or fifteen charged with murder, whereas before that the youngest tended to be in their late teens. Also, it's not only the black kids now, but other kids as well, taking up the gun. We've now got mixed gangs, and it's all about "disrespect". There were mixed gangs before, but most of the respect issues were within the black communities. What you're getting now is that culture spreading into other communities as well, so that now we've got Asian and British gangs with "disrespect". This is becoming a problem for British society as a whole.'

Meanwhile, the shootings and killing continue...

Index

Index

Index

ABBREVIATIONS

PC – Police Constable
DC – Detective Constable
DS – Detective Sergeant
DI – Detective Inspector
DCI – Detective Chief Inspector
D. Supt – Detective Superintendent
DCS Detective Chief Superintendent
Comm. – Commander
ACC – Assistant Chief Constable
Asst. Commiss. – Assistant Commissioner
Commiss. – Commissioner